P9-CMY-267

# THE
# National ⚾ Pastime
## A REVIEW OF BASEBALL HISTORY

## CONTENTS

Editor: James Charlton    Fact Checker: Scott Flatow    Designer: Glenn LeDoux
Designated readers and peer reviewers: Marty Appel, Pete Bjarkman,
Cliff Blau, Bob Dorrill, Joe Elinich, Ed Hartig, Henry Hascup, Alan Kaufmann,
Alan Nathan, Rod Nelson, Bill Nowlin, Lyle Spatz, Fred Stein, Stew Thornley, Fay Vincent

ON THE FRONT COVER: Pirates outfielder Roberto Clemente is tagged out by Cubs catcher Harry Chiti in the first inning of the first game of a June 21, 1955, doubleheader at Wrigley Field (Photo courtesy of George Michael). ON THE BACK COVER: Actors Ronald Reagan and Frank Lovejoy in The Winning Team, and inset, Danny Gardella (National Baseball Library, Cooperstown, NY).

THE NATIONAL PASTIME Number 26. Published by The Society for American Baseball Research, Inc., 812 Huron Road, Suite 719, Cleveland, OH 44115. Postage paid at Kent, OH. Copyright ©2006, The Society for American Baseball Research, Inc. All rights reserved. Reproduction in whole or in part without written permission is prohibited.

# A Note from the Editor

Growing up as a baseball fan, I was well aware of the story that the Brooklyn Dodgers hid the young Roberto Clemente on the Montreal Royals roster so that he could be left unprotected but not in danger of being snatched away by a rival team. Hearing it repeated so often—even by Clemente himself—I was sure that it was as true as Ruth hitting 60 homers in 1927 or DiMaggio hitting in 56 straight games. As Stew Thornley reveals in his beautifully researched cover article, not so fast. It is a readable and compelling rebuttal to the authors, coaches and players who have perpetuated the myth.

Goodness gracious! It wasn't the players' fault that the 1962 Mets lost 120 games: it was management. Keith Olbermann points the finger and pen at Casey and the front office in his amusing indictment of drafts and trades made and not made. He convinced me. But I didn't need any convincing even before reading novelist Darryl Brock's short piece. I think that every reader will agree with him: at most baseball games the decibel sound level can be extraordinarily high.

Bill Nowlin has a doubleheader here. First, he has a one-pager that corrects a piece he wrote several years ago stating that the "Boston Pilgrims" never existed. Turns out they did, but just barely. His second article is an interesting account of a seven-game series of virtual all-star games that took place in the armed forces in 1945. While there was no All-Star game in the major leagues that year, the armed services games played in Hawaii included such stellar players as Ted Williams, Johnny Pesky, Bob Lemon, Stan Musial, Billy Herman, Dick Wakefield, Bob Kennedy and Fred Hutchinson.

Bob Bailey's tantalizing article on General Rosy O'Donnell, who was elected to succeed Happy Chandler as baseball commissioner in 1951, is fascinating. O'Donnell seems to have echoed General Sherman who, when asked if he would accept the Republication nomination for President, replied, "I will not accept if nominated, and will not serve if elected." O'Donnell was elected by a majority of the owners, yet never served as commissioner. If it was because he was on active duty, why did the owners bother to elect him?

Showing my colors, no issue of *The National Pastime* would be complete without an article on the Cubs, and this one is no exception. Richard Puerzer offers up a lengthy account of one of the unique and weirder baseball management decisions: the rotating college of coaches. These are just a few of the wide-ranging articles to be found in this issue of *TNP*.

Jim Charlton
May 2006

# The Chicago Cubs' College of Coaches
## A Management Innovation That Failed

### by Richard J. Puerzer

In any business venture, management often seeks to make changes in everyday operations in order to bring about improvements in overall performance. These changes may range from minor tweaks in normal operating procedures to overhauls of the conventional methods in place. The same is true in professional baseball. Minor management changes may include rearranging the batting order or perhaps the reapportionment of playing time. When a major change in team direction is desired, it often involves the replacement of the manager. Following the 1960 baseball season, Chicago Cubs owner Philip K. Wrigley wished to make a significant change in how his team operated. Team performance warranted such a change, as the Cubs finished in seventh place, having won 60 and lost 94 games, ending up 35 games out of first place. Wrigley wished to change the direction of his team while also expediting the development of players in the Cubs' minor league system. The method he developed and implemented for bringing about this change was revolutionary and radical, defying all previous baseball convention. His idea was to essentially do away with the position of manager, a position which had existed on virtually all professional baseball teams for nearly a century, while increasing the number and changing the roles of his coaches.

On January 12, 1961, at the annual hot stove press luncheon of the Chicago Cubs, Wrigley made several announcements that grabbed the attention of the baseball world. He stated that in 1961 the Cubs would operate without a manager "as that position is generally understood," that the eight-man coaching staff would take turns directing the major league

team, and that those same coaches would also rotate through the Cubs' minor league system.[1] Thus began what became known as the Chicago Cubs' college of coaches. The Cubs would operate using the college of coaches scheme for the 1961 and 1962 seasons, and continued to utilize aspects of it through 1964. These tumultuous years would prove that the primary idea behind the college of coaches, to operate without an individual manager on the major league level and to regularly rotate the responsibilities of coaches throughout all levels of the organization, was a failure. However, there were also positive outcomes resulting from this innovative approach to baseball management. The following is an examination of the ideas behind, and the implementation and the results of, the Chicago Cubs' college of coaches.

### Philip K. Wrigley

PHILIP K. Wrigley assumed ownership of the Cubs in 1932 when, upon the death of his father William Wrigley, he inherited the team. He retained ownership of the team until his own death in 1977.[2] During his long tenure as owner, Philip Wrigley's enigmatic leadership approach wavered between innovation and a rigid adherence to the status quo.

Although Philip Wrigley is best known for successfully continuing the business ventures started by his father, he was an extremely successful, ambitious, and often innovative businessman in his own right. He was one of the forefathers of commercial aviation in the United States, helping to start the company that would become United Airlines.[3] He was also successfully involved in the banking and hotel industries. And of course he led the Wrigley Company, synonymous with chewing gum, following in the footsteps of his father. He continued his father's success in the chewing gum business, aided greatly by his own groundbreaking ventures at the forefront of radio, and later

RICHARD J. PUERZER is an associate professor of Industrial Engineering and Engineering Management at Hofstra University and a member of SABR's Elysian Fields Chapter.

television, advertising. During World War II, Wrigley appealed to patriotic efforts by utilizing advertising relating the chewing of gum to increased efficiency on the job. He also worked closely with the government while still promoting his product. Wrigley's gum was included in army rations, which themselves were packed in Wrigley plants.[4] Efforts such as these made Wrigley's gum ubiquitous throughout the world and allowed the company to not only survive but to flourish in these economically difficult times. Innovative thinking such as this was also evident on occasion in Wrigley's approach to the management of the Cubs.

At times Wrigley was quite revolutionary in his approach to baseball management. In 1938, he hired Coleman R. Griffith, a pioneer in the nascent field of sports psychology, as a consultant to the team. Griffith stayed with the team for two years and pursued many new methods for the analysis of the game in an attempt to build a scientific training program for the team. His work included such techniques as filming players, recommending improved training regimes, the documentation of player progress through charts and diagrams, and changes in batting and pitching practice in order to make the practice sessions more closely resemble game conditions. However, Griffith suffered through rancorous relationships with the two Cub managers he worked with, Charlie Grimm and Gabby Hartnett, and had much of his work undermined by these men. In the end, although he produced over 400 pages of reports, including documentation on the use of novel methods and measures later used throughout professional baseball, his work was for naught.[5]

At other times Wrigley was very traditional in his approach to the management of the team. He was often inclined to loyalty, hiring former Cub players

*School daze? P. K. Wrigley and his "college" of coaches.*

ASSOCIATED PRESS

to be manager, including Gabby Hartnett, Charlie Grimm, Stan Hack, and Phil Cavarretta. Although he participated in the operations of the team, including personnel decisions, he claimed to defer to the judgments of his baseball men in the evaluation of talent.[6] Still, he was often criticized for not attending many games and instead focusing his attention on the operations of the chewing gum company.[7] The one decision which drew the most fire of critics, and arguably had a deleterious effect on the performance of his team, was his refusal to install lights at Wrigley Field. Unlike every other team in major league baseball after 1948, the Cubs played only day games at home. Whether or not playing day games exclusively provided the Cubs with a home field advantage or hurt the team, clearly it was an indication of Wrigley's often inscrutable approach to the management of his baseball team.

Despite the quote attributed to Wrigley, "Baseball is too much of a sport to be a business and too much of a business to be a sport," he made considerable efforts in trying to apply a business approach to the management of the Cubs.[8] The college of coaches system was clearly inspired by the business world and was certainly innovative in baseball. No team had gone without a field manager, a single leader with the authority over, responsibility for, and the accountability for his team's performance in the history of professional baseball.

### The Performance of the Cubs: 1945–1960

DURING the early years of Wrigley's tenure as owner, the Cubs had experienced a fair amount of success, winning the National League pennant in 1932, 1935, and 1938. In 1945, the team won 98 games and the National League pennant, but lost the World Series to the Detroit Tigers. In 1946, the Cubs won 82 games and finished third in the National League. Following 1946, however, the Cubs would not finish over .500 for 14 straight years, including nine seasons when they would finish in last or second to last place in the National League.[9] In these 14 years of futility, the Cubs employed six managers. All but one of these managers was given at least one full season to improve the play of the team. The lone manager that was given less than a full season to manage was Lou Boudreau, who managed only a part of the 1960 season.

The Cubs' managerial situation immediately prior to 1961 foreshadowed the emergence of the college of

coaches. Bob Scheffing managed the team through the 1957, 1958, and 1959 seasons. Despite improvements in the number of wins each season and a good relationship with his players, Scheffing was replaced prior to the 1960 season by Charlie Grimm. He had served as Cub manager twice previously, leading the team to the 1945 pennant. A favorite of Philip Wrigley, Grimm managed only the first 17 games of the season, with the team going 6-11, before he traded jobs with then Cub radio broadcaster Lou Boudreau. Although Boudreau was certainly a seasoned manager, with 15 years of experience under his belt, this switching of roles of broadcaster and manager was unprecedented and certainly unorthodox.

In 1960, the Cubs finished with a record of 60 wins and 94 losses, good for seventh place in the National League, 35 games behind the league-leading Pittsburgh Pirates. Following the season, Wrigley denied Boudreau's request for a two-year contract and supported his return to the radio booth.[10] Thus, the position of manager was once again open.

Clearly the poor performance of the Cubs in the years leading up to the implementation of the college of coaches was strong motivation for the development of the system. The failings of the Cubs during this time were limited to neither the managers nor the many players filling the roster. The problems were systemic; including failures in scouting players, training players at the minor league level, and in organizational decision making. So, in seeking to change team performance, Wrigley decided to not just hire a new manager but to devise a plan to change the club's system of management, and approach to player development, on all levels of the organization.

### The College of Coaches

THE original concept of the college of coaches was probably an assemblage of several ideas. Elvin Tappe, who had served as a backup catcher for the Cubs in the late 1950s and early '60s, claims to have approached Wrigley with the idea of rotating coaches on the minor league level. His suggestion was to have hitting, pitching, and fielding instructors who would rotate around the minor league teams so as to provide uniform instruction to developing players. Tappe pointed out that minor league teams were often managed and/or coached by former pitchers who might not be able to understand the needs of position players or provide the requisite instruction in batting. Tappe's rotating-coach idea would solve this problem by providing specialized instruction to all players. However, Tappe stated, "I never intended it to be used on the big league level," and that "Mr. Wrigley got all carried away."[11] Tappe's scheme would later become commonplace in professional baseball, with specialized roving instructors working throughout the minor league systems of every major league team.[12]

There was clearly a business aspect implicit in the implementation of the college of coaches as well. At the press conference in which Wrigley made his initial justification of the system, he discussed in detail his discomfort with the word "manager." He equated the meaning of the word with that of the word "dictator," and made it clear that "he did not want a dictator."[13] Wrigley illustrated the manner by which managers were, and essentially still are, employed in the major leagues. He pointed out that when a team performs poorly, the manager is made the scapegoat and is often fired. This led him to question the importance of managers given the rate with which they were replaced. He pointed out that managers must be relatively interchangeable given that in the period from 1946 to 1960, 103 managers had been replaced on the major league level.[14] Additionally, he equivocated that the job of managing a baseball team, like that of the presidency of the United States, is too much for one man. Wrigley also pointed out that this team-based approach to leading a ball club was similar to the methods employed by his gum company, and that no one manager was too important to be replaced either due to necessity or preference. In the end, however, Wrigley clarified the essence of the motivation for the change in stating, "We certainly cannot do much worse trying a new system than we have done for many years under the old."[15]

As time passed after Wrigley's initial announcement, it became clear that the college of coaches approach was designed not just to change how the management of the major league team would be accomplished. Wrigley also planned to rotate all of the coaches through the minor league system in hopes of improving and expediting the development of minor league players. This would be accomplished through the training and instruction of players by major league–caliber coaches. Wrigley pointed out that in football, a cadre of specialized coaches was utilized to improve team performance. He believed that this approach could be just as applicable in baseball.[16]

He was also seeking to make uniform the instruction that minor league players received as they ascended through the farm system. Wrigley pointed out that in the current system, minor leaguers "have been transients through several farm clubs and at each new place they receive conflicting advice and coaching." Wrigley announced that eight to 14 coaches would make up the system, and that all of the coaches would be considered equal, and would receive similar salaries of $12,000 to $15,000 a year.[17] Overall, the many changes brought about by the college of coaches were designed to improve the Cubs on the major league level and to make them a competitive ball club. Wrigley termed his approach "business efficiency applied to baseball."[18]

### Computerization

ANOTHER pioneering approach that Wrigley sought to use in concert with the college of coaches was the use of computers for statistical analysis. Wrigley brought several IBM computer cards with him to display at the press conference used to introduce the idea of the college of coaches. The initial application of the technology was to calculate and track the batting averages of Cub hitters against individual opposing pitchers and likewise monitor Cub pitchers' performance against hitters. Wrigley stated that the data the team would track was not new, but that the availability of the information would be expedited through the use of the computer allowing for it to be used in a more timely fashion.[19] In doing this, the Cubs were most likely the first major league team to utilize computer technology.[20]

The utilization of computers was met with skepticism by the press. One writer described it as a tool for providing "modern, if slightly mad, decisions."[21] Another marveled at the possibility of turning to a computer in the dugout and querying the machine as to what strategies to employ. Overall, the Cubs' use of computers was generally scoffed at, although in retrospect they were clearly on the leading edge of data analysis in the baseball world.

### Reaction to the College of Coaches Concept

INITIAL reaction to the college of coaches approach ranged from curiosity to derisive criticism. The press developed a number of names mocking the group of rotating coaches including: the college of coaches, the braintruster bloc, the knights of the Cubs' round-table, the enigmatic eight, the double-domed thinkers, and the nine-headed manager. Although the approach generally became known as the Cubs' college of coaches, Wrigley usually referred to it as the "management team."

John Carmichael of the *Chicago Daily News*, a longtime critic of Wrigley, saw the college of coaches idea as an ulterior motive and means for reviving both Wrigley's and the fans' interest in the Cubs.[22] Meanwhile, a writer for the *Los Angeles Times* belittled Wrigley's efforts, comparing him to "the scientists who are trying to put a man on the moon when they could benefit humanity a whole lot more by discovering a preventative for hangovers."[23] The Cubs' coaching situation even drew the attention of President John F. Kennedy. In a speech on the introduction of automation and the potential problems it presented in terms of unemployment, Kennedy observed, "Chicago, I might add, also provides the exception to this pattern – since it now takes ten men to manage the Cubs instead of one!"[24]

One voice in support of Wrigley's innovative approach was found on *The Sporting News*' editorial page, applauding his "refusal to conform" and stating that they were eager to see how the "experiment" progressed.[25] Another supportive, although anonymous, voice was found at the *Chicago Tribune*, expressing that Wrigley deserved "great credit for trying to overcome his baseball problems in the same calm spirit that he applies to chewing gum problems" and that perhaps he would prove to be the "Einstein of the game."[26] Overall, however, the press was quite critical. Or, as Wrigley would put it: "Newspapers from coast to coast were filled with columns and columns of misinformation, cockeyed speculation, derision, and outright condemnation, none of which is based on a shred of information to what our plan was, but only on the fact that we were going to try something new."[27] Former major leaguer Fred Lindstrom was so moved by the news of Wrigley's idea that he wrote to *New York Times* sportswriter Arthur Daley stating that it was clear to him that Wrigley "had never been exposed to the value of a truly great leader like John McGraw." Daley, in reflecting on the idea of the college of coaches, remarked rather presciently that the Cubs "may be the most coached and least managed team in baseball."[28]

Cub players were initially positive, at least to the press. Richie Ashburn was quoted as saying that the "plan for the minors is really good," although he also admitted to some confusion regarding the overall idea.[29] An interesting, although cynical, perspective on the college of coaches was offered by an opposing player. Jim Brosnan, Cincinnati Reds relief pitcher and author of *Pennant Race*, a diary of sorts of the Reds' 1961 season, remarked that "the psychological aspects of Chicago-style management were admirable," and that "any player who did not like his manager at the start of the year could wait patiently, aware that a change, maybe for the better, was just around the next losing streak."[30]

### The First Year of the College of Coaches

THE initial cadre of nine coaches selected to lead the Cubs were Bobby Adams, Rip Collins, Harry Craft, Vedie Himsl, Charlie Grimm, Goldie Holt, Fred Martin, Elvin Tappe, and Rube Walker. Tappe, Craft, and Himsl had all served the Cubs as coaches the previous year; Grimm had just served as Cubs' manager and announcer; Walker had worked in the Cub farm system for several years; and Collins, Holt, Martin, and Adams were new to the organization. Also, veteran player Richie Ashburn was assigned as the player representative working with the coaches. During spring training, the initial scheme was for each of the coaches to serve as head coach in the squad games using an alphabetical-order rotation.[31]

After the team was at spring training and media scrutiny continued, Wrigley continued to defend the new system. On March 17, the team issued a 21-page booklet, titled *The Basic Thinking That Led to the New Baseball Set-Up of the Chicago National League Ball Club*, to the baseball writers covering the team.[32] Each booklet was numbered so as to ensure that all copies would be returned to the team. Sadly, no copies of this booklet appear to still exist. However, a great deal of its contents was included in the newspaper stories on the Cubs. In the booklet Wrigley continued to assert, "To achieve more and better instruction, we need coaching specialists in the various baseball skills and we can't have them dominated by somebody with a one-track mind, which is what a man with the title of manager usually turns out to be." Likewise, Wrigley wrote, "Analyzing our own situation and the failure of every type of manager, from the hard bitten slave-driver to the inspirational leader, to move the team into a contending position in the last 14 years, we can conclude that individually and collectively the problem is the same for everyone—namely a lack of sufficient amount of quality talent." He also pointed out that expansion in baseball makes these issues all the more critical, as the pool of talent will be spread more thinly among a larger number of teams. After expansion, Wrigley clarified, the number of major league players will increase from 400 to 500 players. Wrigley then pointed out, "It is obvious an accelerated program of development is an absolute necessity to meet our commitments and that it is essential to have more instruction of big league quality in order to turn raw material into the finished product at the fastest rate possible." Wrigley closed by making it clear that the Cubs' goal was to "take the major league club and loosely knit organization of minor league clubs and weld the whole thing into one compact organization, where everyone is of equal importance to our ultimate goal."[33]

Towards the end of spring training, the initial assignment of coaches was determined. Bobby Adams, Harry Craft, El Tappe, and Vedie Himsl were to serve as the initial rotating group of head coaches with the major league team. Meanwhile, Charlie Grimm, Gordie Holt, and Fred Martin would serve as roving instructors throughout the farm system; and Rip Collins, Lou Klein, and Rube Walker were assigned to manage in the farm system. The season began with the naming of Vedie Himsl as the first head coach of the Cubs. Avitus "Vedie" Himsl, 44, was a career minor league pitcher, and had been with the Cubs since 1952. However, his only managerial experience was two years at the helm of the Cubs' Class D League team.[34] It was announced that Himsl would remain head coach for two weeks.

The 1961 Cubs were not a bad lot of players. In fact, the opening day lineup featured three future Hall of Fame players in Richie Ashburn (although he was nearing the end of his career), Ernie Banks, and Billy Williams. That year was Banks' ninth season with the Cubs. At 30 years old, he was the heart of the team, coming off of four consecutive seasons with 40 or more homeruns and 100 or more runs batted in. The 1961 season was Billy Williams' first full season in the majors, and his performance would win him the National League Rookie of the Year award. Also in the starting lineup was Ron Santo, who many argue is deserving of Hall of Fame status. Santo was beginning his second year with the Cubs, and was considered a very promising player. Other prominent players on

the team included George Altman, Frank Thomas, and Don Zimmer. However, the Cubs' pitching corps was weak, and this would be a primary reason for the failings of the team.

The Cubs started the season on April 11 with a 7-1 loss to the Cincinnati Reds. Reds starter Jimmy O'Toole tossed a complete-game four-hitter while Reds' sluggers Frank Robinson and Wally Post hit homeruns.[35] Following this first game of the season, Wrigley seemed pleased with the initial implementation of the system. Still, he claimed that he did not foresee any immediate returns from the program, stating, "This is a long-range plan," and that "it may take several years to bear fruits." He went on to state, "The plan was designed primarily to help our lower-classification clubs and speed our farm products to the Cubs."[36]

Vedie Himsl served as head coach for the initial 11 games of the season, leading the team to a 5–6 record. Although it was predetermined that Himsl would be replaced as head coach and rotate to a role in the minor leagues following the games of April 23, his final two games in this rotation were portentous. The Cubs would surrender a doubleheader sweep to the Phillies by scores of 1-0 and 6-0. In the second game, Phillies pitcher Art Mahaffey struck out 17 Cubs, setting the Phillies' club record for strikeouts in a game.[37] Wrigley's initial plan for rotation of the coaches was to remove the head coach while he was winning so as to "quit while he was ahead." Wrigley believed that "this is a common approach, everywhere but in baseball."[38] Unfortunately for the Cubs, this would be difficult to achieve given their performance.

Following his rotation as manager, Himsl departed for San Antonio, where he would serve as a pitching instructor for the Cubs' AA affiliate. Taking his place as head coach was Harry Craft. The other coaches in the system would remain in their initial roles. As it was with Himsl, it was announced that Craft would also serve as head coach for two weeks.

Harry Craft had managed the Kansas City Athletics from 1957 through 1959. He had joined the Cubs in 1960 as a coach. In taking the head coaching position, Craft announced that he would implement several changes, including rearranging the batting order by moving Ernie Banks from the fifth spot to the third and benching rookie Billy Williams.[39] The Cubs won their first game under Craft on a 10th-inning home run by Don Zimmer, defeating the Cincinnati Reds.[40]

NATIONAL BASEBALL LIBRARY, COOPERSTOWN, NY

*The Cubs' first African American manager and player, Buck O'Neil, with Ernie Banks.*

Craft would remain head coach until May 10, leading the Cubs to a record of 4–8, including losses in the final six games while under his leadership. Craft then rotated to the position of head coach of the AA San Antonio team, replacing Rip Collins, who rotated up to the big league team.

In a surprising move, Vedie Himsl was reappointed as head coach following Craft's rotation to the farm system. It was reported that because of his success in his first rotation and his relationship with the players, the two other holdover Cubs coaches, El Tappe and Bobby Adams, had recommended that Himsl regain the head coaching position.[41] In personally making the announcement that Himsl would return as head coach, Wrigley stressed that "comparative records had nothing at all to do with Himsl's return," but he failed to indicate if there was any predefined limit to Himsl's time as head coach.[42] This move was seen by some as a possible end to the rotating-coach plan, as it had initially called for all of the coaches to take their turn as head coach. It was also speculated that the coaches were not making any recommendations, and that Wrigley and vice-president John Holland had decided that Himsl was in fact a good manager and not in need of replacement.[43] Such speculation on the decision-making processes within the Cubs organization would be the norm for the season.

The team's performance under Himsl's second rotation as head coach would not be nearly as successful as its relatively mediocre record under his first go-round. They began by losing on May 12 to Sandy Koufax and the Los Angeles Dodgers and would go on to but five wins against 12 losses in his rotation, which lasted until May 30.

Some of the deficiencies in team management caused by the rotating coaches system were evidenced in the early season handling of Ernie Banks and Billy Williams. Many of these manipulations were plainly due to the lack of consistency and long-term responsibility in team management by the coaches. Banks was of course regarded as the premier player on the Cubs, but was having a difficult season in 1961. He had aggravated an old knee injury during spring training, and was slowed considerably in the early season. Banks began the season at shortstop, the position he had held down for the previous seven seasons, but played poorly. On May 23, despite considerable pressure from the press to have him move to first base, Banks was shifted to left field, a position he had

never played. Still hobbled by the bad knee, Banks had little range or agility in the outfield and likewise did not have the arm strength necessary to throw out runners. On June 16, Banks was moved to first base, another new position. The Cubs had considerable difficulty filling the first base position in 1961, using a total of eight men at the position.[44] Although he did not require much range at first, he was still no better than adequate. After only seven games at first and a brief time on the bench, Banks was moved back to shortstop.[45] Despite all of these moves, Banks was still a threat at the plate, hitting two homeruns in a game on four different occasions during the season.

Billy Williams, on the other hand, had a fabulous spring training, and was perched to become a star with the Cubs. However, he was also was shifted about considerably in the early season. Despite the fact that he had played primarily as a left fielder in the minors, he began the 1961 season in right field. After 18 games in right, Billy was moved to left field, albeit temporarily. He was shifted between left and right, and was benched for a time, until June 16, when it was passed down from the office of John Holland that Billy was to start and be stationed permanently in left field.[46] Upon his permanent installation in left, Williams went on a tear, hitting a grand slam in his first game and then going on to collect 10 hits in 19 at-bats in the subsequent few games. It was here that he was most comfortable, and went on to field and hit at the level worthy of a Rookie of the Year.

Following Himsl's second rotation, the Cubs would experiment with rotating coaches on an extremely short-term basis. Three separate men would serve as head coach over the course of the next nine days. First up was Elvin Tappe, who was named head coach prior to the game on May 30. Tappe, only 32 years old, had also served as a coach for the previous three seasons. Wrigley stated that he was reluctant to appoint Tappe as head coach until he had some experience. Tappe, however, took full advantage of the opportunity, leading the Cubs to wins over the Phillies in both the games he served as head coach. Tappe then handed the reins back to Harry Craft. Craft was head coach for three days, from June 2 to June 4, and led the Cubs to three wins and a loss to the Reds. Vedie Himsl was then renamed head coach on June 5. He could not maintain the luck of his two predecessors, as the Cubs were 0–3–1 against the Cardinals in the games he served as head coach.

At this point in the season the Cubs were in seventh place in the National League, ahead of only the lowly Phillies, and their record stood at 19 wins and 30 losses. Rip Collins was scheduled to next assume the role of head coach but begged out of the position, preferring instead to work as a coach with the younger players. So, on June 9 El Tappe was once again named head coach.[47] Four days later, it was announced that the Cubs' head-coaching merry-go-round would come to a halt, and that Tappe would remain head coach for the foreseeable future. However, it was also stated that the organization was definitely not giving up on the rotation plan and that it could begin again at any time.[48] Tappe would remain head coach for the next 79 games. During this time the Cubs would continue to rotate their coaches, other than Tappe, throughout the organization. During the 1961 season their AAA team at Houston, AA team at San Antonio, and Class B team at Wenatchee, Washington, all had four men serve as head coaches, including either Harry Craft or Vedie Himsl, who of course also managed the major league team.

El Tappe remained head coach until September 1, when he surrendered the duties to Lou Klein. Tappe was now assigned to begin a trip through the Cubs' farm system and scout the talent. Klein was yet another member of the management team who did not have any major league managerial experience prior to 1961, although he had played in the majors, and was most renowned for being one of the players who had jumped to the Mexican League in the 1940s.[49] Klein had started the season in Carlsbad, coaching the Cubs' Class D team in the Sophomore League—quite a change from the big leagues. From Carlsbad, Klein then went to coach at Houston for a time, and had been with the Cubs since July 18.

Klein would direct the team for 11 games in nine days, with the Cubs tallying a record of 5-6 while under his direction. On September 12, he turned over head coaching responsibilities to El Tappe, who now entered into his third rotation as head coach. Tappe directed the team for the remainder of the season, during which time the Cubs won only five games while losing 11.

Overall, the Cubs would finish the 1961 season in seventh place (ahead of the Phillies), with a record of 64 wins and 90 losses. On the bright side, they did improve upon their 1960 record by four games, and were the only team in the National League to finish with a winning record against the pennant-winning Cincinnati Reds. In looking at the final National League statistics, clearly the pitching and defense were the weak links. They led the league in both errors and runs allowed.[50] Despite his many ailments, Ernie Banks still slugged 29 homeruns. Ron Santo had a very good sophomore season, hitting 23 homeruns and establishing himself as an excellent third baseman. Billy Williams hit 25 homeruns and had 86 runs batted in, earning him the National League Rookie of the Year award. Still, the Cubs had a long way to go to become a pennant contender. Immediately following the season, Wrigley stated that the Cubs would "definitely use the same coaching system next year although there will certainly be some changes in the personnel of the panel."[51]

### Reaction of the Players to the First Year

ALTHOUGH there were no complaints printed in the media from the players during the 1961 season, it is apparent that there was some dissension. When it was suggested to Wrigley that the lack of a single authority affected team discipline, Wrigley admitted, "There were older veterans who did not think much of the coaching system," but "they were fined and brought into line."[52]

The first published criticism from the players, albeit not very strong, came from pitchers Moe Drabowsky and Seth Morehead after they were traded to the Milwaukee Braves just before the start of the regular season. They said that "the system is okay for spring training," but they doubted its merits during the regular season.[53]

The most vocal critic of the coaching system was Cub infielder and team captain Don Zimmer. He ripped into the coaching system in a newspaper article following the 1961 season. He was quoted as saying that it was only natural that the nine coaches would have nine different approaches to baseball. He called the college of coaches idea "a joke and that it was doomed to failure the moment it was created." He explained that he felt the coaches all preferred various players and "treated the players as chessmen, not thinking breathing players."[54] Zimmer did not return to the Cubs after the 1961 season, as he was exposed to the expansion draft and selected by the New York Mets.[55]

### The Second Year of the College of Coaches

PRIOR to the 1962 season, Wrigley continued to reiterate that he intended to keep the rotating-coach system in place. Showing his devotion to the system, he expressed that he believed that the rotating-coach system was working and that the Cubs should have finished in the first division in 1961. However, Wrigley did indicate that in 1962 there would be less shifting around of coaches.[56]

The Cubs started the 1962 season in much the same way they started 1961, with four coaches at the major league level and six additional coaches dispersed throughout the farm system. Taking the place of Harry Craft, who left the Cubs when he was named manager of the expansion Houston Colt .45's, was Charlie Metro. He had never managed on the major league level, but had managed the previous five seasons at AAA, most recently with the Denver Bears of the American Association, a farm team of the Detroit Tigers. He had been quite successful in those five seasons, leading each team to a top three finish in their league. In looking at the five primary candidates to serve in the head coaching job in 1962, it is clear that the Cubs were experimenting with various approaches to player management. El Tappe, Rube Walker, and Bobby Adams were known as laid-back leaders with a teaching approach, while Lou Klein and Charlie Metro were more authoritarian and known as disciplinarians. In describing his managerial approach, Metro said, "I'll never win any popularity contests."[57] Just as teams are often inclined to hire a disciplinarian after the tenure of a soft-stanced manager, the Cubs could rotate men with these disparate management styles without the bother of hiring and firing.

The 1962 Cubs were quite similar to the team fielded in 1961. To start the season, Banks was shifted to first base, but was now more experienced and comfortable at the position. Santo, Williams, and Altman held down their respective positions of third base, left field, and right field respectively. After excellent minor league performances the previousseason, rookie Ken Hubbs was given second base and rookie Lou Brock was stationed in center field. Offensively, the team looked strong. Pitching, however, continued to be a problem. The rotation of Bob Buhl, Don Cardwell, Dick Ellsworth, and Glen Hobbie held little more promise than the previous season's staff. Charlie Metro described the team and its mediocre pitching as "a car missing a wheel."[58]

The 1962 Cubs coaches did shift around far less than in 1961. On the farm level, all of the clubs, save for the D-level club at Palatka of the Florida State League, had only one head coach for the entire season.[59] Coaches were still rotated about the minor league clubs, but served as instructors instead of in a lead role. Likewise, there was considerably less shifting of the coaches on the major league level, as only three men served as head coach.

El Tappe, who had served three rotations as head coach the previous year, started the season in the lead role. The team got off to a rocky start, losing nine of their first 10 and winning only four of the 20 games played under Tappe. Lou Klein then was assigned as head coach on May 1. The team's performance would improve under Klein, but not to the point of anything resembling success. Klein was replaced on June 3, after leading the team to 12 wins and 18 losses. The final head coach for 1962 was Charlie Metro. It was thought inevitable by many that Metro be given ample opportunity to replicate his minor league managerial success with the Cubs. After a month as head coach, Metro approached Wrigley to discuss his rotation to the minor leagues. When asked by Wrigley if he would rotate, Metro said he would go, "but he sure as hell won't like it."[60] It was decided to keep Metro on as head coach, effectively ending the rotation of head coaches on the big league team. He would go on to lead the Cubs for the final 112 games of the season. The Cubs still played poorly, winning only 43 games while losing 69. At season's end, the Cubs finished with a record of 59 wins and 103 losses. They ended up in ninth place, ahead of only the legendarily bad New York Mets, playing in their inaugural season. To their embarrassment, the Cubs finished behind the other new expansion team in the National League, the Houston Colt .45's. On a historic basis, the Cubs' .364 winning percentage in 1962 represented the worst performance in the 87-year history of the club.

In 1962, the college of coaches approach was far more contentious both on the player and the management levels than in 1961. This was especially true during Charlie Metro's tenure. Metro banned golf clubs from the clubhouse after learning that some of the players were playing on the morning of day games.[61] He later criticized several unnamed players and coaches through the press for being "happy losers." This caused clear dissension in the coaching ranks. Metro tried to ban shaving in the clubhouse, but was outvoted by his fellow coaches. He also established a daily 10:00 A.M. coaches meeting, which was poorly received by the other coaches, who had been meeting at night after games. It reached the press that both El Tappe and Lou Klein were very critical of Metro and his approach to team management.[62] At the time, the Cubs had a record of nine wins and nine losses under Metro. Despite the discord among the coaches, Metro received an endorsement from Wrigley, who made it clear that Metro would likely remain as head coach for the entire season.[63] In a later show of support for Metro, all of the other Cubs coaches, except for Metro, were at some point rotated to positions within the farm system.[64] It is interesting that Wrigley, who claimed his disdain for the use of the term "manager" due to an association with the word "dictator," saw fit to support some of the more disciplinarian efforts of Metro. Wrigley continued to support Metro, however, following the season Metro was fired. He was the only coach from the 1962 season to be relieved of his position. In retrospect, Metro was glad for the opportunity to serve as head coach with the Cubs. However, he came to believe that the college of coaches approach "would never work" most especially due to the rotation of pitching coaches, a position he believed that required stability.[65] Despite all of this turbulence, Wrigley remained unmoved in his belief in the college of coaches system, and announced at season's end that it would continue on.[66]

Although the players held their tongues and did not publicly criticize the coaching methods at the time, almost all of the players did disparage it years later. Lou Brock stated, "Fourteen chiefs is an awful lot of brass for just 25 Indians, only eight of whom play every day anyhow. The system was not good for morale, and there was plenty of tendency toward insubordination on the team. The trouble was, how could you know who to insubordinate to?"[67] Pitcher Dick Ellsworth, who finished with a record of 9 wins and 20 losses in 1962, believed that the college of coaches offered "no leadership" and that "the lack of leadership was reflected in how we did on the field."[68] Catcher Dick Bertell remembered the system as "horrible," recalling, "We would go from a manager who would like to bunt and hit-and-run one week to a guy who didn't do any of that the next week." Bertell also thought that "the problem with the Cubs was Phil Wrigley."[69] At the end of the 1962 season, pitcher Don Cardwell went to John Holland and told him that he did not like the system. A week later, he was traded.[70]

### Buck O'Neil's Experiences in the College of Coaches

ONE positive outcome of the college of coaches experiment was the hiring of the first African American coach in the major leagues. John "Buck" O'Neil, who had served the Cubs for seven seasons as a scout and spring training instructor, was named a coach on May 29, 1962.[71] O'Neil had played for and/or managed the Kansas City Monarchs of the Negro Leagues for 17 years. He had distinguished himself as a manager with the Monarchs, and was selected to manage the East–West All-Star game four times. He was responsible for the signing of Ernie Banks and George Altman, who had played under him when he managed the Monarchs. He also signed Lou Brock and was instrumental in the development of Billy Williams. Despite these achievements for the Cubs, O'Neil believes that if it were not for the college of coaches and the additional opportunities it offered, he would not have been named as a coach.[72]

In an interview soon after he was hired as a coach, O'Neil called the college of coaches a "wonderful innovation."[73] Years later, however, O'Neil admitted that he "did not think much of the idea of the college," but he was not going to turn down the opportunity to work as a coach on the major league level.[74]

When O'Neil was hired, it was announced that he would be an instructor with the Cubs, although he would not be a part of the rotating coaches system. Thus he would not have the opportunity to serve as head coach. Later, Cubs vice-president John Holland did state that it was possible that O'Neil might join the rotation and serve as head coach one day, perhaps as soon as the following season.[75] However, it would soon become apparent to O'Neil that this would be unlikely. During one game against the Houston Colt .45's, Cubs head coach Charlie Metro was thrown out of the game. Soon after, his replacement, El Tappe, who had been coaching third base, was also thrown out. Several of the players on the Cub bench, including Ernie Banks, realized that O'Neil should take over as third base coach. This was not to be however, as Fred Martin, the Cubs pitching coach, trotted all the way in from the bullpen to take over third base coaching responsibilities. O'Neil would later find out that Charlie Grimm had previously made it clear to the other coaches that O'Neil was not to coach on the base paths. Grimm apparently told Metro that O'Neil would take over someone's job if he was given the opportunity. Although it was never stated, it is difficult not to assume that O'Neil was kept off the field because of his race. He would never get the chance to serve as first or third base coach, which he would later describe as one of his few disappointments in baseball.[76]

Generally, O'Neil's experiences as the first African American coach and member of the college of coaches were positive. He believed that he "didn't face what Jackie did" with regard to his treatment. O'Neil stated that although he demanded the respect of the players and his peer coaches on the team, he did not face any problems and was on a friendly basis with almost everyone.[77] Following the 1962 season and the firing of head coach Charlie Metro, Doc Young of the *Chicago Defender* promoted the idea that O'Neil be named the next manager of the Cubs.[78] But this was not to be.[79] Although O'Neil would certainly have liked to manage the team, he returned to scouting and special assignments for the Cubs in 1964, and would eventually sign such players as Oscar Gamble, Lee Smith, and Joe Carter to the Cubs. It would be 13 more years after O'Neil integrated the coaching ranks until Frank Robinson was named as the first African American manager in major league baseball, with the Cleveland Indians in 1975.

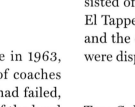

*Manager Leo Durocher*

### The End of the Experiment

AT his annual January press conference in 1963, Wrigley finally gave up on the college of coaches approach. He admitted that the system had failed, stating, "Despite our grand plans, each of the head coaches had his own individual ideas," and "the aim of standardization of play was not achieved because of the various personalities." He added, "The players did not know where to turn," and "the goal was not attained."[80]

In announcing the end of the college of coaches, however, Wrigley was not ready to return the Cubs to a conventional management system. At the press conference, Wrigley introduced the Cubs' newly appointed "athletic director," Robert W. Whitlow. Whitlow, who was 43 years old, was a retired colonel in the United States Air Force. He was a highly decorated

World War II fighter pilot.[81] His most recent position was as the first athletic director of the United States Air Force Academy. Neither the Cubs nor any other major league team had had an athletic director, a position associated with college sports. However, the title of athletic director was a misnomer as it related to the responsibility granted to Whitlow. He was expected to head up the entire organization and answer only to Wrigley.

Whitlow, Wrigley announced, was the "type of man we had hoped to get from among the many coaches brought into the organization the past few years." Whitlow himself announced that his job was to be a "centralized director responsible for the playing end of the game." He also announced that he might sit on the bench in uniform during games.[82] Wrigley did state that there would still be no position with the title manager and that the Cubs would still be led by a head coach. He added that the head coach and all of the other coaches would report directly to Whitlow.

On February 20, Bob Kennedy was named as the new head coach for the Cubs. It was also announced that the 43-year-old Kennedy was expected to remain as head coach for the entirety of the season. Kennedy had served as the general and field manager for the Cubs' AAA club in Salt Lake City the previous year. Kennedy's coaching staff consisted of Lou Klein, Fred Martin, and Rube Walker. El Tappe was assigned as manager at the AAA level, and the other six members of the college of coaches were dispersed throughout the Cubs' farm system.[83]

### 1963 and 1964 to Durocher

THE Cubs responded to the new stability in the coaching ranks and finished the 1963 season with a record of 82–80, their first winning record in 17 years. Tragedy struck the Cubs in February 1964, when second baseman Ken Hubbs was killed in a plane crash. In the 1964 season, the team slipped a bit, finishing with a record of 76 wins and 86 losses. Bob Kennedy and the rest of the Cubs coaches remained intact. The year 1965 however, saw team performance slide further. After 56 games, Kennedy was replaced by Lou Klein. The team finished in eighth place with a record of 72–90.

Wrigley's experiment with Whitlow as athletic

TRANSCENDENTAL GRAPHICS

director was nearly as disastrous as the college of coaches. On one hand, Whitlow was rather forward thinking in his approach. He proposed to study and implement systems of conditioning and "applied psychology." He had a fence erected in center field in Wrigley Field, dubbed "Whitlow's Wall," to serve as a better hitter's background.[84] He also championed Lou Brock as a future star with the Cubs. However, his influence within the Cub organization slowly dwindled. He lost a power struggle with head coach Bob Kennedy toward the end of the 1963 season, when Kennedy essentially told Whitlow to keep away from the players.[85] He developed exercise regimens and purchased special exercise equipment and designed special diets, including powered nutritional supplements, for the players. All of these schemes were soundly avoided and rejected by the players. Finally, following the 1964 season, Whitlow resigned from the Cubs, stating that he "wasn't earning his salary." In commenting on Whitlow's lack of success, Wrigley suggested that Whitlow "was too far ahead of his time" and that "baseball people are slow to accept anyone with new ideas."[86]

A final disaster which is often attributed to the college of coaches was the trade which sent Lou Brock to the St. Louis Cardinals. On June 15, 1964, the Cubs traded Lou Brock, along with pitchers Jack Spring and Paul Toth, for Cardinal pitchers Ernie Broglio and Bobby Shantz and outfielder Doug Clemens. At the time the Cubs had a .500 record and were 1½ games ahead of the Cardinals in the standings. The Cubs, hoping to build on their success in 1963, were seeking more pitching in Broglio, who had won 18 games the previous season, and the veteran reliever Shantz. The trade was well received in Chicago, where the press was happy to be rid of what they perceived as an underachieving Brock.[87] Following the trade, the fortunes of the two teams reversed, with the Cardinals winning the National League pennant and the World Series, and the Cubs finishing in eighth place. Likewise, Brock went on to a Hall of Fame career, collecting 3,023 hits and stealing a then-major league record 938 bases. Broglio hurt his shoulder after joining the Cubs and lost his effectiveness. Although it is clear that Brock suffered in the early part of his career under the college of coaches, he did play more than a full season for the Cubs under a stable management arrangement. The Cubs had simply failed to recognize Brock's potential and gave up on him too soon.

The true end of the college of coaches came on October 25, 1965, with the hiring of Leo Durocher as Cubs manager. In announcing his hiring, a representative of the Cubs stated that the title of the team leader did not matter as long as he had the ability to take charge. Responding to this statement, Durocher, in no uncertain terms, expressed his opinion. He stated, "I'm not the head coach here. I am the manager."[88]

Durocher, after a terrible 1966 season, did lead the Cubs to contention in 1967, 1968, and famously in 1969, when the Cubs lost a substantial lead and subsequently the National League East division title to the New York Mets. It has been suggested that the success of Durocher's Cub teams, and the 1969 team in particular, was due at least in part to the development of such players as Don Kessinger and Glenn Beckert by the rotating-coach system. El Tappe, for one, has stated, "The 1969 team was a team the coaching plan developed."[89] However, this likely overstates the influence of the college of coaches as the vast majority of impact players on that team were with the Cubs before or came to the Cubs after the system was used.

### Conclusions

CLEARLY, the college of coaches, as it was employed, was a fiasco. The system was difficult for both the coaches and the players. The coaches were expected to be familiar and work with not just one but three or four teams over the course of a season. This must have been overwhelming. Likewise, the players were given conflicting orders and advice, and were expected to perform equally under various leadership personalities. Arthur Daley's quote, that the Cubs would be "the most coached and least managed team in baseball," was certainly true.

There were several positive outcomes as a result of the innovative thinking that was behind the college of coaches concept. The more unified approach to player development through the use of roving instructors, consistent teaching, and coaching methods, and a general organizational approach to player development did become the norm in baseball. The use of computer technology, albeit at a very basic level, was certainly prescient. Likewise, the hiring of Buck O'Neil and an interest in the integration of coaches was also, relative to the rest of major league baseball, ahead of its time. In all, the college of coaches experiment was an innovative, tumultuous, frustrating, and, in the end, disappointing time in the history of the Chicago Cubs.

This paper was presented first at the *Seventeenth Cooperstown Symposium on Baseball and American Culture, 2005.*

## The Rotation of the College of Coaches' Head Coaches

### 1961 Rotation

| COACH | BEGAN | ENDED | W | L | T |
|---|---|---|---|---|---|
| Vedie Himsl | April 11 | April 23 | 5 | 6 | 0 |
| Harry Craft | April 26 | May 10 | 4 | 8 | 0 |
| Vedie Himsl | May 12 | May 30 | 5 | 12 | 0 |
| Elvin Tappe | May 31 | June 1 | 2 | 0 | 0 |
| Harry Craft | June 2 | June 4 | 3 | 1 | 0 |
| Vedie Himsl | June 5 | June 7 | 0 | 3 | 1 |
| Elvin Tappe | June 9 | August 31 | 35 | 43 | 1 |
| Lou Klein | Sept. 1 | Sept. 10 | 5 | 6 | 0 |
| Elvin Tappe | Sept. 12 | October 1 | 5 | 11 | 0 |
| TOTAL | | | 64 | 90 | 2 |

### 1962 Rotation

| COACH | BEGAN | ENDED | W | L |
|---|---|---|---|---|
| Elvin Tappe | April 10 | April 30 | 4 | 16 |
| Lou Klein | May 1 | June 3 | 12 | 18 |
| Charlie Metro | June 5 | September 30 | 43 | 69 |
| TOTAL | | | 59 | 103 |

### Overall Team Performance Under Each Head Coach

| COACH | W | L | PCT. |
|---|---|---|---|
| Harry Craft | 7 | 9 | .437 |
| Vedie Himsl | 10 | 21 | .323 |
| Lou Klein | 17 | 24 | .415 |
| Charlie Metro | 43 | 69 | .384 |
| Elvin Tappe | 46 | 70 | .397 |
| TOTAL | 123 | 193 | .389 |

### Notes

1. Edward Prell. "No Manager for Cubs in '61—Wrigley,." *Chicago Daily Tribune,* January 13, 1961, C1.
2. John C. Skipper. *Take Me Out to the Cubs Game: 35 Former Ballplayers Speak of Losing at Wrigley.* Jefferson, NC: McFarland, 2000, 219.
3. Paul M. Angle, *Philip K. Wrigley: A Memoir of a Modest Man,* New York: Rand McNally, 1975, 42–44.
4. Angle, 69–76.
5. For an in-depth description of Griffith's work with the Cubs, see: Christoper Green. "Psychology Strikes Out: Coleman Griffith and the Chicago Cubs." *History of Psychology,* vol. 6, no. 3 (2003): 267–283.
6. Angle, 59.
7. Skipper, *Take Me Out to the Cubs Game,* 220.
8. Jonathan Fraser Light. *The Cultural Encyclopedia of Baseball.* Jefferson, NC: McFarland, 1997, 129.
9. Derek Gentile. *The Complete Chicago Cubs.* New York: Black Dog & Leventhal, 2002. The Cubs did finish at .500, with a record of 77-77 in 1952, good enough for fifth place in the National League.
10. James Enright, "P.K. Defies Critics of 'Coaching College.'" *The Sporting News,* January 25, 1961, 3.
11. John C. Skipper. *Inside Pitch: Classic Baseball Moments.* Jefferson, NC: McFarland, 1996, 42–43.
12. Skipper, *Inside Pitch,* 44.
13. "Confused Cubs Will Start Without Manager." *The Washington Post,* January 13, 1961, A23.
14. "Managers? They Aren't Important." *Los Angeles Times,* January 14, 1961, A2.
15. Prell. "No Manager for Cubs in '61—Wrigley." C1.
16. Jerome Holtzman. "Cubs Concoct 'Coach of Month' Plan to Speed Title Time-Table." *The Sporting News,* January 18, 1961, 9 and 12.
17. Jerome Holtzman. "Inside Story: The Cubs' Curious Experiment." *Sport,* Vol 32 No 2, August 1961, 79.
18. Frank Gianelli. "P. K. Junks 'Minor Leaguer' Tag for Kids." *The Sporting News,* March 8, 1961, 3.
19. Prell, "No Manager for Cubs in '61 – Wrigley," C1.
20. Alan Schwarz. *The Numbers Game: Baseball's Lifelong Fascination with Statistics.* New York: Thomas Dunne, 2004, 136. Although Schwarz writes that the Cubs did not use computers until about 1963.
21. "Confused Cubs Will Start Without Manager." *The Washington Post,* January 13, 1961, A23.
22. John P. Charmichael. "Cub Minority Stockholder Gives Views on P. K.'s Plan." *The Sporting News,* January 25, 1961, 3.
23. Al Wolf. "Cub Pilot Plan Poses Problem." *Los Angeles Times,* February 15, 1961, C2.
24. "'Cubs Exception to Pattern of Automation,' JFK Says." *The Sporting News,* April 20, 1963, 5.
25. "P. K.'s Coach Stint May Fool 'Em." *The Sporting News,* January 18, 1961, 9.
26. "Wrigley's Reasoning." *Chicago Daily Tribune,* March 22, 1961, 12.
27. Edward Prell. "Wrigley Blasts 'Obsolete Baseball Policies.'" *Chicago Daily Tribune,* March 17, 1961, C1.
28. Arthur Daley. "The Revolving-Door System." *New York Times,* February 1, 1961, 44.
29. "Richie 'Confused' by Wrigley Plan." *The Sporting News,* January 25, 1961, 10.
30. Jim Brosnan. *Pennant Race.* New York: Harper & Brothers, 1962, 77–78.
31. Jerry Holtzman. "Drott and Drabowsky Start Comeback Bids." *The Sporting News,* March 8, 1961, 3.
32. "Wrigley Details Cubs' Philosophy." *The Washington Post,* March 18, 1961, A13.
33. Prell. "Wrigley Blasts 'Obsolete Baseball Policies.'" C1.
34. Angle, 132.
35. Edward Prell. "Reds Rout Cubs, 7-1; Braves Lose, 2-1." *Chicago Daily Tribune,* April 12, 1961, C1.
36. Jerry Holtzman. "Five-Man Board Acts as Bruin Brain Trust." *The Sporting News,* April 19, 1961, 21.
37. "Mahaffey Strikes Out 17 Cubs as Phillies Sweep Double-Header." *New York Times,* April 24, 1961, 40.
38. Frank Gianelli. "P. K. to Shelve Head Coach Before Loss Streak Mounts." *The Sporting News,* March 8, 1961, 3.
39. Edward Prell. "Baseball Spotlight on Chicago." *Chicago Daily Tribune,* April 25, 1961, B1.
40. "Cubs Beat Cincy on Zimmer's Homer in 10th." *The Washington Post,* April 27, 1961, D9.
41. Edward Prell. "Himsl Supplants Craft At Cubs' Helm." *Chicago Daily Tribune,* May 12, 1961, C1.
42. James Enright. "Switch Back by Wrigley in Coach Board." *The Sporting News,* May 17, 1961, 1.
43. Edward Prell. "Himsl Recall Indicates End of Cubs' Multiple Coach Plan." *Chicago Daily Tribune,* May 13, 1961, C1.
44. This information and much of the other statistical information was drawn from www.retrosheet.org.
45. Bill Libby. *Ernie Banks: Mr. Cub.* New York: G.P. Putnam's Sons, 1971, 83–85.
46. Billy Williams and Irv Haag. *Billy: The Classic Hitter.* New York: Rand McNally, 1974, 75–76.
47. "Rip Collins Ducks Turn as Field Boss of Cubs." *The Washington Post,* June 9, 1961, C5.
48. "Cubs Shelve Rotating Head Coach System." *The Washington Post,* June 14, 1961, C2.
49. "Lou Klein Named Cubs' Head Coach." *The Washington Post,* September 1, 1961, D1.
50. Statistics were taken from *Official Baseball Guide—1962,* Compiled

by J. G. Taylor Spink, Paul A. Rickart, and Clifford Kachline. St. Louis, MO: Charles, C. Spink & Son, 1963.

51. Edgar Munzel. "P. K. to Shake Up Cubs' Board of Tutors, Continue Plan in '62." *The Sporting News*, October 11, 1961, 20.

52. Munzel. "P. K. to Shake Up Cubs' Board of Tutors." 20.

53. Jerome Holtzman. "Inside Story: The Cubs' Curious Experiment," *Sport*, Vol 32 No 2, August 1961, 78.

54. Edgar Munzel. "Zimmer Rips Cub Coaching Setup as Flop," *The Sporting News*, October 25, 1961, 22.

55. Don Zimmer with Bill Madden. *Zim: A Life in Baseball*. New York: McGraw-Hill, 2001, 53.

56. Edward Prell. "Owner of Cubs Sees the Light! May Illuminate Wrigley Field." *Chicago Daily Tribune*, January 12, 1962, C1.

57. Richard Dozer. "Hurling Aids Out of Consideration." *Chicago Daily Tribune*, February 28, 1962, C1.

58. Charlie Metro with Tom Altherr. *Safe By a Mile*. Lincoln, NB: University of Nebraska Press, 2002, 250.

59. *Official Baseball Guide—1963*, Compiled by J. G. Taylor Spink, Paul A. Rickart, and Clifford Kachline. St. Louis, MO: Charles, C. Spink & Son, 1964.

60. Metro with Altherr, 251.

61. Metro with Altherr, 252.

62. Richard Dozer. "Showdown Near Among Staff of North Siders." *Chicago Daily Tribune*, June 23, 1962, C1.

63. David Condon. "Wrigley Indorses Metro as No. 1 Man!" *Chicago Daily Tribune*, June 23, 1962, C1.

64. "Latest Cub Shift Moves 4 Coaches." *Chicago Daily Tribune*, August 23, 1962, D3.

65. Charlie Metro, phone interview with Richard J. Puerzer, March 2, 2006.

66. Richard Dozer. "Cubs Fire Metro; Coach Plan Stays." *Chicago Daily Tribune*, November 9, 1962, C1.

67. Lou Brock and Franz Schulze. *Stealing Is My Game*. Englewood Cliffs, NJ: Prentice Hall, 1976, 53.

68. Skipper, *Take Me Out to the Cubs Game*, 103.

69. Skipper, *Take Me Out to the Cubs Game*, 118–119.

70. Skipper, *Take Me Out to the Cubs Game*, 125.

71. "Cubs Sign Buck O'Neil As First Negro Coach." *New York Times*, May 30, 1962, 12.

72. Sean D. Wheelock. *Buck O'Neil: A Baseball Legend*. Mattituck, NY: Amereon House, 1994, 82–83.

73. "First Negro Coach In Majors." *Ebony*, Vol. 17 No. 10, August 1962, 29–31.

74. John "Buck" O'Neil, phone interview with Richard J. Puerzer, February 3, 2005.

75. "Vice Prexy Says O'Neil May Head Cubs Eventually." *Ebony*, Vol. 17 No. 10, August 1962, 32–33.

76. O'Neil interview. A similar account of this situation is found in: Buck O'Neil with Steve Wulf and David Conrad. *I Was Right on Time*. New York: Simon and Schuster, 1996, 213–214.

77. O'Neil interview.

78. A. S. "Doc" Young. "An Open Letter to Cub Owner Phil Wrigley." *The Chicago Defender*, March 30, 1963, 20.

79. O'Neil, Wulf, and Conrad, 215.

80. Edward Prell. "Col. Whitlow Takes Over—Cubs Appoint Athletic Director." *Chicago Daily Tribune*, January 11, 1963, C1.

81. Jerome Holtzman. "Whitlow Attacks Cub Defeat Pattern." *The Sporting News*, April 20, 1963, 5.

82. Prell. "Col. Whitlow Takes Over—Cubs Appoint Athletic Director," C1.

83. Edward Prell. "Cub Coaching Staff Stops Revolving!" *Chicago Tribune*, February 21, 1963, D1.

84. C. C. Johnson Spink. "Cub Colonel Loses Rank to Kennedy." *The Sporting News*, September 7, 1963, 7.

85. Spink, "Cub Colonel Loses Rank to Kennedy," 7.

86. Jerome Holtzman. "Whitlow Takes Walk—'Game Not Ready for Him'." *The Sporting News*, January 23, 1965, n.p.

87. Brock and Schulze, 61.

88. Light, 174.

89. Skipper, *Take Me Out to the Cubs Game*, 116.

# Dizzy Dean, Brownie for a Day

## by Ronnie Joyner

IT ain't braggin' if you can back it up. That was the reply of one Jay Hanna "Dizzy" Dean when questioned about his lack of humility when it came to discussing his formidable talent as a big league pitcher for the St. Louis Cardinals' Gas House Gang of the 1930s. Ol' Diz was from a time when superstars were usually quiet, humble men, so his brash confidence was somewhat of a sensation to Depression-era baseball fans—but they ate it up, as Dean almost always made good on his bold predictions of success.

Diz dominated National League batters from the early to mid-'30s, setting countless records while, through his zany antics, further etching himself into American folklore as a truly original character. His meteoric rise finally stalled, however, when the old soupbone he'd ridden to greatness failed him in 1937. On track for another 25-win season, Dean started the '37 All-Star game only to suffer a broken toe when he was struck by an Earl Averill line drive. He rushed himself back into the Cards' rotation before he was fully healed, and subsequently altered his pitching motion to favor his injured foot. The results were devastating as the change in his delivery caused him to develop bursitis in his throwing shoulder, a condition that would plague him for the few short years he continued to pitch.

By the spring of 1941, Ol' Diz wasn't doing so much bragging anymore, mainly because he could no longer back it up. Nine months after his All-Star mishap of 1937, Dean was dealt to the Cubs, where he struggled to a 16–8 record in 42 games from 1938–40. Following a tough 1941 spring training and a poor showing in his only start of the season on April 25, the Cubs had seen enough. When May 14 arrived, or "Axe Day" as some called it because it was the day for roster cut-downs, Dean was given his outright release. Diz's subsequent statement that he "was through" insofar as the Big Show was concerned stamped a sad finality on the playing days of the 31-year-old from Lucas, Arkansas—or so everybody thought.

On September 28, 1947, over six years since he'd thrown his last professional pitch, Dizzy Dean took the mound as the starting pitcher for the St. Louis Browns in their last game of the campaign, a season-closing Sunday afternoon contest against the Chicago White Sox at Sportsman's Park. The events that led Diz to don the brown and orange of St. Louis' other big league team, and the events of the game itself, just served to enhance the already colorful legacy he'd crafted for himself.

Following his release from the Cubs back in 1941, Dean flirted with the idea of embarking on a new career as a pitching coach, but that plan was quickly abandoned when Diz was approached about a different opportunity, something that would turn out to be his second true calling—broadcasting. Dean joined KMOX radio, where he worked with partner Johnny O'Hara broadcasting both Cardinals and Browns home games from 1941 to 1946. He was an immediate success, connecting with listeners through his exuberant personality and purely original homespun sense of humor. Fans loved Ol' Diz's incorrect use of the English language. A melee was a "melly." A conflict became a "confliction." A base runner didn't slide into third, he "slud."

KMOX listeners also found Dean's original creations for typical baseball situations amusing. When players and umpires argued, they were "disputers." If Diz strongly agreed with something said by his on-air partner, he'd exclaim, "You ain't just a-woofin', broth-

RONNIE JOYNER *is a graphic artist living in Charlotte Hall, Maryland. Joyner's baseball illustrations can be seen regularly in* Sports Collector's Digest, *as well as in publications of the Philadelphia Athletics, St. Louis Browns (where a version of this article first appeared), and Washington Senators historical societies. He has co-authored recent autobiographies by Don Gutteridge, Virgil Trucks, and original Met Frank Thomas.*

er!" He coined the phrase "a sluggers' fest" to describe a game with unusually prolific offensive output. And, to Dean, a bases-loaded, two-out, bottom-of-the-ninth situation meant "there's a lotta nerve-wrackin' goin' on out there." Diz occasionally stirred things up with his sometimes candid observations, but his down-home demeanor usually allowed the incident to be quickly diffused. One anecdote has it that Dean once observed a young couple "neckin'" in the bleachers, to which Diz, while on the air, is reported to have said, "That young feller is kissin' her on the strikes and she's kissin' him on the balls."

On January 11, 1947, Cardinals owner Sam Breadon announced that he had created a new six-station radio network to broadcast all Cardinals games, home and away. Despite being named by *The Sporting News* as the best baseball announcer of 1946, Breadon also announced that Dean was out, replaced by Harry Caray and Gabby Street as the Cards looked to create a more "conventional" and "dignified" broadcast.

"They can't do that to me," said an outraged Dean. But as he came to the realization that they could and, in fact, did, he accepted his new exclusive position with the Brownies and said, "Well, now I'm a fella with two home teams. I can root for them Cards and support the good ol' Brownies, too. And that's what I'm gonna do. You know, these Browns have a great organization and it'll be fun doin' their games again."

Dizzy quickly learned that watching the Browns lose game after game was a little more difficult than he had imagined. "Boy, you earn your dough watchin' these fellas," he once said. The Cardinals, a perennial pennant contender, had previously acted as a buffer for Dean, but without their games to counter the losing of the Brownies, Dean eventually grew weary. He became increasingly more critical of the Browns as the summer of '47 wore on. Dizzy, referring to Al Zarilla (.224) and Les Moss (.157), posed the on-air question, "What're they doin' up in the big leagues if they can't swing a bat no better than that?"

Brownie pitchers weren't exempt from Ol' Diz's scrutiny, either. He wondered on-air how Jack Kramer (11–16), Sam Zoldak (9–10), Bob Muncrief (8–14), and Ellis Kinder (8–15)—guys with losing records—had the gall to ask for their paychecks.

By September, with just a few weeks left in the campaign and the Browns looking at a possible 100-loss season, Dean began intensifying his criticism. "Gosh, folks," he told his listeners, "I haven't pitched since 1941, but I feel sure I could go out there today and do better than a lot of these throwers who are drawin' big salaries as major league pitchers." Diz repeated his theory on a number of occasions over the course of the next week, then took the whole subject to a new level when he volunteered to pitch "for nothin'" in the last week of the season to convince the public that he was serious. The idea quickly caught fire with fans, who besieged Browns management with requests to "let Diz make good on his boast." This was still the pre-Veeck era of the Browns, so the full-out circus atmosphere had yet to evolve, but even Bill DeWitt, the Browns general manager at that time, knew a good attendance-drawing gimmick when he saw one. When the Browns returned from their last road trip of the season on Monday, September 22, DeWitt signed Dean to a 1947 contract for a salary of $1, the minimum salary required to make the document binding. They then agreed to pencil Dizzy in as the starter in the season finale, to be played six days later.

The buzz created by the news of Dean's upcoming appearance generated speculation of a big turnout at Sportsman's Park for the game. Rumors were swirling that the $1 contract was a mere formality and that Dean was actually paid $1,000 for his impending one-game gig. He played it close to the vest, however, refusing to divulge any details and saying, "This is the first baseball contract I signed without first turnin' it back for more money. Everybody was satisfied with the contract the Browns offered me."

NATIONAL BASEBALL LIBRARY, COOPERSTOWN, NY

There's no question that the Browns brass were hoping that Dizzy would provide their lowly franchise with one last chance to make the turnstiles click in 1947. The Browns' futility on the field up to that point in the season had a devastating effect on their attendance, and with only four games left on the schedule they had yet to draw 300,000—less than half of what they drew in 1946. Then things got worse. Only an embarrassing 315 paid to see the Browns lose a 9–1 contest to the Indians on September 24, a league low for 1947. That dubious achievement only served to increase the hopes that Diz would be the Browns' temporary deliverance from their attendance woes.

At the age of 37 in 1947, Ol' Diz wasn't exactly the picture of physical fitness. A skinny 6-foot 2-inches back in his glory days with the Cardinals, Dean now had the "gait and gut of somebody 10 years older," —that according to Robert Gregory's 1992 book, *Diz: The Story of Dizzy Dean and Baseball During the Great Depression*, which was very helpful in the writing of this article. That wasn't about to discourage Dean, though. Even in his prime, Dean wasn't known for his conditioning. He had always relied on his God-given ability, and on was quite often reported to have let fly with a hard one without sufficiently warming up his famous right arm. So, in keeping with that tradition, Diz's preparation for his return to the mound was minimal—he threw a round of batting practice to the Brownies and then declared, "I'm ready!"

On September 28, 1947, 15,916—many of them holdovers from the Gas House Gang days of the mid-1930s—paid to see if Diz was, in fact, ready. When asked before the game how he would manage to juggle his broadcasting and pitching duties, Dean casually replied, "Well, I sorta figure my partner Johnny could handle the first three innings while I'm doin' the pitchin'. If I ain't doin' so well after that, I'll come up and broadcast the rest of it." Dizzy then followed with a statement of amazing foresightedness considering the popularity of today's reality television. "But I'll stay in as long as I can," he said, "and if Johnny wants me to spell him a while I guess I could put a walkie-talkie on my back and do my broadcastin' between pitches." Needless to say, if that had happened the audio would have been priceless.

Dizzy had hinted that he would most likely only pitch three innings, but Browns manager Muddy Ruel made it clear that while he didn't approve of the whole Dean stunt, Diz would be allowed to go as long as he wanted to. After the top of the first inning was completed, Diz looked good enough to make some folks wonder whether he could go a full nine, and at the end of his work that day he even made a believer of Ruel. White Sox leadoff man Don Kolloway opened the game with a ground ball behind second base that Browns second baseman Johnny Berardino stopped, but not in time to make a throw to first. The threat was quickly snuffed, however, when Dizzy got Sox right fielder Bob Kennedy to hit into a 6-4-3 double-play—Vern Stephens to Berardino to Walt Judnich. Chicago left fielder Dave Philley then rolled out to Berardino to end the inning.

Dizzy's broadcast booth complaints about the Browns' inability to hit came back to roost as St. Louis failed to score in the home half of the first against White Sox starter Eddie Lopat, but he seemed unfazed as he strolled back out to the mound for his second inning of work. Sox first baseman Rudy York, a dangerous hitter with 21 home runs, opened the second with a flyout to Browns center fielder Paul Lehner. Ol' Diz appeared to be in some trouble when he allowed a single to Chicago center fielder Thurman Tucker, followed by a base on balls to shortstop Jack Wallaesa, but he again got out of the jam courtesy of another double-play ball when he induced Sox third baseman Cass Michaels to hit into another 6-4-3 job.

Dean's new teammates again failed to score any runs in the bottom of the second, but not to worry—Diz appeared to be getting stronger in the top of the third. He set down the Pale Hose in order as catcher Mike Tresh flied to Browns right fielder Ray Coleman, followed by center field flyouts off the bats of Lopat and Kolloway. Seemingly determined to validate Dean's statements about their anemic offense, the Browns did not score in their half of the third inning.

Dizzy's pitching performance alone through three innings would have been enough to send the Browns' third-largest crowd of the season home happy, but leave it to Ol' Diz to give them something extra. As he walked to the plate to open the bottom of the third for his lone at-bat of the game, here's how *The Sporting News* described the scene:

> Always one to give the customers some kind of show while doing his pitching chores, Dean didn't miss this opportunity to get a laugh out of his public. When he went to bat, he carried a black-striped bludgeon to the plate, only to have it

ruled out as "illegal" by Umpire Cal Hubbard. Diz walked back to the rack, pulled out a gaudier red-colored stick and took his place at the plate. The bludgeon had been sent to Dean by the Southwest MFG. Co., makers of bats, as a gag. He swung at the first pitch and singled. Later, trying to reach second on a teammate's infield grounder, Diz was forced, but slid into the bag as in days of old, and came off the diamond limping.

Despite a pulled leg muscle, Dean hobbled to the mound for the top of the fourth for what would prove to be the last time in his storied career. If Dean's wife, Pat, had got her way, however, Ol' Diz may never have gone back out to the hill. While her husband was still limping off the field following his slide into second, Pat leaned over the dugout rail and hollered to Ruel, "He's proved his point—now get him out of there before he kills himself!"

Kennedy opened the frame with a single to left, but was stranded as the "Great One" got Philley and York on long flies to center. Diz then closed the inning by retiring Tucker on a drive to Brownie left fielder Jeff Heath. As Dean limped off the mound, he must have known that he was through. He flashed a warm smile and good-naturedly waved his cap as he made his way to the dugout, obviously happy with the fact that he had, as Pat had said, proved his point. The fans at the

*Hold on to your hats, baseball fans, because Ol' Diz is getting out of the frying pan and into the fire.*

park knew they were witnessing something special, and they bade farewell to the old Cardinal great with resounding cheers. His Brownie teammates greeted him in the dugout with smiles and congratulations, to which Dean grinned and said, "I'm goin' back to my retirement!" He then called on trainer Doc Bauman for one final rubdown.

Dean's work on the hill that day was impressive. He wasn't as fast as he'd been back in the days when he was "foggin' 'em through" for the Cardinals, but he kept the White Sox off balance with near-perfect control. In four complete innings, Dizzy threw but 39 pitches, facing just 14 batters and allowing no runs. Les Moss, Dean's catcher that day, said that Diz simply set the Sox hitters down with his "good control and that big ol' flat curve." The rest of the game was played out of mere formality—the crowd had already seen what they'd come to see. For the record, though, Glen Moulder relieved Dizzy and went the rest of the way. He pitched well for four frames, but Chicago roughed him up for five runs in the ninth inning, sending the Browns to defeat, 5–2—their 95th loss of the season and good enough for another last-place finish.

Dizzy left immediately after the game for his home in Texas, but not before reporters got one last statement from him. "I still believe I can pitch good enough to win games today," Diz said, full of his old swagger, "but I don't intend to try it," he added hastily. "I have a contract as a radio announcer and I'm gonna stick to that job." Before Dean could resume his broadcasting career, however, there were some loose ends that needed to be tied. In an article entitled Dizzy Goes Back to Minors—To Get Free Agency, this is how *The Sporting News* explained the details involved in closing out Dean's career:

> Dizzy Dean, who swore he never would become a minor leaguer after his major league career was over, unwittingly found himself one for a few days, during the time it took to unwind some baseball red tape. Under the rules, Jerome Herman, who signed a $1-a-year contract and pitched four scoreless innings for the Browns against the White Sox the last day of the season, could not be given his unconditional release, since

there is a lid on waivers for that purpose after September 25, three days before Dizzy went to the pitchers' mound. It was necessary for the Browns to release him outright to their Toledo American Association farm after getting waivers. The Mud Hens, in turn, obtained the necessary Association waivers to make him a free agent.

The iconic status Dean had achieved during his heyday with the Cardinals still had a hold on baseball fans across America, so there was always a great deal of interest in anything relating to him. As the newspapers and radio spread word around the country of Dean's success on the mound for the Brownies, fans were amazed. As for the $1-a-year contract—people weren't buying it. They knew that Ol' Diz was just too smart to let management make off with all the dough. Dizzy stuck by the story that he did it "for nothin'," but statements from players left people wondering. Vern Stephens, for one, was sure that Dean had cleaned up from his performance with the Brownies, and upon his return home to Long Beach, California, he told *Long Beach Press-Telegram* reporter Frank Blair that Dizzy "undoubtedly received a percentage of the gate for his part in luring fans through the turnstiles."

When the 1948 season began, Diz was back in his familiar seat in front of the KMOX microphone broadcasting Browns games. He remained there through 1949, but in 1950 he joined the New York Yankees television broadcast team of Mel Allen and Curt Gowdy because he was fed up with the "humpty-dumpty" Browns. Television was the future, and Dizzy knew it. "Well, folks," Dean said, bidding farewell to his radio public, "I'm through talkin' about things you ain't seein'." And with that, the old country boy left for the bright lights of New York City.

Dean remained in broadcasting through the mid-1960s, a run which included a particularly successful 11-year stint as the star of the *Game of the Week* telecast. St. Louis baseball fans were ecstatic when Dizzy was elected to the Hall of Fame in 1953, but the happy group wasn't limited to Cardinals fans. Because Dizzy once bragged—and then backed it up—while wearing brown and orange flannels, Ol' Diz was already a Hall of Famer in the hearts of Brownie fans.

# The '62 Mets

## Blame Weiss and Stengel

## by Keith Olbermann

THE 1962 New York Mets were a lot worse than they looked.

That's an outlandish statement to make about a team that won just 40 of 160 games.

But even among baseball historians, few realize that nearly a quarter of those precious few victories came during a two-week burst in May in which the Mets won nine of 12.

Subtracting that run, they were actually 31–117.

Even the human symbol of the '62 Mets' futility, Marv Throneberry, has had his very rough edges dulled by time and nostalgia. Many have heard of the day Throneberry was called out for not having touched first on a triple, and of how a coach's protest was muted when the umpire mumbled, "He also missed second." But the anecdote has blunted the true terror of Throneberry's performance in that game, the first of a doubleheader against the Cubs at the Polo Grounds on June 17.

Throneberry drove in two runs with his first-inning should-have-been-a-triple, but conceivably cost the Mets another, since Charlie Neal followed his not-so-fancy footwork with a solo home run. But in the top of the inning, during a rundown play, he had also committed that most rare and foolish of errors, fielder's obstruction—when the player without the ball in a rundown play just stands there in the base path and lets the runner slam into him. That Throneberry gaff led directly to four unearned Chicago runs.

Just to top it off, in a game that theoretically could have been 8–4 Mets, New York rallied to score two runs in the bottom of the ninth to trail 8–7. They got the tying run to first with two men out before their last batter struck out—Throneberry, of course.

KEITH OLBERMANN *joined SABR in 1984. He hosts MSNBC's primetime newscast* Countdown *and co-hosts an hour of the* Dan Patrick Show *on ESPN Radio. His latest book,* The Worst Persons In The World, *is published by John Wiley & Sons.*

If the agonies he caused were not enough, there was pitcher Craig Anderson. The "3" in his 3–17 won-lost record seems to preserve for him a shred of dignity. It doesn't. Anderson was not only 0–11 as a starter, but his last two relief victories came in one double-header—on May 12.

At that point Anderson's record stood at 3–1.

For the next four and a half months Anderson and the blighted Bob Miller would combine to go 0–28—until Miller won his only game of the year, on the season's penultimate day, September 29.

The next day, of course, saw the ignominious farewell of Mets catcher Joe Pignatano. In what would be his last major league at-bat, Pignatano lined into a triple play. Less well remembered is that both the base runners in the play, Richie Ashburn and Sammy Drake, were also in their final big league games. Hall of Famer Ashburn's career, in fact, ended at that moment—Drake would replace him in the field for the bottom of the eighth inning.

So the Mets were bad. However bad you think they were, they were worse.

But why?

The clue may have been contained in that career-evaporating triple play into which Pignatano hit. He, Ashburn, and Drake were hardly the only men to sing their finales with the '62 Mets. Of the 45 players who stumbled through all or parts of the season, 19 of them would never play another season in the majors—and 10 of those guys were under the age of 30.

The players were bad.

The men who chose the players were worse.

Though there was little criticism of it at the time, Met management's obsession with bringing in former Dodgers and Yankees as gate attractions has forever after been blamed. The Houston Colt .45s, born in the same expansion draft, went for more of a mixture of middle-level veterans and prospects, and won

24 more games than did the Mets, to finish a fairly respectable eighth.

The Mets, under the control of future Hall of Famers George Weiss and Casey Stengel, seemed instead to go for players they had heard of during their much more successful tenure across the Harlem River with the Yankees. Their Opening Day line-up featured no fewer than four former Brooklyn Dodgers (Roger Craig, Gil Hodges, Charlie Neal, and Don Zimmer). Clem Labine was in the bullpen, and Pignatano would be added before season's end—as would ex-Yankees Throneberry and Gene Woodling. The original Met plan for '62 had called for two more familiar faces, the ex-Dodger pitcher Billy Loes, and the former Giant ace Johnny Antonelli. The latter even rode on the Mets float in the 1961 Thanksgiving Day parade. Antonelli had the presence of mind to retire before spring training began, and Loes was so ineffective in early practices that he was returned to San Francisco, and then released.

But surely even a Rotisserie-like fascination with guys Weiss and Stengel might have "remembered from a couple of years ago" can't explain the continuing death march of the '62 Mets. The worst teams always get slightly better as veterans fade and get moved out, and Weiss certainly wasn't loath to unload some of the disasters: Zimmer, Labine, Gus Bell, Jim Marshall, Hobie Landrith, Joe Ginsberg, Bobby Gene Smith, and Herb Moford were all gone before summer.

It may have been the transactions the Mets didn't make that doomed them to the modern record for futility.

This is dangerous territory for the researcher. Just because Team A obtains Player X doesn't mean that Team B should, or could have, nor that Player X would have produced as well as he did with Team A. But the pattern of the roster moves the Mets made concurrently with those by other major league teams in 1962 suggests that, at best, Weiss and Stengel were asleep at the switch.

A column in the April 27, 1962, edition of the *New York Times* quotes an unnamed Mets spokesman about the decision not to bid for a player just released by a local rival. "If he couldn't help the Yankees," the spokesman asked rhetorically, "how could he have been any help to us?"

"He" was Robin Roberts, cut loose in the Bronx after having not even pitched in the first two weeks of

*The 1962 Mets passed on Robin Roberts (left) and Don McMahon (right) in favor of pitchers like Dave Hillman. Mediocre players like Marv Throneberry (below) became conspicuous members of the team that redefined futility.*

the Yankees season. To be fair, Roberts had seemingly bottomed out the year before in Philadelphia, when he struggled with a knee injury to a 1–10 record.

Ignored by the Mets—not deemed worthy of more than an anonymous quote—Roberts instead went to Baltimore, where he managed to win 37 games over the next three seasons, and would continue to pitch solidly if not spectacularly in the majors until 1966. As the *Times* noted, on the same day they passed on Roberts, the Mets picked up pitcher Dave Hillman from Cincinnati. Hillman managed to produce a 6.32 ERA in 13 appearances in New York, the last of his major league career.

Having eschewed one National League ace of the '50s, the Mets promptly went out and traded for another one: Wilmer "Vinegar Bend" Mizell. The cost wasn't great—they got him even-up for third-string first baseman Jim Marshall. But while the Mets were making that move on May 6, the Colts were preparing to obtain reliever Don McMahon from Milwaukee in a straight cash deal (it was consummated the same day the Mets traded for Throneberry). Weiss and Stengel should have remembered McMahon—he pitched against them six times in the World Series of '57 and '58.

Mizell was a robust 0–2 with a 7.34 ERA in New York, dropped into long relief after just two calamitous starts. These were his last games in the majors. By contrast, McMahon pitched until 1974.

At about the same time, the Reds were giving up on a left hander who had bounced back and forth between Cincinnati and triple-A. His name was Mike Cuellar, and he had 185 wins ahead of him with four pennant winners, but the Mets couldn't be bothered with his sudden free agent status—they were too busy coaxing the Indians into trading them catcher Harry Chiti for a player to be named later (who, as most everyone knows, would prove to be himself).

The then traditional May 15 cut-down date could have been a shopping day for the talent-starved Mets. But, of course, they'd just traded for Throneberry and had no roster room to sign, say, the pitcher released outright by the L.A. Angels—Joe Nuxhall. Nuxhall had also been released six weeks earlier by Baltimore (while the Mets were trying to decide whether or not to hang on to Butterball Botz, Aubrey Gatewood, or Howie Nunn). The Mets passed again; Nuxhall instead went back to Cincinnati, where, after a brief rehab stint in the minors, he managed a 20–8 record over the next season and a half, and a 46–28 mark over the last five years of his career.

Stengel and Weiss did, however, give a long look to another pitcher released by the A's—ex-Yankee Art Ditmar. Ultimately, they didn't sign him, either.

Soon after, the Mets got rid of the rapidly aging 33-year-old outfielder Gus Bell. But on June 15, they replaced him with 39-year old outfielder Gene Woodling, a Stengel favorite from a decade before.

The missed bargain-basement opportunities continued at a rate of about once a month. The Mets

bought Pignatano—their seventh catcher of the season—from the Giants on July 13. A few days later, the Phillies released veteran pitcher Frank Sullivan. The Mets passed. Sullivan finished the year 4–1 with a 3.24 ERA for Minnesota. Pignatano finished the season (and his career) by hitting into a triple play in his last major league at-bat.

In August, Cincinnati gave up on former Cubs starter Moe Drabowsky, and waived him out of the National League—the Mets again passing—to Kansas City. Drabowsky was no superstar, but he did pitch until 1972, going 54–50 with 51 saves over the rest of his career. Instead, the Mets managed to buy minor league pitcher Larry Foss from the Pirates. He'd make five September appearances with New York (0–1, 4.63) and vanish from the majors.

Hindsight is a wonderful and unfair tool with which to criticize the always dicey business of trying to improve a moribund ball club. But we're not blaming Weiss and Stengel for failing to swap for the serviceable veterans who were traded that season, like Bob Buhl, Charlie Maxwell, Pedro Ramos, or Bobby Shantz, or even prospects like Don Lock and Steve Hamilton. We're not even questioning how their expansion cousins signed amateurs in that pre-draft summer like Joe Morgan, Rusty Staub, Jerry Grote, and Jim Wynn, while their own scouts came up with Ray Apple, Paul Deem, and Ed Kranepool. We're not even noting that Grote, Staub, and Wynn had already made it to Houston's 1963 spring camp, while Weiss and Stengel auditioned instead the likes of more '50s Yankee flash-in-the-pans like Bob Cerv and Johnny Kucks.

We're talking about buying Dave Hillman instead of signing Robin Roberts.

McMAHON: TRANSCENDENTAL GRAPHICS    OTHERS: NATIONAL BASEBALL LIBRARY, COOPERSTOWN, NY

*Casey Stengel gestures for a southpaw during one of many, many, many calls to the bullpen in 1962.*

# Professional Baseball and Football
## A Close Relationship

### by Brian McKenna

THE National Football League and baseball have enjoyed a close relationship from the beginning. To capitalize on the popularity of baseball, pro football teams have, at times, adopted major league names: Boston Braves, Brooklyn Dodgers, Cincinnati Reds, New York Giants, New York Yankees, and Pittsburgh Pirates. The Jets picked their name to rhyme with the Mets when they moved into Shea Stadium. Similarly, the Chicago Bears chose their moniker to draw a link with the local Cubs. Boston owner George Preston Marshall rented Braves Field, so he took on their name. It wasn't until he moved the club to Fenway Park that he changed the nickname to Redskins. A closer relationship unfolds with a study of the men who played both games.

### The Hall of Famers

IN 1919, George Halas, a former football star at the University of Illinois, played five games in right field for the New York Yankees. The following year, Babe Ruth would occupy that slot and Halas would be among the original contingent to form the American Professional Football Association, which in 1922 would be renamed the National Football League. By '22, Halas had assumed ownership of the Decatur Staleys, moved them to Chicago, and changed their moniker to the Bears. He would play for, manage, and administer the team until his death in 1983, the only man associated with the NFL throughout its first 50 years.

Halas is one of eight NFL Hall of Famers tied to major league baseball. The others include Red Badgro, Paddy Driscoll, Cal Hubbard, Greasy Neale, Ernie Nevers, Ace Parker, and Jim Thorpe. Badgro

BRIAN McKENNA *grew up and lives in Baltimore. A lifelong baseball fan, his first book* Early Exits: The Premature Ending of Baseball Careers *will soon be released from Scarecrow Press.*

sandwiched a NFL career around two seasons as a part-time outfielder for the St. Louis Browns in 1929–30. Driscoll's 13 games with the Chicago Cubs in 1917 ended his amateur career as a star halfback and kicker at Northwestern University. Three years later, Driscoll became a charter member of the NFL as quarterback and halfback for the Staleys and Chicago Cardinals.

Cal Hubbard was a star end, tackle, and linebacker for Centenary College in Louisiana and Geneva College in Pennsylvania, earning All-American recognition in 1926. The following year he turned pro, signed with the New York Giants, and helped them win the NFL championship. Halas, for one, claimed that Hubbard was the best lineman he ever saw, certainly the most feared of his era.

During the off-season, Hubbard began umpiring in the minors and was promoted to the American League in 1936. While hunting birds after the 1951 baseball season, Hubbard was struck in the eye with a shotgun pellet. The injury forced his retirement; though, he stayed as a supervisor until 1970. Hubbard is the only man concurrently enshrined in the Baseball, College Football, and Pro Football Halls of Fame.

Greasy Neale starred in baseball, football, and basketball at West Virginia's Wesleyan College. He joined the Cincinnati Reds in 1916 and later starred in the infamous 1919 World Series, hitting .357. Football was his calling, though. While still playing baseball, Neale played football professionally and coached at Washington and Jefferson, a small Pennsylvania college that attained substantial national recognition and a Rose Bowl berth under Neale's guidance. The longtime college coach joined the NFL with the Eagles in 1941 and won the NFL championship in 1948 and '49.

Ernie Nevers' first major league hit came off fireballer Walter Johnson; however, he is best known in baseball for giving up two home runs to Babe Ruth during the famed 1927 season. A 6–12 record and 4.64 ERA did not distinguish Nevers on the ball field. The gridiron was another matter. He was recognized by Pop Warner as the finest football player he ever coached, much to the dismay of Jim Thorpe fans.

Nevers' reputation was made in a hard-fought contest against Knute Rockne's Four Horseman of Notre Dame in the 1925 Rose Bowl, though his Stanford team lost 27–10. Missing most of the season with two broken ankles, Nevers taped up to compete in all 60 minutes of the game.

After turning pro, Nevers became a storied fullback with the Duluth Eskimos and Chicago Cardinals in the NFL during 1926–31. On Thanksgiving Day 1929 Nevers executed perhaps the finest individual performance in NFL history. He scored all the points for the Cardinals in a 40–6 rout over the Chicago Bears. Nevers rushed for six touchdowns and kicked four extra points. To date, no one has surpassed his point total; it is the NFL's oldest surviving significant record.

Ace Parker hit a pinch home run in his first at-bat in the bigs for the Philadelphia Athletics in 1937. Playing baseball and football full-time, the infielder decided to concentrate on football in '39, though he did sneak away during the spring and summer to swing a bat in the minors through 1952.

Jim Thorpe is generally regarded as the finest male athlete of the 20th century. He initially gained fame as a two-time All-American halfback at the Carlisle Indian School. At the 1912 Summer Olympics in Stockholm, he won the pentathlon and decathlon, a feat no other iron man has duplicated. Unfortunately, the Amateur Athletic Union stripped his medals and amateur status in early 1913 after it was discovered that Thorpe had played Class-D baseball in 1909–10.

John McGraw stepped in and signed the Olympian to a three-year contract with the New York Giants in February 1913. Retiring with a career .252 batting average over six seasons, Thorpe's baseball highlight may have come with the winning hit against Hippo Vaughn in the 10th inning of the famous double no-hit game on May 2, 1917.

Thorpe helped reorganize the Canton Bulldogs in 1915, beginning his professional football career. In the years prior to the development of the NFL, Thorpe enjoyed his most productive seasons on the gridiron. He could do everything well: run, pass, kick, catch, and tackle. Thorpe is credited by many with reviving the pro game and almost single-handedly improving its financial future.

Thorpe later served as figurehead president of the American Professional Football Association. The fledgling league used his popularity to gain credibility. During the 1920s Thorpe wore the uniform of eight different teams.

### NFL Players and Officials

In all, 68 men have donned the uniforms of MLB and the NFL, plus one that played strictly in the AFL. Of those, Brian Jordan has played significantly more baseball games than the rest and, conversely, Deion Sanders has done the same between the goal posts. Vic Janowicz became the first Heisman Trophy winner to play in the majors in 1953, after signing a bonus contract with the Pittsburgh. After 83 games and a .214 batting average, Janowicz left the Pirates in '54 to join the Washington Redskins. His football career was over two years later after a near-fatal auto accident during training camp.

Hugo Bezdek is the only man to manage in MLB and coach in the NFL. Bezdek, who never played baseball but did work as a scout on the West Coast and as Pittsburgh's business manager, was hired by Barney Dreyfuss to manage the Pirates during 1917–19. Tom Brown, who appeared with the 1963 Senators, was the first major leaguer to play in the Super Bowl. The defensive back helped the Packers take the first two. Across the line that first championship game was running back Mike Garrett with Kansas City. Garrett, the 1965 Heisman Trophy winner, became a huge feather in the American Football League's cap when he signed with the Chiefs for five years and $450,000. When his contract expired, Garrett left football to join the Pittsburgh Pirates organization but quit after being traded to the Padres, never reaching the bigs.

Charlie Dressen, Bo Jackson, and Deion Sanders are among the bigger names to play in both pro leagues. Manager Dressen won 1,008 games in 16 seasons with five different major league clubs, including two pennants with the Brooklyn Dodgers in 1952–53. He also played quarterback for two NFL teams in 1920–23.

Bo Jackson was one of the premier athletes of the 20th century. In 1985 he won the Heisman Trophy as a running back for Auburn University, rushing for 1,786 yards and 17 touchdowns. He was named MVP in both the 1983 Sugar Bowl and 1984 Liberty Bowl. The Tampa Bay Buccaneers made him the #1 pick in the NFL draft in 1986, but Jackson opted to sign a $7 million deal with the Kansas City Royals instead. Then Bo announced his intention to play football as well and signed with the Los Angeles Raiders.

As a testament to his skills, Jackson was the first man to play in both the All-Star and Pro Bowl Games. On a routine tackle during a 1991 playoff game, Jackson suffered a career-ending injury that required hip-replacement surgery. He was able to return to baseball in 1993, becoming the first professional athlete to compete with an artificial hip.

Sanders was drafted by the Kansas City Royals out of high school but chose Florida State University instead. There he starred in baseball, football, and track and field, qualifying for the 1988 Olympic trials as a sprinter. As one of the top defensive backs in the country, Sanders was named All-American twice.

In 1988 Sanders was selected by the Yankees in the amateur draft. The NFL Atlanta Falcons drafted him the following year. He played both sports for eight years, then retired from baseball. In September 1989 Sanders became the first athlete to hit a home run and score a touchdown for major league teams in the same week. Sanders earned two Super Bowl rings in the 1990s, becoming the first man to play in both the Super Bowl and the World Series. Sanders is recognized as one of the all-time great cornerbacks.

Others of note include Carroll Hardy, the only man to pinch-hit for Ted Williams. It happened in 1960 after Williams fouled a ball off his foot. Hinkey Haines played 28 games in the outfield for the Yankees' first world championship team in 1923 and two games in the World Series. A running back out of Penn State, Haines led the league in touchdowns for the champion New York Giants in 1927.

Minor league legend Ox Eckhardt played fullback for the Giants during the 1928 season. He left the gridiron for the promise of a baseball career. Though he had only two brief stays in the majors, Eckhardt batted .367 in 14 seasons in the minors. From 1925 to 1940, he collected nearly 2,800 hits and five batting titles.

Reserve catcher Charlie Berry played 11 seasons in the American League from 1925 to 1938. He also played in the NFL for two seasons with the Pottsville Maroons in 1925–26. Berry later umpired in the American League for 21 years and refereed in the NFL for 24 seasons. He was the head linesman during the famous 1958 championship game. Syracuse University fullback Ron Luciano made the Detroit Lions roster in 1959–60, but never made it off the injured reserve list.

Dusty Boggess umpired in the National League from 1944 to 1962. He also refereed over 500 games in the NFL and scouted for the Steelers. Fellow umpire Frank Umont was a tackle for the New York Giants in 1943–45. Longtime umpire, farm director, and general manager Billy Evans joined the Cleveland Rams as general manager in 1941. Umpire Jim McKean played at quarterback and kicker in the Canadian Football League.

*While Jim Thorpe is perhaps more highly regarded for his gridiron successes than those he achieved on the baseball diamond, he is an icon of American sports history and a trailblazer of the multi-sport athletic career.*

SPORTS-PHOTOS.COM

Catcher Mike Wilson appeared in five games for the Pittsburgh Pirates in 1921. He also donned football gear professionally prior to the existence of the NFL. Later, Wilson became an assistant to NFL Commissioner Bert Bell and supervisor of officials. Red Kellett played nine games in the infield for the Red Sox in 1934. In 1953 he was hired as general manager by the Baltimore Colts. From there until his retirement in late 1966, Kellett build one of the powerhouses of the NFL.

### Negro Leagues

Jackie Robinson's UCLA teammate Kenny Washington and Woody Strode beat Robinson to the bigs when they joined the Los Angeles Rams in 1946. The NFL had not fielded an African American player since 1933. Three Negro Leaguers, Bobby Marshall, Sol Butler, and Joe Lillard, played during the early years of the NFL.

Bobby Marshall played first base and managed in the Negro Leagues in 1909–11. At 40 years old in 1920 the former University of Minnesota star joined Rhode Island in the NFL. Playing end, he reappeared in the league for three games with Duluth in 1925.

Pitcher Sol Butler appeared in a few games for the Kansas City Monarchs in 1925, posting a 1–0 record. The back out of Dubuque played 23 games in the NFL during 1923–26, rushing for a pair of touchdowns.

Pitcher-outfielder Joe Lillard toiled on the diamond from 1932 to 1937 with the Chicago American Giants, among others. During the off-season in 1932 and '33, Lillard played for the Chicago Cardinals as a halfback, punt returner, and kicker. As roster sizes shrank during the Depression, Lillard and Pittsburgh Pirates tackle Ray Kemp would be the last African Americans in the NFL until after World War II.

Jackie Robinson played professional football in the Pacific Coast Football League in 1941 and '44 with the Los Angeles Bulldogs. The PCFL was a place African Americans found work waiting for the NFL to integrate. Robinson's teammate with the Bulldogs, Ziggy Marcell, also played in the Negro Leagues.

### Early Professional Football

Professional football initially developed from a rivalry among Pittsburgh area clubs in the 1890s. However, the first major hotbed was in Ohio at the end of the decade. The four-way antagonism between Latrobe, Canton, Massillon, and Greensburg later spurred the development of the modern game.

Ed Abbaticchio played fullback for Latrobe in 1895–1900. He is reputed to be the first to boot a spiral punt. Since baseball bred a much more hospitable lifestyle, Abby played 28 games at third base for the Phillies in 1897–98 and was later picked up by the Boston Braves in 1903. Ballplayer and future president of the Players' Fraternity, Dave Fultz, also played pro football in Pittsburgh at the turn of the century.

Dave Berry, one of football's foremost coaches and promoters, formed the Latrobe, Pennsylvania, team in 1895. Suffering financial hardship, Berry encouraged Phillies owner John Rogers to form a football team in 1902 to create a rivalry. This was during the NL's war against the upstart AL, a battle which was especially acrimonious in Philadelphia due to the loss of Napoleon Lajoie, Bill Bernard, Chick Fraser, and Elmer Flick to the crosstown Athletics.

A's owner, Ben Shibe, wasn't about to be outdone. He recruited his manager, Connie Mack, and famed University of Pennsylvania tackle Blondy Wallace to build a better team. A couple more clubs signed up and the first professional football league was established, called the National Football League. The league folded after only one season when the Athletics pulled out after losing $4,000. However, it did make an impact. During the season the aptly named Philadelphia Athletics won the first professional football night game, under a crude lighting system aligned along the sidelines. Christy Mathewson, a former halfback at Bucknell, played punter for the Pittsburgh All-Stars, and it is unclear whether guard Rube Waddell saw action, though he did suit up for the A's. Fred Crolius, on loan from the Pirates, was a teammate of Mathewson.

Pennsylvania clubs may have established the first professional football league in 1902, but the true development of the pro game grew out of an Ohio rivalry between Massillon and Canton which began in earnest the following year. Charlie Moran, formally a college standout, took over the reins of the Massillon Tigers as player-coach in 1905. In 1927 he also led the Frankford Yellow Jackets in the NFL. Moran umpired in the National League for 23 years between 1918 and 1939 after brief stints as both ends of the battery for the St. Louis Cardinals in 1903 and '08. Fellow umpire Cy Riger lined up at right tackle for the pioneering Tigers in 1903.

Charlie Follis, a catcher for three seasons with the

Cuban Giants, joined the Shelby football club of the Ohio League, where he played beside and later against Branch Rickey. On September 15, 1904, with Shelby the halfback became the first African American to officially sign a professional football contract.

Here, an interesting chain developed which linked integration in both professional football and baseball. Follis, the first African American professional football player, was a teammate of Rickey, who hired the first acknowledged African American professional baseball player in organized baseball in the 20th century, Jackie Robinson. Robinson, in turn, was a UCLA teammate of Kenny Washington, who, along with Woody Strode, reintegrated the NFL in 1946.

### American Football League, 1926

IN 1925 George Halas signed running back Red Grange to a Bears contract and began barnstorming. Their trip throughout the country helped popularize the sport. Grange's agent, C.C. Pyle, saw an opportunity to showcase his star and formed the short-lived American Football League. Major leaguers Garland Buckeye, Johnny Mohardt, and Al Pierotti played in the AFL.

### All-American Football Conference, 1946-1949

THE administration of the Brooklyn Dodgers of the AAFC was run, at various times, by baseball men William Cox, former Phillies owner; Branch Rickey; and Freddie Fitzsimmons. Rickey added Pepper Martin to the roster after seeing him fooling around kicking a football. The 44-year-old Martin was successful during the preseason but developed an injury and never played during the season despite the team's hopes.

Hall of Famer Ace Parker played in the AAFC, as did Pete Layden and fullback Jim Castiglia. In 1948-49 tailback Herman Wedemeyer played for the Los Angeles Dons and Baltimore Colts. He then played baseball for the PCL San Francisco Seals' farm club in Salt Lake City in 1950. Wedemeyer went on to serve in the Hawaiian state congress and found a recurring role on the television show *Hawaii Five-O*.

### American Football League, 1960-69

TOM Yewcic played quarterback, halfback, and punter for the Boston Patriots during 1961–66. Prior to that, he played a game at catcher for the Detroit Tigers in June 1957. AFL founder Lamar Hunt was a backer of Bill Shea's aborted Continental League.

### The Minor Leagues

YANKEES power-hitting prospect Ken Strong suffered a career-ending wrist injury in 1931. He originally broke the bone against the center-field fence making a catch, but it was misdiagnosed as a sprain. After the season, a doctor performed surgery on his right wrist but removed the wrong bone. Strong had lost the flexibility needed to play baseball. On 1930 he went deep four times on June 8 in an Eastern League game and set the season mark with 41 round trips while also batting .373 and knocking in 130 runners.

The 200-pounder had starred at New York University during their successful 1926–28 campaigns. Strong returned to football and became a Hall of Fame halfback and kicker for the Staten Island Stapletons and New York Giants.

Other NFL Hall of Famers to play in the minor leagues are Sammy Baugh, John Elway, Joe Guyon, Don Hutson, Bobby Layne, Art Rooney and Charlie Trippi. Canadian Football League Hall of Famer Lionel Conacher also played in the minors.

*Footballer Ace Parker hit a home run in his first major league at-bat.*

*Ernie Nevers (inset) scored all the points for his Chicago Cardinals team on Thanksgiving Day, 1929: an NFL record that stands to this day.*

SPORTS-PHOTOS.COM

Among the recent NFL men to have played in the minors you'll recognize Cedric Benson, Bubby Brister, Isaac Byrd, Quincy Carter, Elway, Kay-Jay Harris, Doug Johnson, John Lynch, Mewelde Moore, Vernand Morency, Jay Schroeder, Akili Smith, Chris Weinke, and Ricky Williams.

Baseball and football share a common link at the executive level as well. Joe Carr, Bob Howsam, and Edward Bennett Williams are among the many that have helped shape both industries. Future professional athletes tend to excel at many sports before they focus on their career path. Many baseball men shined on the gridiron in college and found a spot in the College Football Hall of Fame or local galleries, such as Charlie Caldwell, Chuck Essegian, Bob Harvey, Jackie Jensen, Dutch Meyer, Homer Norton, and Jack Thornton, to name a few. For these reasons the two sports will always share a bond. There are sure to be many more in the future, some learning their trade as you read.

---

*Special thanks to Mark Ford of the Professional Football Researchers Association for finding many of my errors and sparking the thought process.*

## Bibliography

Barber, Phil and John Fawaz. *NFL's Greatest: Pro Football's Best Players, Teams and Games.* New York: Dorling Kindersley Publishing, 2000.

Carroll, Bob, Michael Gershman, David Neft, and John Thorn. *Total Football II: The Official Encyclopedia of the National Football League.* New York: HarperCollins, 1999.

Daly, Dan and Bob O'Donnell. *The Pro Football Chronicle.* New York: Collier, 1990.

Grosshandler, Stanley. *The Grosshandler Lists* from *The Coffin Corner Newsletter.* North Huntingdon, PA: Professional Football Researchers Association, Vol. 27, No. 5, 2005.

James, Bill. *The New Bill James Historical Baseball Abstract.* New York: Free Press, 2001.

Johnson, Lloyd. *The Minor League Register.* Durham, NC: Baseball America, 1994.

—— and Miles Wolff. *The Encyclopedia of Minor League Baseball*, 2nd ed. Durham, NC: Baseball America, 1997.

Kriegel, Mark. *Namath: A Biography.* New York: Viking Penguin, 2004.

MacCambridge, Michael. *America's Game: The Epic Story of How Pro Football Captured a Nation.* New York: Random House, 2004.

Maher, Tod and Bob Gill. *The Pro Football Encyclopedia.* New York: Macmillan, 1997.

National Football League. *NFL 2005 Record & Fact Book.* New York: Time Inc. Home Entertainment, 2005.

Peterson, Robert W. *Pigskin: The Early Years of Pro Football.* New York: Oxford University Press, 1997.

Pietrusza, David, Matthew Silverman, and Michael Gershman. *Baseball: The Biographical Encyclopedia.* New York: Total Sports, 2000.

Porter, David L. *Biographical Dictionary of American Sports: Football.* New York: Greenwood Press, 1987.

Shatzkin, Mike and Jim Charlton. *The Ballplayers: Baseball's Ultimate Biographical Reference.* New York: Arbor House, 1990.

Thorn, John, Phil Birnbaum, Bill Deane, Rob Neyer, Alan Schwarz, Donald Dewey, Nicholas Acocella and Peter Wayner. *Total Baseball: The Ultimate Baseball Encyclopedia*, 8th ed. Wilmington, DE: Sport Classic, 2004.

Whittingham, Richard. *What a Game They Played: An Inside Look at the Golden Era of Pro Football.* New York: Simon & Schuster, 1984.

profootballreference.com

thebaseballcube.com

## Drafted Players, by MLB

| Player | Team | Year | Player | Team | Year | Player | Team | Year |
|---|---|---|---|---|---|---|---|---|
| Bill Bradley | DET-A | 1965 | Steve Bartkowski | BAL-A | 1974 | Kerry Collins | DET-A | 1991 |
| Mike Garrett | PIT-N | 1965 | Danny White | CLE-A | 1975 | Mark Brunell | ATL-N | 1992 |
| Mike Garrett | LA-N | 1966 | Anthony Davis | MIN-A | 1975 | Lawyer Milloy | CLE-A | 1992 |
| Ken Stabler | NYY-A | 1966 | C. Holloway (CFL) | ATL-N | 1975 | John Lynch | FLA-N | 1992 |
| Ken Stabler | NYM-N | 1967 | C. Holloway (CFL) | ATL-N | 1976 | Akili Smith | PIT-N | 1993 |
| Archie Manning | ATL-N | 1967 | Jay Schroeder | TOR-A | 1979 | Josh Booty | FLA-N | 1994 |
| Dan Pastorini | NYM-N | 1967 | Dan Marino | KC-A | 1979 | Kerry Collins | TOR-A | 1994 |
| Ken Stabler | HOU-N | 1968 | John Elway | KC-A | 1979 | Duante Culpepper | NYY-A | 1995 |
| Noel Jenke | BOS-A | 1969 | Turner Gill | CHI-A | 1980 | Lawyer Milloy | DET-A | 1995 |
| Johnny Rogers | LA-N | 1969 | Bubby Brister | DET-A | 1981 | Tom Brady | MTL-N | 1995 |
| Ray Guy | CIN-N | 1969 | John Elway | NYY-A | 1981 | Ricky Williams | PHI-N | 1995 |
| Archie Manning | CHI-A | 1970 | Jack Del Rio | TOR-A | 1981 | Chad Hutchinson | ATL-N | 1995 |
| Anthony Davis | BAL-A | 1971 | Turner Gill | NYY-A | 1983 | Isaac Byrd | STL-N | 1996 |
| Steve Bartkowski | KC-A | 1971 | Rodney Peete | TOR-A | 1984 | Quincy Carter | CHI-N | 1996 |
| C. Holloway (CFL) | MTL-N | 1971 | Deion Sanders | KC-A | 1985 | Doug Johnson | TAM-A | 1996 |
| Archie Manning | KC-A | 1971 | Brian Jordan | CLE-A | 1985 | Kay-Jay Harris | TEX-A | 1997 |
| Archie Manning | CHI-A | 1971 | Greg McMurtry | BOS-A | 1986 | Antwaan Randle-El | CHI-N | 1997 |
| Ray Guy | HOU-N | 1971 | Brian Jordan | STL-N | 1988 | Marques Tuiasosopo | MIN-A | 1997 |
| Joe Theismann | MIN-A | 1971 | Rodney Peete | OAK-A | 1988 | Vernand Morency | COL-N | 1998 |
| Ray Guy | ATL-N | 1972 | Deion Sanders | NYY-A | 1988 | Chad Hutchinson | STL-N | 1998 |
| Dave Logan | CIN-N | 1972 | Rodney Peete | OAK-A | 1989 | Drew Henson | NYY-A | 1998 |
| Danny White | CLE-A | 1973 | Greg McMurtry | DET-A | 1990 | Michael Vick | COL-N | 2000 |
| Ray Guy | CIN-N | 1973 | Rodney Peete | DET-A | 1990 | Ronnie Brown | SEA-A | 2000 |
| Danny White | CLE-A | 1974 | Chris Weinke | TOR-A | 1990 | Roydell Williams | CIN-N | 2000 |
| Danny White | HOU-N | 1974 | Kerry Collins | DET-A | 1990 | Mewelde Moore | SD-N | 2000 |
| Anthony Davis | BAL-A | 1974 | Rob Johnson | MIN-A | 1991 | Cedric Benson | LA-N | 2001 |

## Major Leaguers Who Played in the NFL

| Name | MLB | #G | NFL | #G |
|---|---|---|---|---|
| Cliff Aberson | 1947–49 | 63 | 1946 | 10 |
| Red Badgro | 1929–30 | 143 | 1927–36 | 94 |
| Norm Bass | 1961–63 | 66 | 1964 | 1 |
| Gene Bedford | 1925 | 2 | 1925–26 | 3 |
| Charlie Berry | 1925–35 | 709 | 1925–26 | 20 |
| Howard Berry | 1921–22 | 15 | 1921 | 4 |
| Larry Bettencourt | 1928–32 | 168 | 1933 | 2 |
| Lyle Bigbee | 1920–21 | 43 | 1922 | 3 |
| Josh Booty | 1996–98 | 13 | 2002 | 1 |
| Tom Brown | 1963 | 61 | 1964–69 | 71 |
| Garland Buckeye | 1918–28 | 108 | 1920–26 | 40 (AFL–10) |
| Bruce Caldwell | 1928–32 | 25 | 1928 | 10 |
| Ralph Capron | 1912–13 | 3 | 1920 | 1 |
| Jim Castiglia | 1942 | 16 | 1941–48 | 40 (AAFC–2) |
| Chuck Corgan | 1925–27 | 33 | 1924–27 | 30 |
| Shorty DesJardien | 1916 | 1 | 1920–22 | 9 |
| D.J. Dozier | 1992 | 25 | 1987–91 | 43 |
| Chuck Dressen | 1925–33 | 646 | 1920–23 | 12 |
| Paddy Driscoll | 1917 | 13 | 1920–29 | 118 |
| Ox Eckhardt | 1932–36 | 24 | 1928 | 11 |
| Steve Filipowicz | 1944–48 | 57 | 1945–46 | 21 |
| Paul Florence | 1926 | 76 | 1920 | 9 |
| Walter French | 1923–29 | 398 | 1922–25 | 10 |
| Wally Gilbert | 1928–32 | 591 | 1923–26 | 17 |
| Norm Glockson | 1914 | 7 | 1922 | 1 |
| Frank Grube | 1931–41 | 394 | 1928 | 11 |
| Bruno Haas | 1915 | 12 | 1921–22 | 11 |
| Hinky Haines | 1923 | 28 | 1925–31 | 53 |
| George Halas | 1919 | 12 | 1920–28 | 105 |
| Carroll Hardy | 1958–67 | 433 | 1955 | 10 |
| Drew Henson | 2002–03 | 8 | 2004– | 7+ |
| Chad Hutchinson | 2001 | 3 | 2002– | 16+ |
| Bo Jackson | 1986–94 | 694 | 1987–90 | 38 |
| Vic Janowicz | 1953–54 | 83 | 1954–55 | 22 |
| Rex Johnston | 1964 | 14 | 1960 | 12 |
| Brian Jordan | 1992– | 1408+ | 1989–91 | 36 |
| Matt Kinzer | 1989–90 | 9 | 1987 | 1 |
| Bert Kuczynski | 1943 | 6 | 1943–46 | 5 |
| Pete Layden | 1948 | 41 | 1948–50 | 10 (AAFC–21) |
| Jim Levey | 1930–33 | 440 | 1934–36 | 13 |
| Dean Look | 1961 | 3 | 1962 | 1 |
| Waddy MacPhee | 1922 | 2 | 1926 | 10 |
| Howie Maple | 1932 | 44 | 1930 | 8 |
| Walt Masters | 1931–39 | 8 | 1936–44 | 12 |
| Bill McWilliams | 1931 | 2 | 1934 | 5 |
| Johnny Mohardt | 1922 | 5 | 1922–26 | 42 (AFL–14) |
| Ernie Nevers | 1926–28 | 44 | 1926–31 | 54 |
| Ossie Orwoll | 1928–29 | 94 | 1926 | 3 |
| Ace Parker | 1937–38 | 94 | 1937–46 | 56 (AAFC–12) |
| Jack Perrin | 1921 | 4 | 1926 | 6 |
| Al Pierotti | 1920–21 | 8 | 1920–29 | 47 (AFL–5) |
| Pid Purdy | 1926–29 | 181 | 1926–27 | 17 |
| Dick Reichle | 1922–23 | 128 | 1923 | 6 |
| Deion Sanders | 1989–97 | 609 | 1989– | 173+ |
| John Scalzi | 1931 | 2 | 1931 | 7 |
| John Singleton | 1922 | 22 | 1929 | 5 |
| Red Smith | 1927 | 1 | 1927–31 | 37 |
| Evar Swanson | 1929–34 | 518 | 1924–27 | 27 |
| Jim Thorpe | 1913–19 | 289 | 1920–28 | 52 |
| Andy Tomasic | 1949 | 2 | 1942–46 | 15 |
| Luke Urban | 1927–28 | 50 | 1921–23 | 32 |
| Joe Vance | 1935–38 | 15 | 1931 | 11 |
| Ernie Vick | 1922–26 | 57 | 1925–28 | 27 |
| Tom Whelan | 1920 | 1 | 1920–21 | 20 |
| Hoge Workman | 1924 | 11 | 1924–32 | 19 |
| Ab Wright | 1935–44 | 138 | 1930 | 4 |
| Tom Yewcic | 1957 | 1 | 1961–66 | 0 (AFL–77) |
| Russ Young | 1931 | 16 | 1925 | 4 |

## Drafted Players, by the NFL

| Name | Team | Year | Pos |
|---|---|---|---|
| Bob Finley | PIT-N | 1937 | b |
| Ace Parker | Brooklyn Dodgers | 1937 | b |
| Babe Barna | Philadelphia Eagles | 1937 | e |
| Sam Chapman | Washington Redskins | 1938 | b |
| Allie Reynolds | New York Giants | 1939 | rb |
| Eric Tipton | Washington Redskins | 1939 | b |
| Ferrell Anderson | Brooklyn Dodgers | 1939 | g |
| Snuffy Stirnweiss | Chicago Cardinals | 1940 | b |
| Jim Castiglia | PIT-N | 1941 | b |
| Andy Tomasic | PIT-N | 1942 | b |
| Steve Filipowicz | New York Giants | 1943 | b |
| Bert Kuczynski | Detroit Lions | 1943 | e |
| Don Lund | Chicago Bears | 1945 | b |
| Alvin Dark | Philadelphia Eagles | 1945 | b |
| Walt Dropo | Chicago Bears | 1946 | e |
| Joe Tepsic | PIT-N | 1946 | b |
| Walt Dropo | NY Yankees (AAFC) | 1947 | e |
| Lloyd Merriman | Chicago Bears | 1947 | b |
| Lloyd Merriman | LA Dons (AAFC) | 1947 | b |
| Jerry McCarthy | Chicago Bears | 1947 | e |
| Jerry McCarthy | CHI Rockets (AAFC) | 1948 | e |
| Bill Renna | Los Angeles Rams | 1949 | c |
| Red Wilson | Cleveland Browns | 1950 | c |
| Jay Van Noy | Los Angeles Rams | 1950 | b |
| Ed White | Washington Redskins | 1950 | e |
| Al Lary | New York Yankees | 1951 | e |
| Vic Janowicz | Washington Redskins | 1952 | b |
| Harry Agganis | Cleveland Browns | 1952 | qb |
| Haywood Sullivan | Chicago Cardinals | 1953 | b |
| Earl Hersh | Philadelphia Eagles | 1953 | b |
| Laurin Pepper | Detroit Lions | 1953 | b |
| Steve Korcheck | San Francisco 49ers | 1954 | c |
| Tom Yewcic | PIT-N | 1954 | qb |
| Laurin Pepper | PIT-N | 1954 | b |
| Paul Giel | Chicago Bears | 1954 | b |
| Carroll Hardy | San Francisco 49ers | 1955 | b |
| Norm Cash | Chicago Bears | 1955 | rb |
| Tom Gastall | Detroit Lions | 1955 | b |
| Em Lindbeck | Los Angeles Rams | 1956 | qb |
| Charlie Dees | Los Angeles Rams | 1956 | t |
| Gordon Massa | New York Giants | 1957 | c |
| Ron Luciano (umpire) | Detroit Lions | 1959 | t |
| Jim Hickman | Boston Patriots | 1960 | t, g |
| Dean Look | Denver Broncos | 1960 | qb |
| Jake Gibbs | Cleveland Browns | 1961 | qb |
| Jake Gibbs | Houston Oilers (AFL) | 1961 | qb |
| Tom Brown | Green Bay Packers | 1963 | b |
| Merv Rettenmund | Dallas Cowboys | 1965 | hb |
| Steve Renko | Oakland Raiders (AFL) | 1966 | qb |
| Tom Paciorek | Miami Dolphins (AFL) | 1968 | db |
| John Stearns | Buffalo Bills | 1973 | db |
| Dave Winfield | Minnesota Vikings | 1973 | te |
| Rick Leach | Denver Broncos | 1979 | qb |
| Kirk Gibson | St. Louis Cardinals | 1979 | wr |
| Bo Jackson | Tampa Bay Buccaneers | 1986 | rb |
| D.J. Dozier | Minnesota Vikings | 1987 | rb |
| Bo Jackson | Los Angeles Raiders | 1987 | rb |
| Deion Sanders | Atlanta Falcons | 1989 | db |
| Brian Jordan | Buffalo Bills | 1989 | db |
| Mike Busch | Tampa Bay Buccaneers | 1990 | te |
| Josh Booty | Seattle Seahawks | 2001 | qb |

# Wallace Goldsmith, Boston Sports Cartoonist

## by Ed Brackett

WHILE searching through the pages of the *Boston Globe* from the years 1905 through 1920, I noticed a particular feature of the baseball coverage that you don't see today, the use of a cartoon to accompany the written account of a game. It was suggested to me that perhaps a cartoonist was employed due to the lack of photographs in the sports pages of that era. I can agree with that to some degree; however, I am of the opinion that they were used primarily to provide a different perspective to the reporting of the games.

The reporter's job was to produce a detailed account of the game's proceedings. He had virtually unlimited space to create a complete description of the game. If a team was to score 25 runs, the reader would get a description of how each one crossed the plate. The story would be written in his personal style, but it is still a narrative of all the significant plays and events to give the reader the entire story.

The cartoonist, on the other hand, had a limited space in which to create his work, so he had to make a condensed version of the story. Because the scenes depicted were entirely of his choosing, he created an interpretation of the game that resulted in a summary more like that of a fan than reporter. The artist also had the power to satirize, and it was a duty which he seemed to relish. For example, an umpire will be drawn with daggers coming out of his eyes as he's arguing with a player. On a play in which a fielder hopelessly misplays a batted ball, he will be shown in a confrontation with a baseball that has come to life saying, "You can't catch me."

Wallace Goldsmith produced cartoons for the *Boston Globe* from 1909 to 1919, and his creations were primarily of sporting topics. The subjects he covered were numerous, with the competition levels ranging from the local schoolboy to the professional ranks. Aside from his work of sporting subjects, he created editorial cartoons of Boston city politics as well as national issues such as the women's suffrage movement or President Wilson's foreign policies. He also made cartoons of local interest such as scenes from around the city on a record hot day or the winning species from the Boston poultry and dog shows. His work in this genre would compare favorably to any artist who specialized in political cartoons and would do so today if created using current topics.

He was the creator of a comic strip whose main character, Mr. Asa Spades, is a bumbling black man who gets caught up in adventures that revolved around the events of the day. This is an item that certainly wouldn't be published today, but in an advertisement from 1910 it was hailed as a cartoon that "should be read by every man, woman and child in New England."

The main focus of Mr. Goldsmith's work was the coverage of the Red Sox and Braves. He traveled with the Red Sox to the spring training destinations of Hot Springs, Arkansas, and Redondo Beach, California, to provide daily reports of the workouts. During the baseball season his cartoons were reviews of the previous day's game for whichever team was playing at home in Boston. His cartoons usually consist of a large sketch that serves as a highlight of a thrilling play or sequence of plays which should allow the viewer to make an instant judgment of the game's outcome. This large sketch is surrounded by three to six smaller sketches depicting some great plays and not so great plays, along with such incidental moments as a boisterous spectator in the stands or a park employee reclaiming a foul ball from a fan.

ED BRACKETT *is a Cad Designer for Atrium Medical Corp. in Hudson, NH. He is a member of the Massachusetts Baseball Umpire Association and can be seen calling games in the Merrimac Valley. This is his first article published by SABR.*

## FENWAY PARK ALLIES TAKE NEW HEART WHEN REINFORCEMENTS FROM TROY ARRIVE

*By WALLACE GOLDSMITH.*

*May 26, 1915: Reds at war with Braves*

He was always among the corps of writers providing coverage of the World Series games. In an advertisement introducing the staff of reporters and experts covering the 1914 fall classic, here is the brief summary that accompanied his picture.

> Everybody knows Goldsmith's baseball cartoons and his cleverness in picturing happenings on the baseball field, and during the World Series no bit of humor will escape his eye.
>
> When he draws a likeness of a ball player you know who it is, and his sketches of the champions will be characteristic attitudes truer to life than would be possible in any photograph. Goldsmith will see the crucial plays in every game and will picture them in his graphic and funny way.

As an indication that Mr. Goldsmith was considered an important member of the *Boston Globe* staff, I make reference to an ad for a contest open to local children to acquire new subscribers. The *Globe* published a list of different features as selling points for them to recommend to potential customers while canvassing their neighborhood. Among the various suggested columns and editorials were features that would be of interest to baseball fans, "the funny and graphic cartoons" of Wallace Goldsmith.

In an example of how writer Timothy Murnane and Wallace Goldsmith interpreted the same event, I refer to an incident reported on May 27, 1914, in a game between the Red Sox and Cleveland. There was a play at second base in which the Red Sox Del Gainor was tagged out by Napoleon Lajoie, a product of the hidden-ball trick. Umpires Jack Sheridan and Oliver Chill each made call reversals on the play and caused protests from both teams. Here is how Murnane reported the incident:

> There was quite a mixup at the base, and when Umpire Jack Sheridan looked, he saw Lajoie holding the Boston runner off the base and declared him out. This caused a sharp cry of protest from the Boston players, who argued that Lajoie pushed Gainor off the base, and as Sheridan had been caught looking anywhere but where the ball was he turned to the umpire at the plate for advice.
>
> Umpire Chill waved his hand, as much as to say that the man was safe. Then Sheridan turned around and waved Gainor safe. At this stage nearly the whole Cleveland outfit, headed by the irate Frenchman from Woonsocket headed for the umpire at the plate.
>
> Chill evidently saw them coming, for he immediately changed his mind and commenced to wave the player out. Umpire Sheridan then made his third decision, and this time was in full accord with the umpire in charge of the game, the pair of them having made five decisions on one play and pulling a juicy bone about the size of Bunker Hill Monument.

The cartoon Goldsmith produced was titled ONE WAY TO UMPIRE: IF YOU DON'T SEE IT, GUESS IT. In it Lajoie is shown tagging a prostrate Gainor with base umpire Sheridan having his back to the play while he is dreaming of lying on the beach. Plate umpire Chill is looking away from the play, dreaming of women and saying, "How lovely the ladies look in their summer garb."

I believe that Mr. Goldsmith created his best work in 1914, 1915, and 1916, so I have included six examples from those years that will showcase his talent.

# ILLUSTRATING HOW SEEMINGLY SURE HITS ARE STOLEN WITH THE WORST OF INTENTIONS

## By WALLACE GOLDSMITH.

*May 23, 1916: Thrilling win for Red Sox*

The cartoon from May 23, 1916, is what I consider a typical example of a game recap. This was a close game which was decided in the ninth inning when Tilly Walker scored on Harold Janvin's single to left to give the Red Sox a 2–1 win over the Detroit Tigers. You will always notice certain distinguishing features utilizing a bit of artistic license. Smoke rings coming off a bat indicates a mighty blast or a puff of smoke off a glove means the fielding of a hot liner. Dotted lines track the flight of the ball; in this case you can see two examples of the ball leaving the bat and the return throw from a fielder. The players are constantly making some kind of statement, such as Janvin's excitement over his hit or Gardner's disappointment about his groundout. The fans have something to say also, the gent shouting, "It's the dinner bell blow" certainly lets us know that the hit has ended the game.

The main element of a Goldsmith cartoon is his use of humor and sarcasm, especially when used to show the ineptitude of the opposing team. The cartoon from April 28, 1916, reviews a game in which the Braves defeated the Giants 3–2. The incident to poke fun at occurred in the fifth inning when umpire Bill Klem was so annoyed by the chatter coming from the New York bench that he banished all players to the dressing room. Only manager John McGraw and the batboy were allowed to remain in the dugout as shown in the small sketch. The scene of the players filing out across the field is portrayed as a parade with McGraw riding atop an elephant and the whole group being trailed by a circus wagon. In the sixth inning, John McGraw was ejected for using offensive language, apparently taken from the book he is holding, titled "McGraw's Vocabulary."

While the battles of World War I were being fought in Europe, Mr. Goldsmith often integrated a war theme into his work. The cartoon from September 3, 1914, illustrates when the Miracle Braves took the lead in the pennant race. A Brave is overhead snatching the flag from the New York Giants in an airship named "The Stallings Zeppelin" in reference to the Boston manager George Stallings. He is dropping two bombs, one labeled first game and the other labeled second game, which represents the Braves winning both ends of a doubleheader from the Phillies. In the background is a Brooklyn player setting off a mine, signifying their win over the Giants, all events which combined to cause the change in the standings.

In the cartoon that appeared on May 16, 1915, an Indian is shown getting blasted out of his canoe by a torpedo launched from a submarine piloted by a Pirate. You will notice that the canoe is named "9th" and the torpedo is labeled "6 hits in a row." In this game the Braves were leading Pittsburgh by a score of 6 to 4 when, in the ninth inning, the Pirates had a string of six consecutive hits and scored six runs to eventually win the game 10–6.

Equipment was often fashioned as weaponry, as in a cartoon from April 18, 1916, which shows Walter Johnson getting shot to pieces by a Gatling gun with barrels made of baseball bats. In that game the Red Sox batters tagged Johnson for 11 hits in his six innings of work, and Boston won by a score of 5–1.

One feature of the cartoons that really made an impression that this was a different era is the complete lack of political correctness and portrayals of seemingly acceptable stereotypes. There are many humiliating representations of Native Americans. When the Boston Braves won, they were shown as Indians on the warpath, shooting arrows at a foe or wielding knives and tomahawks. When they lost, they were the poor souls who have been relocated to a reservation, bent over a campfire with an empty pot hanging over it.

During the war years players of German descent were sometimes pictured with spiked helmets like the ones worn by the German soldiers in the trenches of France. In the cartoon from May 26, 1915, Cincinnati's players Buck Herzog, Fritz Von Kolnitz, and Fritz Mollwitz are shown in this capacity and acting quite militaristic in the sketch where they are ordering the ball to roll foul.

I believe that you really must admire Wallace Goldsmith's portfolio of work at the *Boston Globe*. His cartoons reviewing the Red Sox and Braves games are impressive because he produced these pieces on a daily basis with each one being a unique and clever essay of the game. He was truly an imaginative and talented man.

# AFTER GEN McGRAW'S INVADING HOST PARADED, JOHN JOINED THE RETREAT

### By WALLACE GOLDSMITH.

*April 28, 1916: Giants make grand exit*

# BRAVES LAND A COUPLE OF BOMBS ON THE GIANTS

## By WALLACE GOLDSMITH.

*September 3, 1914: Braves take the lead*

# RARELY HAS THE PEERLESS SIR WALTER
## BEEN SO COMPLETELY RIDDLED WITH SHOT
### By WALLACE GOLDSMITH.

*April 18, 1916: Walter Johnson shot to bits*

# About the Boston Pilgrims

by Bill Nowlin

My 2003 article, "The Boston Pilgrims Never Existed" was published in *The National Pastime* (#23) and covered the year 1903 press accounts in five Boston dailies and three other newspapers. I failed to find even a single reference to a Boston baseball team known as the Pilgrims.

On December 18, 1907, owner John I. Taylor decided that his 1908 team would wear red stockings and be known as the "Red Sox," as they have been since that time on.

A handful of readers have approached me, pointing out newspaper stories in the intervening years (between 1903 and 1908) where the team was indeed called the Pilgrims. Tom Spaulding was the first, and then Charlie Bevis, Glenn Currie, and Ed Coen all directed me to items they had located. Using SABR's access to ProQuest, I undertook a fresh look.

The first references to the Pilgrims, and the most frequent, turn up in the *Washington Post*. The moniker seems to have been one that writers for the *Post* enjoyed more than those in other cities, and around June 1906 there appear occasional usages. The first time I could find the *Boston Globe* use the term in a baseball story was an April 26, 1907, sports page cartoon declaring "There is no joy in Pilgrimville" following a particular defeat administered the Boston ball club by the Athletics. The *Globe*'s game account on May 15 used the nickname in both the fourth and fifth paragraph.

There is another mention of "Pilgrims" in the July 12, 1907, story and about another 10 uses before the year was out, more or less a baker's dozen of mentions in the one year—many fewer than in the *Washington Post*. The first use in the *Chicago Tribune* was found in the June 21, 1907, edition. The *Times* used the word "Pilgrims" an indicated 182 times during the 1907 baseball season, but never once in connection with baseball.

The 1907 *Boston Journal* interchangeably referred to the team as the Americans or Pilgrims throughout 1907, though more often as the Americans. The *Boston Herald* used the Pilgrims fairly frequently as well, probably a little more than half the time.

My conclusion? Sometime in 1906, perhaps influenced by the name of a touring soccer team, the *Washington Post* began to apply the nickname "Pilgrims" to Boston's American League baseball team, and during 1907 it caught on sufficiently in some Boston newspapers to be a short-lived nickname for the team. Had your time machine landed in 1903, and you were to ask, "Hey, how 'bout them Pilgrims?", Boston's baseball fanatics might not have understood the allusion. If you stuck around to catch a few more seasons, in 1907 they likely would have—though the 1906 team (49–105) is not one that any fan found engaging. And after the spring training suicide of skipper Chick Stahl, the 1907 team suffered through four managers while winning only 59 games. Taylor was no doubt right in thinking it was time to refashion the team, even as to its name.

So, the Boston Pilgrims actually did exist, at least in the minds of some writers for a while in 1907. By no means is there any indication that the nickname was commonly used, though it appears it might have been sufficiently familiar to have been understood at the time. It remains a wonderful name, but its appeal seems to have grown dramatically as the decades have passed. For clarity, Boston Americans remains unchallenged as the choice until 1908 and the Red Sox.

# Danny Gardella and the Reserve Clause

## by David Mandell

**D**ANNY Gardella's 24 home runs and three seasons of major league baseball may be forgotten, but his impact remains. Today's players enjoy independence and wealth unimaginable to previous generations. While Curt Flood, Andy Messersmith, and Dave McNally are often credited with winning free agency for baseball players, the battle of an outfielder from the Bronx, New York, opened the door.

Born in New York City on February 26, 1920, Gardella worked in shipyards and played in Bronx sandlot leagues. In the minor leagues Gardella made a name for himself as a strong hitter and risky fielder for the Jersey City Giants. On May 13, 1944, he homered for Jersey City and was called up to the New York Giants the next day. He played his first games in a doubleheader in Pittsburgh and three days later hit two singles and a triple against the Cubs. In June he hit a dramatic homer to defeat the Cubs, putting Hall of Famer Joe Medwick on the Giants bench. In his first two seasons Gardella batted .250 and .272 with 18 home runs in 1945. His older brother Al joined him for 16 games with the Giants.

As the 1946 season approached, the major leagues looked forward to the first season after World War II, with many stars returning from military service. Owners presumed that the players would quietly accept salaries dictated to them. Baseball's reserve clause bound a player to his team, and unless released, a player was forbidden to negotiate with any other team. The player either accepted what was offered or sat out the season in hopes that the owner would meet his demands. Under a 1922 United States Supreme Court ruling, major league baseball enjoyed immunity from anti-trust laws.

In 1946 things changed. Major league baseball

DAVID MANDELL *practices law in New London County, Connecticut, and is a lifelong Giants fan.*

faced its first serious challenge since the collapse of the Federal League decades earlier. Jorge Pasquel, the oldest of five brothers and three sisters, and President of the Mexican baseball league, decided to compete for the services of major league players. With a family fortune estimated at 60 million dollars, the Pasquels had the means to challenge the majors. Starting as cigar manufacturers, they now owned banking, ranching, and exporting businesses. Jorge Pasquel was so confident that he offered to bet skeptics two million dollars that his league would finish the season. Pasquel envisioned teams in Mexico City, Monterrey, San Luis Potosi, Toreon, Tampico, Veracruz, and Puebla stocked with American players. His brother Bernardo served as vice president.

When the New York Giants assembled for spring training in Miami, Danny Gardella stunned the baseball world. His contract of $4,500 had expired and the Giants offered $5,000 for the new season, assuming that the reserve clause would give him no choice but to accept it. But the 25-year-old Gardella had other plans. On February 18 he signed a five-year deal to play in Mexico, along with teammates Nap Reyes, Adrian Zabala, and Luis Olmo of the Dodgers. He defiantly told reporters, "You may say for me that I do not intend to let the Giants enrich themselves at my expense, by selling me to a minor league club after the shabby treatment they have accorded me. So I have now decided to take my gifted talents to Mexico."

On February 22 he became the first American player to arrive in Mexico. He told Mexican fans "I'm mighty glad I'm no longer connected with the New York Giants. They are paying me more so why shouldn't I play in Mexico?"

Major league baseball responded quickly. On March 10 Commissioner Happy Chandler warned players that they faced a five-year suspension if they played in Mexico. The Mexican season opened on

*Danny Gardella*

TRANSCENDENTAL GRAPHICS

March 23, and Gardella hit a two-run homer as his Veracruz Blues defeated the Mexico City Reds before 33,000 spectators. Mexico's president Manuel Avila Camacho threw out the first ball. Eight days later, second baseman George Hausmann and pitcher Sal Maglie announced that they would be leaving the Giants for Mexico. Dodger catcher Mickey Owen was next to sign with Pasquel, for a $12,500 bonus. Giants owner Horace Stoneham, who later moved the Giants from New York to San Francisco, denounced the players' disloyalty, saying, "So long as they wanted to go to Mexico, the quicker they went, the better. We no longer have any use for them."

Gardella was undaunted by his former owner's comments. On April 21 he hit two home runs against Monterrey. Pasquel kept up his raids on major league talent. April 26 saw him sign two more Giants, pitchers Harry Feldman and Ace Adams. By now eight Giants had "jumped" to Mexico. Mexican baseball achieved another milestone on May 16, when Babe Ruth attended a game and praised Pasquel for bringing top baseball to Mexico. At the July 9 all-star game Gardella hit two home runs and Admiral William F.

Halsey tossed out the first ball. The all-star game represented the high-water mark of Pasquel's Mexican league. Tensions soon rose between the highly paid imported major leaguers and the Mexican and Cuban players who had dominated Mexican baseball. In one game a fight erupted over a hard tag at the plate by catcher Mickey Owen on left fielder Claro Duany. Gardella and Ramon Heredia joined in. It was soon apparent that Mexico's small stadiums made maintaining the salaries of the Americans a challenge.

As the season wore down, Pasquel promised no further forays into the major leagues and by the next season his other American stars, Max Lanier, Ace Adams, Harry Feldman, George Hausmann, and Roy Zimmerman were gone. The Mexican league enacted limited payrolls and a mandatory number of Mexican citizens per team. Commissioner Chandler was unmoved. His ban still stood. Former Mexican League players, desperate to return to the majors, were reduced to barnstorming or playing abroad. Gardella played in Drummondville, Quebec, and worked as a hospital orderly in Mount Vernon, New York, earning 36 dollars per week. As the 1947 season passed with the ban on jumpers reaffirmed, Gardella was determined to rejoin the majors.

Gardella filed a federal suit against major league baseball seeking $300,000 in damages. His attorney, Frederic A. Johnson, accused the major leagues of violating the Clayton and Sherman anti-trust laws through its reserve clause, which permanently bound a player to his employer. An experienced constitutional lawyer, Johnson once served as law secretary for Judge Joseph Crater, the vanishing judge. Crater's last courthouse statement was "Don't forget to turn the lights out, Johnson," before leaving to dine out and take his fateful taxi cab ride. A law school classmate of Commissioner Chandler, Johnson was eager to challenge the reserve clause. Major league baseball used the same defense that had proven successful at the United States Supreme Court in 1922. Claiming that organized baseball was not interstate commerce but merely an amusement, it moved to dismiss the case. On July 14, 1948, U.S. District Judge Henry Goddard agreed.

Baseball rejoiced in the dismissal, but Gardella and Johnson weren't finished. They appealed to the United States Court of Appeals for the Second Circuit and drew a panel of appellate judges that included two of the most respected judges of the era, Learned

*Major league baseball's unequivocal interpretation of Danny Gardella's eligibility sparked an early battle over the reserve clause. Some ballplayers of note—including the aged Joe Jackson, himself banned—were reluctant to come to Gardella's aid; Most were apathetic; one was hostile. From left: Commissioner Happy Chandler, Joe Jackson, Bob Lemon, and Sal Maglie.*

JACKSON: TRANSCENDENTAL GRAPHICS  MAGLIE: ASSOCIATED PRESS
OTHERS: NATIONAL BASEBALL LIBRARY, COOPERSTOWN, NY

Hand and Jerome Frank. Appointed by President William Howard Taft as a trial judge in 1909, Hand was named as an appellate judge by President Calvin Coolidge in 1924. Jerome Frank was appointed chairman of the Securities and Exchange Commission by President Roosevelt in 1939 and nominated by Roosevelt as a federal appeals judge in 1941. Both judges were frequently mentioned as potential Supreme Court justices.

In a two to one decision, the Second Circuit reversed the dismissal on February 9, 1949, and ordered Gardella's case to trial. Hand and Frank voted with Gardella while Judge Harrie B. Chase sided with baseball management. Owners and general managers feared the end of the reserve clause and predicted the demise of professional baseball. Giants' attorney Edgar Feeley said the farm system would be destroyed and only a handful of top-salaried players would benefit. Branch Rickey, the Dodger general manager who signed Jackie Robinson, was not generous toward Gardella. Rickey warned that the reserve clause was opposed by players of communist tendencies. Cleveland Indians owner Bill Veeck was more circumspect, saying only, "I don't have the legal background necessary to say anything."

Gardella drew scant support from his fellow players. Fellow Mexican Leaguer Mickey Owen stated, "Danny is enjoying the notoriety of his damage suit. I hope he loses it." Stan Musial said, "I don't know much about the case but I think baseball has done all right for over a hundred years the way it is." Pitcher Bob Lemon added, "I can't see where it will do ballplayers any good."

Gardella and Johnson looked forward to the next round in court. Johnson promised to go right to trial. Gardella refuted the charges that he was damaging the national pastime. "They say I am undermining the structure of the baseball contract," he said "Let's say I'm helping to end a baseball evil. That's what it amounts to as far as I am concerned." Gardella received an unexpected boost when the United States Justice Department announced that it would begin an investigation of major league baseball and the antitrust laws.

Shoeless Joe Jackson, banned for life from the majors, remained neutral. "I'm sixty-one years old," he said "and it would not mean anything to me one way or the other."

Jumpers Max Lanier, Fred Martin, and Sal Maglie filed their own suits to gain reinstatement, but their cases were not as strong as Gardella's, who was not under any contract with major league baseball. Despite Gardella's win in the appeals court, he was still banned. United States District Court Judge Edward Conger refused to issue an injunction imposing reinstatement, and on June 3, 1949, the Second Circuit Court of Appeals ruled that Gardella must wait for his trial before it would intervene. Faced with the prospect of lengthy litigation and the end of the reserve clause, major league baseball decided to end the suspensions if players terminated their litigation.

On June 5, 1949, Chandler allowed the jumpers to return, and on August 27 Lanier and Martin dropped their suits. Gardella refused to withdraw his. With a November trial looming, attorney Johnson announced that under no circumstances would Gardella apply for reinstatement. Johnson deposed Commissioner Chandler, and both sides prepared for the trial. On October 7 at World Series headquarters in Brooklyn's St. George Hotel, Gardella surprised everyone by announcing that he was withdrawing the lawsuit and joining the St. Louis Cardinals for the 1950 season. Cards president Fred M. Saigh denied that Gardella received any cash for ending his case.

Gardella's stay with the Cardinals was short and unhappy. He played only one game for the Cards, going hitless in one at-bat. On April 25 the Cards sold him to Houston, a minor league team in the Texas League. On June 15 he returned to the Bronx, his baseball career over. Asked if he had received money to give up his claim, he said only, "You may say that Gardella was paid something to drop his suit. That is all." The Cardinals denied any blacklisting of Gardella, claiming that all major league teams had passed on his services.

Gardella was publicly silent until 1961, when he revealed that he received a $60,000 settlement from baseball to withdraw his lawsuit. "I felt like I was getting paid off, but being a poor man I felt more or less justified. It wasn't like I had a lot of money and was being paid off," he explained. Legal fees ate up about half of his award.

Following his baseball career Gardella worked in various jobs, including factory work, movers, truck driving, and sweeping. He died in Yonkers, New York, on March 6, 2005, at age 85, leaving 10 children and 27 grandchildren.

Gardella's attorney Frederic A. Johnson died at age 90 in 1985. After the Gardella case he continued practicing law for many years and served as an editor for the *New York Law Journal*. An ardent baseball fan throughout his life, he attended many games, and in 1982 he told reporters at Shea Stadium that he had seen about 1,000 games.

Jorge Pasquel died in a private plane crash on March 7, 1955. His Mexican league dissolved in 1953 and its remnants merged into organized baseball.

Baseball owners ousted Commissioner Chandler in 1951. Chandler returned to Kentucky politics and was elected governor again. In 1982 he was inducted into the Baseball Hall of Fame. He died on June 15, 1991. Chandler is remembered as the commissioner who oversaw the introduction of pensions and minimum salaries for players and the end of segregation in the majors. In comparison to his predecessor, Kenesaw Mountain Landis, he was seen as a players' commissioner.

Judge Learned Hand took senior status as a judge on June 1, 1951, and died on August 18, 1961. Judge Jerome Frank died on January 13, 1957, still an active judge at the Second Circuit Court of Appeals. Despite the respect they earned as appellate judges, neither was ever nominated to the U.S. Supreme Court.

Gardella's efforts to free baseball players of the reserve clause are barely recognized, perhaps because his lawsuit was settled and the issue was left for another day. Would he have been successful before the United States Supreme Court? No one will ever know, but owners were not taking any chances. Although he was termed a jumper, Gardella had not broken his contract. That placed him in a much stronger position than the other players who went to Mexico. In contrast to players who lost challenges, Gardella may have had the support of the United States government. Its announcement of an investigation of major league baseball surely spurred the resolution of his claim. Major league baseball would have been asking the Supreme Court to overrule two of the most esteemed judges in the lower courts, Hand and Frank. It is no surprise that major league baseball did not want the Gardella case before the Supreme Court.

In this era of free agency it would be unthinkable for any professional sport to bind a player to one team for his entire career. That this is so is due largely to the efforts of an unheralded outfielder from the Bronx.

# Bringing Home the Bacon
## How the Black Sox Got Back into Baseball

by Jacob Pomrenke

For the residents of Macomb, Illinois, it was a scene straight out of the movie *Field of Dreams*. The infamous "Black Sox" had mysteriously showed up in their town, on their field, ready to play.

Only they did not emerge from a mystical cornfield on the horizon, but rather a friend's automobile parked behind the grandstand. And "Shoeless" Joe Jackson wasn't the only one wanting to play; he brought his former major league teammates Eddie Cicotte and Charles "Swede" Risberg as well.

Just five weeks removed from the "Trial of the Century" (before there was even such a designation), a trial in which they were acquitted by a cheering jury and then promptly banished from the game by baseball's new commissioner, the three disgraced ballplayers were back in uniform for the first time.

The date was September 11, 1921.

Exactly one year earlier, Jackson, Cicotte, and Risberg were at Comiskey Park in Chicago—as they had been for most of the previous decade—battling for the American League pennant late in the season.[1] They did not realize that these were the final games of their professional careers.

On September 28, 1920, Cicotte walked into White Sox owner Charles Comiskey's office and confessed that he had plotted to "throw" the 1919 World Series to the Cincinnati Reds, an admission that sent shock waves around the country. Jackson followed Cicotte to testify to a grand jury convened in Chicago to investigate gambling in baseball. Under pressure from Comiskey and his lawyer, both players admitted their involvement in the fix, implicating six other teammates: Risberg, Lefty Williams, Chick Gandil, Happy Felsch, Fred McMullin, and Buck Weaver.

In February 1921, indictments were handed down against seven of the eight ballplayers (McMullin was spared for a lack of evidence) and two of the gamblers; a criminal trial began in June. Under a national spotlight, it took just over five weeks before the jury declared them not guilty of conspiracy on August 2. But their fate was sealed that same night. As they toasted their freedom in a party with members of the jury at a local Italian restaurant,[2] newly appointed baseball commissioner Kenesaw Mountain Landis was busy preparing a statement:

"Regardless of the verdict of juries, no man who throws a game, no player that entertains proposals or promises to throw a game, no player that sits in a conference with a bunch of crooked gamblers, where the ways and means of throwing a game are discussed, and does not promptly tell his club about it, will ever play professional baseball."[3]

Suddenly, their careers were over. None of them would ever set foot in a major league park again.

Cicotte, the oldest of the eight players, was just 37 years old. His only livelihood had disappeared, as had that of his teammates. Lacking any outside work experience and without the benefit of much more than an elementary education—McMullin had gone to high school in Los Angeles, but Weaver had quit school in the eighth grade and the famously illiterate Jackson was working by the time he was eight years old[4]—their prospects for the future were not bright.

So the "Eight Men Out" did the only thing they knew how: they went looking for a game.

Over the next decade they would travel throughout the country and even into Canada and Mexico just to play baseball for a living. Their road trips would not be to Detroit, Boston, and Washington anymore, but to dots on the map such as Douglas, AZ, Bastrop, LA, and Waycross, GA.

They played together and apart, for one semi-

JACOB POMRENKE, *a member of SABR since 1998, is a journalist who lives in San Bernardino, California. This is his first contribution to* The National Pastime.

pro game at a time and for whole seasons in outlaw leagues. They were celebrated and cheered by some fans, jeered and ridiculed by others. They stirred up controversy everywhere they played. It was a nomadic life that most of the players kept up for the rest of the 1920s and, for Weaver, Risberg, and Jackson, even into the 1930s. But barred from professional baseball—and taking grief from Commissioner Landis, who threatened to suspend anyone caught playing against the Black Sox—it was all they had left.

This is how Jackson, Cicotte, and Risberg found themselves suiting up for a game in a rural town in western Illinois less than five weeks after they stood on trial for conspiring to "fix" the World Series. The stakes here were much different, but they were just as meaningful to the towns involved—this was for the championship of McDonough County.

SINCE their inception in the early 19th century, the towns of Colchester and Macomb were engaged in a spirited battle on political, economic, and cultural levels. The county seat (Macomb) and the mining town on the outskirts (Colchester), connected at the time by one paved road and separated by just seven miles, were no different from thousands of other budding communities around the nation. And like the rest of America, nowhere was their rivalry more intense than on the baseball field.

By the end of World War I, both the Colchester and Macomb teams were very competitive around western Illinois, regularly beating the likes of surrounding communities such as Industry, Rushville, and Bushnell, as well as Negro traveling teams from Galesburg and Monmouth, and other barnstorming squads that passed through the area.

On June 19, 1921—eight days before the Black Sox trial began in Chicago—the McDonough County rivals met up at Colchester's Red Men Park for an early season grudge match. The field, on the north-

*Swede Risberg, left, and Joe Jackson, right, were banned from the major leagues in 1921, but played baseball in semipro leagues around the country until the early 1930s.*

RISBERG: NATIONAL BASEBALL LIBRARY, COOPERSTOWN, NY    JACKSON: TRANSCENDENTAL GRAPHICS

east side of town, was maintained by the Colchester team's sponsor, a fraternal group called the Improved Order of Red Men.

It was a good day to root for the home team. Colchester's 14–1 win caused *Colchester Independent* editor J. H. Bayless to write:

> Once upon a time, a bunch of nice young men in the city of Macomb had a dream. They dreamed that they were ball players and could beat most any team in these parts. . . . They undertook to use the Colchester Redmen [sic] as their first stepping stone to fame and fortune, but alas and alack, their plans miscarried and they were trampled on, figuratively speaking.[5]

The over-the-top boasting surely did not sit well with Macomb's proud civic leaders, adding a painful insult to the bruised egos they sustained in the loss. Macomb vowed the two-game series on Independence Day weekend would not have the same result.

Colchester predicted, as was the custom for many town teams in those days, that Macomb would find a way to improve its team for the next game—and they were right. Not a single one of the nine players who took the field for Macomb on July 3 had been with the team two weeks earlier.

Macomb's desire to win even overstepped racial boundaries. The new shortstop and cleanup hitter was Adolph "Ziggy" Hamblin, a black player from Galesburg who was a three-sport star at nearby Knox College.[6] Nearly 25 years before Jackie Robinson joined the Brooklyn Dodgers, employing a talented black player for an important game was not an unprecedented step for some semi-pro teams. Macomb also added, among others, a hard-hitting third baseman, "Boots" Runkle, a second baseman from Knox College named Welch, and an outfielder from Monmouth College who used the alias "Johnson."

Macomb's additions had the desired effect, as Colchester managed just five hits in a 3–0 loss. The second game, on July 4, was just as well-played, but Colchester pulled this one out to win 4–2 in the 13th inning on a two-run home run by one of their own new players, a right fielder named Marks.[7]

Both teams showed up at Red Men Park the following Sunday for what was supposed to be the deciding third game (apparently the June 21 result was discounted because both lineups had turned over so much). Macomb brought in another minor leaguer named Switzer, who had reportedly played for the Rock Island club of the Three-Eye League. Colchester took advantage of Ziggy Hamblin's absence—which was noted but not explained by the local newspapers—to win going away, 8–4.[8]

TEN days after that decisive third game in Colchester, the *Macomb Journal* published an Associated Press article about the Black Sox trial in Chicago, which garnered national headlines all summer long.

As the trial dragged on throughout July 1921, Shoeless Joe Jackson bided his time with friends at his successful South Side poolroom and cigar store on 55th Street in Chicago, which he had owned and operated for about a year. Students from the nearby University of Chicago popularized the hangout, which also may have been frequented by Henry "Kelly" Wagle on his trips to the big city. Wagle was a 35-year-old Colchester supporter who placed more than a rooting interest in the team's games against Macomb—usually a few dollars or more.

In Colchester, Wagle cultivated his image as a philanthropic businessman, generous to one and all, raised by an upstanding family, respected around town—and he was all of those things—but everyone knew what he really was: a bootlegger. Prohibition had opened the doors to organized crime in America's small towns, and Wagle was one of the most successful at his chosen profession this side of Al Capone. In fact, he soon became friends with the notorious mob boss, and Wagle often drove one of his flashy automobiles—in 1921 alone, he owned a black Ford, a white Cadillac, and a blue Marmon[9]—across Illinois' rural highways to meet Capone. In those years Wagle acquired most of his alcohol from a supplier at 35th and Halsted streets in Chicago,[10] about eight blocks from Comiskey Park, and near where many of the White Sox lived. The sociable Wagle no doubt struck up conversations with the players and likely even slipped them a quart of "booze" from time to time.

It was an especially difficult summer for the ballplayers, because baseball had turned its back on the "Eight Men Out." However, they still had plenty of opportunities to play for money—even in Chicago, where they passed the hat around the bleachers at White City Ball Park on Sunday afternoons before the trial began in July. Hundreds of fans showed up at the corner of 65th Street and South Park Avenue each weekend to see Jackson, Cicotte, Risberg, Gandil, and Williams, on a team promoted as the "South Side Stars," play the likes of the local Elks Club, the "Nebraska Indians," and the "Woodlawns."[11]

The Black Sox did not lack for offers to play in other cities, either. The *Boston Globe* reported that more than 50 towns had invited one or more of the players to a Sunday game, even as the trial was going on. The article stated that Jackson was "sought by half a dozen Wisconsin towns," Williams was wanted by "several Iowa points," and Cicotte had turned down several requests "as to whether he could pitch tomorrow [July 25]."[12]

While some more lucrative—and nearby—offers were eagerly accepted, many were turned down for various reasons, not the least of which being the very real possibility of jail time. So mostly they stayed at home in Chicago: Jackson managing his poolroom, Weaver tending his drugstore, Cicotte taking care of his family, all laying low on the South Side.

When Kelly Wagle asked for their assistance and athletic expertise in his hometown of Colchester, the request was met with indifference at first. But Wagle had a charming way of disarming even the most guarded of exiled ballplayers, and his advances did not go unnoticed. There would be money in it for the players, of course, and no hassles other than the customary catcalls from the bleacher bums when they showed up for the game—nothing they weren't used to by now. All Wagle asked was that the players not tell anyone but him if they chose to accept.

In the meantime, Lefty Williams was receiving a similar offer from backers of the Macomb team. Wagle had known about this ahead of time, having made it his habit as a bettor to be prepared for situations before they occurred, but he figured that Williams would not want to leave his wife, Lyria, in Chicago and travel to Macomb (250 miles away) for a game so soon after the trial. Wagle's assessment was accurate: the left hander would not be pitching for Macomb or Colchester, not now, not ever.

But Jackson seemed willing to listen to Wagle's offer, as did Risberg and Gandil, the two purported ringleaders of the 1919 World Series fix.[13] Cicotte was also interested; after declining most non-Chicago offers from various promoters during the summer, "Knuckles" said he wouldn't mind suiting up, too.

First, however, there was another game to play. WHILE Colchester was busy courting the Black Sox,

Macomb was securing the services of a right-handed fireballer who called himself "Frank Smith." Although his identity was never revealed, it was reported that Smith was a former hurler in the Three-Eye League and a St. Louis Browns farmhand. While his background and his pedigree remained a mystery, his talent was decidedly not. After joining Macomb in mid-July, Smith dominated in his first two starts over Bushnell and Industry, leading the *Macomb Journal* to boast that it was the clear—if unofficial—champion of McDonough County.

A game was scheduled for August 21 at Red Men Park, and talk soon began to swirl that both teams were trying to recruit more "ringers" for the highly anticipated contest. On August 18, the *Macomb By-Stander* reported that "rumor had it" Colchester was on the verge of bringing in players from Chicago—which was only half right. Colchester showed up for the game with two players from the *University of Chicago*, catcher Clarence Vollmer and a top semi-pro pitcher called "Adams."

Macomb countered with another minor leaguer, Jimmie Connors of Rock Island's Three-Eye League club, who played first base for Macomb. Now their roster was comprised of four collegiate players and three minor leaguers, including the pitcher. It was an imposing lineup and also a successful one. Frank Smith was his usual impressive self against Colchester, "a complete master of the situation from beginning to end" in a 4–0 shutout.[14]

It was "the most sensational game played in the mining city in the last decade," boasted the *Macomb Journal*—an exhibition worthy of an encore. A fifth and final game had already been scheduled, for September 11 at Macomb, before the 1,300 spectators had even cleared the grounds.

The upcoming "championship" game was the talk of both towns immediately afterward, and it would continue to be so until September 11—three weeks away. J. H. Bayless made a seemingly innocuous remark near the end of his game story in the *Colchester Independent*: "We believe that we can improve the team a little with some of our home boys." Bayless wasn't aware that the same idea had already passed through Kelly Wagle's mind.

IN the *Macomb Journal*, just below the box score signifying Macomb's victory over Colchester, was a small box labeled, "This Time Last Year." The final item mentioned that the Chicago White Sox were leading the American League standings one year ago—on August 22, 1920.

But that didn't matter to Joe Jackson, Eddie Cicotte, and their six former White Sox teammates—their major league careers were over for good. Commissioner Landis, a federal judge in Illinois since 1905, had laid down his own brand of the law when the law had failed to find the players guilty of any crime. His announcement that banned the players for life came just hours after the verdict was handed down in Chicago.

Organized baseball quickly made it clear that the "Eight Men Out" would not be welcomed back. The National Association, the game's ruling body, announced that it would not allow any of the Black Sox to play in the minor leagues, while many semi-pro leagues, such as the Lake Shore League in Sheboygan, WI, voted against the players' participation as well.[15]

The residents of McDonough County, however, had no such referendum on which to vote for or against the "baseball crooks." Kelly Wagle was very good at keeping a secret—his darkest one would not be uncovered until a year after his death.

Wagle's early efforts to secure the Black Sox had paid off. In addition to Jackson, Cicotte, and Risberg, Chick Gandil had also agreed to play against Macomb for a reasonable fee—in advance, of course. They had learned from their bungled World Series fix, when only Cicotte had received, on demand, a payment before game one. Gandil had spent the rest of the Series begging the gamblers for the money he had promised his teammates, with little success.

The Black Sox did not always ask for their money up-front; they knew that usually they could rake in far more by passing the hat around the bleachers during the game. But because their participation was to be unveiled on the day of the game, there would not be enough time to promote their presence, which was sure to bring in a larger crowd. While no records exist showing how much Wagle offered to pay the players, they likely received about $250 apiece, give or take a bottle of whiskey. That was the equivalent of two weeks' salary for a major league player making $6,000 per year, and easily affordable for Wagle. He planned to make much more on the game itself.

Money—whether it was because they were paid poorly or they simply were greedy—was a prime motivating factor for the Black Sox to consider fixing the World Series back in 1919. It was also the reason the players were willing to suit up for Colchester against Macomb. Because of their suspensions, they no longer were receiving paychecks from the White Sox. Jackson, Weaver, and Felsch later sued the team for back pay owed to them, but not until 1924, when it was getting harder for them to make ends meet simply by playing semi-pro and outlaw games around the country. A hundred dollars or two for an afternoon's work was easily worth the effort.

MEANWHILE, baseball fever was rising throughout McDonough County as the calendar turned to September.

Macomb's confidence was high in the days leading up to the "championship" game on September 11. The *Journal* wrote, "With a team not considered as fast as this, they defeated the Colchester importations before, and they believe they can do it again."[16]

By all accounts, Colchester's team had not changed. They still had "the three Chicago players engaged that they secured before, according to the dope from that city."[17] None of the three newspapers in McDonough County even hinted at the possibility that "the three Chicago players" were any different from Vollmer, Adams, and a semi-pro catcher by the name of "Kid" Standard, a distant relative of Dr. A. P. Standard, the newly elected president of the Macomb Fairgrounds Association. Kelly Wagle's secret was secure.

On Saturday, September 10, Wagle was busy meeting four out-of-towners who had arrived on the 6:18 P.M. train from Kansas City. It was Jackson, Cicotte, Risberg, and the catcher, Standard. Chick Gandil had also traveled with them from Oklahoma but missed the train in Kansas City after calling on some friends between connections. Before the ballplayers could be noticed by anyone in town, Wagle quickly whisked them up to Bushnell, a small community 15 miles northeast of Macomb, where they spent the night.

Finally, after all the hype that had been building for four months, it was time for the big game between Colchester and Macomb—a game that would be talked about in McDonough County for years to come.

SUNDAY, September 11, 1921, arrived quietly but with great anticipation. Game time was set for 3:00 P.M. at the Macomb Fairgrounds, and a typically large crowd was expected there when the unofficial championship of McDonough County was to be decided.

As the fans trickled in to the ball field, where additional wooden bleachers had been set up down the foul lines to accommodate the throng that would reach 1,611, they noticed nothing out of the ordinary. Adams was warming up with Clarence Vollmer on one side of the diamond, while Frank Smith was on the other side loosening up his arm with his catcher, a minor leaguer named Wilson. Members of the Macomb team joked with some Colchester players, asking them "if they wouldn't strengthen up a little in order that the fans could be insured [sic] of a good game." They didn't know what they were in for.

After a long pregame workout, and the crowd had gotten settled, three players in "rather seedy-looking uniforms" with World War I stars on their jerseys emerged from Kelly Wagle's automobile behind the grandstand. They began to play catch amidst "a painful silence" as the spectators strained to recognize their vaguely familiar faces.

Then umpire McPherron—whom Colchester tried to keep out of the game because he had once played for Macomb years before—stepped to home plate and announced the pitching matchups for both teams: "Battery for Colchester, Cicotte and Standard; Macomb, Smith and Wilson."[18]

According to J. H. Bayless in the *Independent*, it was "the surprise of a lifetime, as no one could conceive of the bigness of the deal, not thinking Colchester was able to handle a deal of this magnitude."

After the initial shock set in, the Macomb fans jeered lustily and team promoter Art Thompson protested that the game should not be played with the "blackest of the Black Sox" present. Noting the red, white, and blue rings on Cicotte's stockings—similar to those worn by the White Sox during the 1917 World Series—one heckler shouted, "You've got a lot of guts to wear those colors." During the game, Jackson was "frequently reminded of his record of working in the ship yards instead of Uncle Sam's army during the war" when he came to bat.[19]

The Black Sox players, however, had heard it all before and were not fazed by the negative reaction they received from the Macomb side. The Macomb fans had reason to be distressed. As the game began, it was clear that Cicotte was as sharp as he had ever been in the American League. A roster of college boys and imported minor leaguers, even though it had dominated the local competition all summer, was no match for the knuckleballer's dazzling array of pitches—the emery ball, drop ball, and, of course, his famous "shine" ball—which had helped him win 208 games, including 35 shutouts, since 1908.

J. H. Bayless explained: "Cicotte simply toyed with the batters, not passing a man and striking them out when necessary. (Connors) of Rock Island, the idol of Macomb fans, struck out every time he was at bat. . . . Not a Macomb man reached second except McPherron!"[20]

Cicotte allowed just four singles—all but one of those coming to the bottom half of the order—and struck out 10. He beared down especially hard on Wilson, per request of Kelly Wagle, who had bet that the Macomb catcher would not record a hit. Wilson struck out all three times and did not so much as register a foul tip.

Jackson and Risberg were equally impressive in the field. On one base hit by Boots Runkle to left, Jackson "loafed" a little to bait Runkle into trying for second, which he did. But "old Joe tried out his good right arm and Risberg did the rest." For his part, Risberg chased one high fly deep into the outfield and made a running catch over his shoulder that brought many cheers from the Colchester side.[21]

The presence of the Black Sox even seemed to elevate the play of their teammates, as Clarence Vollmer and Kid Standard each recorded two hits and the third baseman, Boyle, had a double and two singles. Cicotte gave his club the lead in the second inning, as Hamblin muffed his hard grounder to short, letting Standard score with the first run. Risberg also drove in the former Chicago ace with a run in the fourth. Jackson (who had an off-day, going 1-for-5 with a strikeout), Adams, and Vollmer all scored, while every starter but John Kipling recorded a hit.

Colchester's 5–0 victory was a decisive one, and the debate over its legitimacy had already begun long before the game was over.

Both Macomb newspapers were heavy-handed in their criticism of Colchester, noting, "They allowed a desire to win a game to override their better judgment on sportsmanship in general. . . . It is certain that the local team will not again play against those players whom Judge Landis has barred from professional baseball because of their alleged crookedness."[22]

The *By-Stander* added: "Colchester won a ballgame yesterday and Macomb lost one—but both teams lost something that means a lot more than winning or losing. . . . It is not 'sport' to engage or play these men

NATIONAL BASEBALL LIBRARY, COOPERSTOWN, NY   INSET: TRANSCENDENTAL GRAPHICS

*Eddie Cicotte, who was 208–149 in 14 years for Boston and Chicago (AL), expressed regret for his role in the 1919 World Series scandal. He disappeared from the public eye after he was banned for life in 1921.*

who have sold out their clubs and their friends. If the 'Black Sox' are 'out in the sticks to get the money,' as one player put it, the *By-Stander* won't give any of its space to help them do it."[23]

Colchester fans—and in particular, the unabashed *Independent* editor, J. H. Bayless—were nothing short of ecstatic after "pulling over a fast one" on the county seat. He wrote: "A mighty cheer went up from those from Colchester, Industry, Rushville, Bushnell and nearly every place except Macomb. . . . Even when Cicotte, Risberg and Jackson—men of worldwide reputation, perhaps the best there is—were making apparently impossible plays, the Macomb fans refused to be moved to cheers. We don't wonder, for they are a hard bunch of losers.

"The Colchester Redmen Base Ball team are champions of McDonough County!"[24]

### Epilogue

SPEEDING out of the Macomb Fairgrounds after the game, with the Black Sox and Kid Standard in tow, Kelly Wagle could not have been more satisfied with his celebrated accomplishment.

But his story—and the players'—was one of dark secrets and tragic endings.

The skeleton in the players' closet was, of course, well-known. They would pay for their sins every time they stopped on a ramshackle field in some rural town, knowing that their skills were more suited for a well-manicured diamond in a major league city.

Shoeless Joe Jackson, by far the most famous of the banished eight, went back to his dry-cleaning business in Savannah, GA, and was largely forgiven by the Southern people he so dearly loved. They still considered Jackson one of their own, and his smashing line drives and circus catches earned him great acclaim when he led his Americus, GA, team in the independent South Georgia League to the "Little World Series" championship in 1923. He was "the biggest attraction the league ever had."[25]

Later, he moved back home to Greenville, SC, and opened a successful liquor store on the west end of town. He finally stopped playing baseball in 1933, at age 45, but continued teaching youngsters the game and stayed involved in the game. A few years later, he was invited to serve as chairman of the protest board for the Western Carolina Semi-Pro League, and he held the post for the rest of his life.[26]

Jackson continued to deny his involvement in the Black Sox scandal and said, "I know in my heart that I played to the best of my abilities."[27] He died of a heart attack on December 5, 1951, just days before he was to appear on a television special to publicize his case for reinstatement.

Eddie Cicotte stayed around Chicago for another year and played ball with Risberg (and sometimes against Felsch, Weaver, or Williams) on a barnstorming team called the Ex-Major League Stars in 1922. But he and Risberg had a falling-out that summer after Cicotte demanded his money up-front and the shortstop responded by punching him in the mouth, knocking out two of his teeth![28]

After 14 years in the big leagues and another two years playing exhibition games in Illinois, Minnesota, and Wisconsin, Cicotte had grown tired of being away from his family all the time, so he moved back home to his farm outside Detroit. He continued playing ball on infrequent occasions, but made his living as a paymaster at a Ford motor plant in Highland Park, MI, and spent his final years raising strawberries.[29]

He disappeared from the public eye until 1963, when Eliot Asinof's authoritative work on the 1919 World Series scandal, *Eight Men Out*, was published. He gave several interviews thereafter and expressed regret for his role in the scandal. Cicotte died quietly at age 84, on May 5, 1969, in Farmington, MI.

Swede Risberg moved to Rochester, MN, and bought a farm there in the early 1920s. But he spent the rest of the decade touring the northern part of the country and Canada—often playing with or against Happy Felsch—during the summer.

Like many barnstorming stars, Risberg found that more money could be made as a pitcher and, while he had pitched professionally only in the low minor leagues as a teenager, he spent most of his post-major league career on the mound. His travels took him to Duluth and Hibbing, MN (1922–24), Scobey, MT (1925), Watertown and Lignite, SD (1926–27), Manitoba and Saskatchewan (1927–29), Jamestown, ND (1929–30) and Sioux Falls, SD (1931–32) before he finally hung up his spikes for good.[30]

In 1927, he and Chick Gandil were "the center of baseball controversy" after claiming that the entire White Sox team had paid members of the Detroit Tigers to intentionally lose games to them 10 years earlier. Judge Landis called for an investigation and they went to Chicago, along with dozens of other major league stars—including their ex-Black Sox teammate, Buck Weaver—to testify in the matter. But Weaver failed to corroborate their story, instead making a dramatic plea for his own reinstatement, and Landis dismissed the charges.[31] Quietly, Risberg returned home to Minnesota.

The Great Depression hit Swede and his family hard, as it did millions of other Americans, and they lost their home, a car agency, a hotel, and their farm.[32] Risberg worked many odd jobs for the next two decades—including shoveling corn for a dollar a day in Sioux Falls, SD—before opening a successful nightclub called Risberg's on the California-Oregon border. He worked as a correspondent for the *Red Bluff Daily News* during the 1970 World Series, providing analysis on Brooks Robinson, Pete Rose, Jim Palmer, and Johnny Bench, et al (although he erred on his prediction of Cincinnati to win).

Risberg remained in good health over the years, despite walking with a decided limp for most of his life. An old spike wound that had never healed forced him to get surgery—still a risky procedure before World War II—which gradually deteriorated the circulation below his knee. Later in life, after moving in with his son Robert's family in Red Bluff, Risberg's leg was amputated and he spent his final years in a wheelchair at a convalescent home. He died of cancer on his 81st birthday, October 13, 1975, the last surviving member of the Black Sox. Unlike most of his banished teammates, he never claimed innocence or applied for reinstatement from baseball.[33]

Kelly Wagle, the mastermind of Colchester's most memorable victory, continued circumventing the law throughout the Roaring Twenties, doing his best to avoid prosecution by the various civic leaders brought in to "clean up" McDonough County.

He was arrested for the first and only time in 1927, when he spent six months in jail for illegally possessing and transporting liquor. But soon he was back to bootlegging, expanding his operation all the way to Iowa, Nebraska, and Missouri with the help of several partners.[34] But with greater success also came threats to that success, and Wagle had a history of using the same violent methods favored by his friend Al Capone to dispel those threats.

Back in 1919, Wagle had quietly followed his wife, Beulah, to Omaha, NE, after she had sold $1,400 worth of his alcohol to a bootlegger from Galesburg and left town with her lover. On November 20, a woman's body was found with a bullet wound in her head, lying facedown at the bottom of an embankment near a little-used country road outside of Omaha.[35] The *Omaha Bee* published a gruesome photograph of the corpse asking for help in identifying her, but no one was able to. The crime remained unsolved . . . for 11 years. In 1930, two enterprising reporters for the *Omaha World-Herald*, with the help of a *Chicago Tribune* staffer, located Beulah's father in nearby Carthage, IL, and finally confirmed (through dental records) the identity of the "Omaha Mystery Girl": Beulah Wagle.[36]

By then, however, Kelly Wagle was dead—murdered in a drive-by shooting on the streets of Colchester on April 8, 1929. His death was never officially solved, but as his widow, Blanche, told a local newspaper later, "Everybody knows who did it." Wagle's gangland-style death—orchestrated by his former partner-turned-chief rival, Jay Moon, who was engaged to Kelly's sister—was reminiscent of something put on by Al Capone, such as the infamous "St. Valentine's Day Massacre" that occurred in Chicago earlier that year.

It also signaled the end of an era for Colchester.

The death of the most notorious man in McDonough County brought about a revitalized effort to enforce Prohibition and stop the violence and lawlessness of the bootlegging days. After the 18th Amendment was repealed in 1933, Colchester voted not to allow alcohol sales four years later—and the town has been dry ever since.[37]

Macomb discontinued its Independence Day fair in 1928, and the Fairgrounds was sold to the city's Board of Education two years later. All the buildings were removed, except for an old horse barn in the southwest corner of the grounds. The baseball field where the Black Sox had once played became the high school's athletic facility for the next decade, but it fell into disrepair and was abandoned by World War II, then deeded to the state for an armory site.[38]

But the extraordinary events that took place on September 11, 1921, were never forgotten. Decades later, the famous Black Sox game was said to be the "most exciting thing that ever happened in Colchester," according to Tom Smith, who operated the Princess Theatre there until it closed down in 1954.[39] Some might say it remains so today.

Because for one day, at least, Macomb was a major league city with major league baseball. And for that one day, because of the slick ingenuity of Henry "Kelly" Wagle, the Colchester Red Men team was the champion of McDonough County.

## Notes

1. "1920 Chicago White Sox." BaseballLibrary.com.
2. Asinof, Eliot. *Eight Men Out*, New York: Henry Holt & Co., 1963; 273.
3. *Chicago Tribune* (August 4, 1921).
4. Gropman, Donald. *Say It Ain't So, Joe.* New York: Lynx Books, 1988; 17.
5. *Colchester Independent*, June 23, 1921.
6. Hallwas, John. "Bootlegger notes." Western Illinois University library archives.
7. *Colchester Independent*, July 7, 1921; *Macomb Journal*, July 5, 1921.
8. *Colchester Independent*, July 14, 1921; *Macomb Journal*, July 20, 1921.
9. Hallwas, John. *The Bootlegger.* Urbana, Ill.: University of Illinois Press, 1998; 180.
10. *Ibid* 178.
11. Classified advertisements, *Chicago Tribune*, June 18, 1921; June 25, 1921; July 2, 1921.
12. *Boston Globe*, July 24, 1921.
13. Gandil, Arnold, as told to Melvin Durslag. "This is My Story of the Black Sox Series." *Sports Illustrated*, September 17, 1956.
14. *Macomb Journal*, August 22, 1921.
15. *Los Angeles Times*, August 6, 1921; *Chicago Tribune*, August 7, 1921.
16. *Macomb Journal*, September 9, 1921.
17. *Ibid.*
18. *Colchester Independent*, September 15, 1921.
19. *Macomb Daily By-Stander*, September 12, 1921.
20. *Colchester Independent*, September 15, 1921; *Chicago Tribune*, April 23, 1962.
21. *Macomb Daily By-Stander*, September 12, 1921; Hallwas, 186.
22. *Ibid.*
23. *Ibid*; *Macomb Daily By-Stander*, September 16, 1921.
24. *Colchester Independent*, September 15, 1921.
25. Gropman, 204; Bell, John, *Shoeless Summer.* Carrollton, GA.: Vabella Publishing, 2001.
26. Gropman, 218; *New York Times*, December 6, 1951.
27. Bisher, Furman. "This Is the Truth", *Sport*, October 1949.
28. *Chicago Tribune*, June 23, 1922; *Los Angeles Times*, June 4, 1922.
29. *New York Times*, May 9, 1969.
30. Muchlinski, Alan. *After the Black Sox: The Swede Risberg Story.* Bloomington, IN: AuthorHouse, 2005. *Washington Post*, January 10, 1927; Lardner, John. "Remember the Black Sox?" *Saturday Evening Post*, April 30, 1938.
31. *Chicago Tribune*, January 5–7, 1927; March 13, 1927; *New York Times*, October 16, 1975.
32. Muchlinski, 108.
33. Smith, Red. "Last of the Black Sox." *New York Times*, November 2, 1975.
34. Hallwas, 228.
35. *Ibid* 164.
36. Hallwas, 258; *Chicago Tribune*, August 24, 1930; *Washington Post*, August 24, 1930.
37. Hallwas, 266.
38. Western Illinois University archives, "Macomb Fairgrounds."
39. *Chicago Tribune*, April 23, 1962.

# "Why, They'll Bet on a Foul Ball"
## The Southern Association Scandal of 1959

### by Warren Corbett

CHATTANOOGA Lookouts first baseman Jess Levan was the last man to be banned from professional baseball for trying to fix games.

The uproar surrounding Levan's banishment in 1959 revealed evidence linking other players to widespread gambling in Southern ballparks. The Southern Association scandal was either, as *The Sporting News* dismissed it, "relatively insignificant,"[1] or a potentially lethal danger that was deftly covered up by baseball authorities.

The story has a whistle-blower, but it has no resolution. That's because the story has no Judge Landis. No Bart Giammati. No John Dowd. Nobody who followed the evidence wherever it led. The baseball authorities were eager to let the story die.

The whistle-blower was Sammy Meeks, veteran infielder and first-base coach for the Mobile Bears. Meeks told baseball investigators that Levan had approached him in a Mobile hotel before a series between the two teams and introduced him to a gambler. Meeks was offered an unspecified amount of money to participate in a scheme that amounted to sign-giving rather than sign-stealing: from the coach's box, he was to watch the Lookouts' shortstop, Waldo Gonzalez. If Gonzalez stood erect, it signaled a fastball; if he crouched, it meant a curve.

Meeks said he declined to take money, but agreed to relay the signs to Mobile batters because he thought it would give his team an edge.

While Meeks, Levan, and the gambler were talking in the hotel bar, another Mobile player, shortstop Andy Frazier, joined the conversation. Frazier agreed to take the signs from Meeks.[2]

In the first game of a June 6 doubleheader, Frazier said, Meeks tipped him on two pitches—and both tip-offs were wrong. Mobile won the game, 7–3, when first baseman Gordy Coleman hit a grand-slam home run off Chattanooga's Jim Kaat, but there was no evidence that Coleman knew what was coming.[3]

The 35-year-old Meeks was released by Mobile June 18 and joined Chattanooga two days later. Shifting his loyalty to his new club, he told Lookouts' catcher Ray Holton about the incident. Holton alerted manager Red Marion and Marion reported it to the team's president, Joe Engel. The information was relayed to George Trautman, president of the National Association of Professional Baseball Leagues, the governing body of the minors.

Trautman sent his assistant, Phil Piton, to meet Engel, Southern Association President Charlie Hurth, and the Lookouts in Nashville July 3.[4]

The executives questioned all Chattanooga players under oath, with a stenographer recording the interrogations, in a five-hour session at Nashville's Andrew Jackson Hotel[5] and uncovered more evidence against Jess Levan.

Jim Heise, a 26-year-old right-handed pitcher, revealed that Levan had approached him twice asking whether he wanted "to make a little money" by serving up fat pitches. Heise said he declined.[6]

Another pitcher, 22-year-old left hander Tom McAvoy, testified that Levan had approached him in Mobile and asked "whether he would like to throw a game." McAvoy said he thought Levan was joking.[7]

Jess Levan was a first baseman—like fixers Chick Gandil and Babe Borton 40 years earlier—who had failed to stick in three brief big league trials. The six-foot left-handed slugger from Reading, Pennsylvania, signed his first professional contract in 1944, but lost the next two years to military service.[8] The Phillies gave him nine at-bats as a 20-year-old in 1947, and then he disappeared into the minors except for a 1950 spring training tryout with the Browns.[9] He was a

WARREN CORBETT, *a former batting champion of the Bearden, Tennessee, Little League, is the editor of a trade publication in Washington.*

career .316 hitter in the minors.[10] A .412 average in 29 games with Charlotte brought him to the parent Washington club's attention in 1954. Charlotte's manager, the cracker-barrel wit Ellis Clary, said, "I wrote to Calvin Griffith that Levan could do him some good if hitting was still going to be a part of baseball."

The next spring, Washington owner Clark Griffith likened him to Hall of Famer Goose Goslin, the best hitter in the franchise's history, saying, "His kind don't come along very often." Manager Chuck Dressen and *Washington Post* writer Shirley Povich touted him as the Nats' answer to World Series pinch-hitting hero Dusty Rhodes. Povich said Levan was "not much outfielder and not much first baseman." Dressen quipped that his best position was "at bat."[11]

With President Eisenhower in the stands on opening day in 1955, Levan lined a game-tying pinch single.[12] But he delivered only two hits in 15 at-bats over the next month,[13] and went from Dusty Rhodes to "hit the road." He returned to the minors. At 28, his days as a prospect were over.

In July 1959, shortly before his 32nd birthday, Levan was in his fourth season with AA Chattanooga and was the club's all-time home run leader with 83.[14] He was batting .337.[15]

Questioned by Hurth, Engel, and Piton, he first denied Sammy Meeks' accusations, but acknowledged that he had introduced Chattanooga players to "an individual unknown to him, but obviously a gambler . . . Levan was to receive an unstated amount of money for his services." He insisted he never received any money and "he knew nothing of any program to throw games by the deliberate tipping of signs."

As to Heise's testimony, "Levan admitted the contacts, but continued to insist that he did not know the real purpose of them." He denied McAvoy's accusation altogether.

Levan's questioners then asked, in effect, "C'mon, you must have known that this gambler wanted to fix games." Levan replied, "Yes, sir, I'll agree."

With that, Levan ended his baseball career.

When confronted by Sammy Meeks, he confessed to a scheme involving signs tipped by Gonzalez, the 25-year-old Cuban shortstop. Gonzalez, called into the room, reluctantly admitted that Levan had discussed the idea with him, but denied taking part.[16]

When the interrogation was finished, Southern Association President Hurth announced that Levan and Gonzalez were suspended indefinitely for "failure to report a bribery attempt by a gambler." But he said there was no evidence that either man took any money. The case was forwarded to the National Association for a final ruling.[17]

The suspensions spurred several sportswriters to ask questions about gambling, a subject that was obviously familiar to them.

On July 28, Bob Christian of the *Atlanta Journal* reported that the suspensions "could be just one scratch on the surface of gambling activities involving Southern Association players." Christian's story was not about game fixing; he focused on gamblers in the stands who bet on foul balls. Relying on a source "masked in deepest secrecy," he charged that players on "several if not all teams" in the league cooperated with gamblers by deliberately fouling off pitches.

"Betting on foul balls has become increasingly popular in the league's parks, replacing much of the 'action' that formerly was placed on 'fly balls,'" he wrote. He quoted odds set by bookies on whether a player would hit a foul, such as "three-to-one on [one of] the next three pitches" or "three-to-two on any pitch."

Christian continued, "Betting on Southern Association baseball, once big business, has declined steadily this year." He quoted an unnamed gambler in one league city: "I used to handle $60,000, maybe $70,000, on a good weekend. But this year I don't think that I handled that much for the whole season [through July]."[18] The league's shrinking attendance is the likely explanation; the 1959 attendance of just over 600,000 for eight teams was the lowest since the war-shortened 1918 season.[19] By September both the Atlanta and Chattanooga franchises were threatening to fold.[20]

The next day Bud Shrake of the *Dallas Times-Herald* chimed in, quoting a former Southern Association player as saying that Chattanooga's Engel Stadium was "nothing but a gambling casino."[21] The anonymous player added that deliberate fouling of pitches "has been done by some players in the league for years."[22]

Shrake said one player, later identified as shortstop Jack Caro, then with Dallas (Texas League), reported "a stranger" had offered him $700 in 1953 to hit three straight fouls, but he refused, partly because he didn't think he could do it.[23]

*Chattanooga Times* sports editor Wirt Gammon, sticking up for his hometown, tried to play down the allegations. He said his contacts in the gambling community reported that betting on foul balls was just "dollar-exchanging"; the bets seldom amounted to more than $20.[24]

The allegations against Jess Levan were not about foul balls. On July 30, National Association President Trautman handed down his ruling: "For admittedly acting as liaison for a gambler in a program designed to throw Chattanooga games, Jesse Levan is hereby placed on the permanently ineligible list."[25]

Trautman said Levan was the first man to be banned for life since a player in the Carolina League in 1948. He declined to identify that player on the grounds that he had become "a respectable citizen." (The player was pitcher-manager Barney DeForge of the Reidsville club.[26])

Waldo Gonzalez, who did or did not relay his catcher's signs, was suspended for one year.[27] Trautman justified the lenient sentence because both Levan and Gonzalez testified that Gonzalez refused to pass the signs.[28]

No other player was disciplined, either because they did not go along with the attempted fix or because they thought it a joke or, in the case of Andy Frazier, who received misleading signals, because he "told the truth."[29]

Trautman's public statement is long and detailed, but it conceals more than it reveals. The statement records nothing beyond what the players said. Levan's contention that he did not know the gambler in Mobile is not challenged. There is no indication in the public record that Levan or anyone else was asked to name the gambler. There is no indication that he was questioned about how he hooked up with this mystery man or about the identity of those who put him up to his earlier approaches to pitcher Jim Heise. Trautman's statement does not reveal any effort to examine Levan's bank records to confirm his claim that he took no money.

The Chattanooga Times' Gammon reported, "Testimony brought out, but did not reveal for publication, [the gambler's] first name, his type of build, and what European stock he comes from. Will they catch him?"[30] No.

In fact, Trautman's ruling was written to reassure the public that Levan was merely a lone rogue, if a stupid one. In his first finding, Trautman asserts that after "intensive" questioning, all other Chattanooga players were found innocent.

He mentions no interrogation of other Mobile players besides Frazier and Meeks.

In the next paragraph, he declares, "No proof was obtained at this hearing, or elsewhere as the investigation progressed, that a game or games had actually been 'thrown.'"[31] If the investigation did progress "elsewhere," Trautman's statement does not say where or how.

Levan denied the charges. "If Meeks was approached, he was approached by a gambler. I did not approach him," he said. "I have never been a contact man for any gambler who tried to throw Chattanooga games, as I understand I have been charged. . . . This thing has been quite a shock. . . . I never approached anybody with a proposition to throw a Chattanooga ball game."[32]

"Levan plans to hock his car to hire a lawyer to appeal his life suspension," The Chattanooga Times reported.[33] An appeal was a vain hope; Commissioner Ford Frick had already commented, "It looks as if they had them dead to rights."[34]

Trautman later disclosed that Levan had given further testimony in July, recounting that he and other players had been approached by gamblers in 1959 and asked to throw a doubleheader between Chattanooga and Mobile. He said the players refused. Again, no gamblers were named.[35]

The banishment of Levan had its "say it ain't so" moment. That was the headline above a UPI story in the August 2 Atlanta Journal: "Say It Ain't So, Jesse." It recounted how 10-year-old Lookouts batboy Bo Short, vacationing with his family in Daytona Beach, Florida, learned of his favorite player's disgrace. "It's like a bad dream," he told UPI, "choking back tears." Bo had gone to spring training with his father, Chattanooga Times sportswriter George Short, and Levan had helped him with his homework: "He told me I had to study my lessons and do the right thing."[36]

The scandal also produced the ritual hand-wringing. The Chattanooga Times reported, "The FBI is on this case."[37] The Chattanooga district attorney asked for a transcript of the ballplayers' testimony.[38] A Mobile newspaper called for a grand jury investigation.[39] Atlanta Journal reporter Bob Christian was invited to tell what he knew to a Georgia grand jury.[40]

No further reports on any of those investigations ever appeared.

But that was not the end of it. As a result of the news stories about betting on foul balls, Trautman's assistant Phil Piton conducted another round of interviews in August with former Southern Association players. Jack Caro of Dallas admitted that he was the player who turned down $700 to hit foul balls. Caro said he told about it after the Levan case was publicized, but at the time he thought it was a joke. Piton said Caro was the only player to admit knowledge of such activities. He was not disciplined.[41]

In November, Trautman decreed a second lifetime ban, this time for the only player who admitted taking money from gamblers. Former major league catcher Joe Tipton had confessed to the baseball investigators that he received payoffs for hitting foul balls while he was playing for Birmingham against Chattanooga in 1957. His take: $50 from Jess Levan, an additional $75 received in the mail. Tipton said Levan had put him up to it.

Tipton also revealed that he had been approached in Birmingham in 1958 by a gambler who said he was from Chattanooga, and who asked him to persuade other players to hit foul balls for money. Again, no gambler was named.

The 37-year-old Tipton was out of baseball by 1959. Trautman said he had come forward "because of his desire to clear his conscience."[42]

Trautman also announced that Levan's appeal had been denied.

And that *was* the end of it. Jess Levan was banished, claiming all the while that he never received any money. Joe Tipton was banished for taking the piddling sum of $125.

Levan's gambler contacts? No follow-up. Betting in other parks? No follow-up. The Chattanooga ballpark was "a gambling casino?" No follow-up. An examination of *The Sporting News* and several daily newspapers for a year after the scandal turned up no additional stories.

In its year-end roundup of baseball activities in 1959, *The Sporting News* dismissed the incident as "a blown-up gambling scandal in the minors that promised to shake the foundations of the game yet proved relatively insignificant. . . . [T]he probe led to the uncovering of little gambling activity and that directed to betting on foul balls."[43]

Not that gambling and baseball were strangers, 40 years after the Black Sox and 30 years before Pete Rose. *The Sporting News* published the Las Vegas betting line on the 1960 major league pennant races: Yankees, 4–5; Braves 7–5.[44] In July 1960, Chicago police arrested 20 bleacherites in a gambling raid at Wrigley Field. The "Baseball Bible" reported, "Hundreds of dollars were wagered, sometimes just on the umpire's calls on balls and strikes." Commissioner Frick had called the cops after finding that "gambling conditions at the Cubs' park were among the worst in the majors."[45] There were many other published reports of police raids on gamblers in major and minor league parks in the 1940s and 1950s.[46]

The story of the Southern Association scandal went away, but the gamblers in the ballparks did not. Four years later, Ed Doherty, a veteran baseball executive who was general manager of the Nashville Vols (then in the Sally League after the Southern Association folded), pointed the team's new play-by-play broadcaster toward a group of men sitting behind the third-base dugout. "They're gamblers," Doherty warned. "I don't want you to mention them on the air."

The young announcer had heard of the Black Sox and naively believed that Commissioner Kenesaw Mountain Landis had driven the gamblers out of baseball. "What do they bet on?" he asked.

"They'll bet on anything," Doherty replied. "Why, they'll bet on a foul ball."[47]

---

### 15 MEN OUT

Jess Levan and Joe Tipton were among 15 minor league players banned on gambling-related charges from 1920 to 1959. The others:

#### Merry Christmas, Babe

First baseman William Baker "Babe" Borton of the Pacific Coast League Vernon Tigers and Harl Maggert, William Rumler, and Gene Dale of Salt Lake City were kicked out in 1920 for allegedly fixing the 1919 PCL pennant race.

Opposing players testified that Borton had offered them bribes "to lay down in games against Vernon, so Vernon could win the pennant"—as it did.[48]

Borton confessed, but sloshed gasoline on the fire: He claimed his Vernon teammates had raised a pool to pay off their opponents. His teammates denied it. League president W. H. McCarthy believed Borton was covering for a gambling syndicate that had put up the money.

In December a Los Angeles County grand jury indicted Borton, Maggert, Rumler, and Nate Raymond, an alleged gambler from Seattle, for criminal conspiracy to fix games. The grand jury named two dozen people who allegedly put up a bribe pool of $3,995, including Roscoe Arbuckle (the real name of silent-film star Fatty Arbuckle, a part-owner of the Vernon club) and S. Goldwyn. (Samuel Goldwyn, the "G" in MGM, was a pioneer movie producer.)

On Christmas Eve a judge dismissed the charges because fixing games was not a crime under California law.[49]

Salt Lake City pitcher Gene Dale never spoke to the grand jury or to baseball investigators. Borton named him as one who had taken payoffs.[50]

Borton, 32, had played regularly for St. Louis of the Federal League in 1915 and had trials with three American League teams. Maggert, a 37-year-old outfielder, had played briefly in the majors as far back as 1907. Outfielder Rumler, 29, had played part-time in three seasons with the Browns. (He was later reinstated.[51]) Dale, 31, had pitched in the majors with the Reds and Cardinals.[52]

*Last man out: Jesse Levan in a 1948 photo.*

### A Gloomy Right hander

PITCHER Julio Bonetti of the PCL Los Angeles Angels was released in 1941 for associating with gamblers. A private detective hired by the team saw Bonetti take a handful of cash from an alleged gambler a few hours before he started, and lost, a game. Bonetti at first denied it, but eventually said he had placed a bet on a horse race for the gambler. He insisted he did not throw the game.

Sinker-balling right hander Bonetti, 28, had won 20 games for the Angels in 1939. He had a tryout with the Cubs the following spring, but was sold back to Los Angeles. A sportswriter said he had been "gloomy" because he didn't think the Cubs had given him a fair chance. He won 14 games for the Angels in 1940 and seven in 1941 before he was released.[53] The published record does not show that he was officially banned; he was in the Army the next year.[54]

### "Fooling Around"

OUTFIELDER Hooper Triplett of the Sally League Columbus (GA) Cardinals was banned in 1946 for betting $20 against his team. Triplett claimed he was only "fooling around." His statements and those of others hinted he was drunk when he placed the bet.

Triplett was the 26-year-old brother of former big league outfielder Coaker Triplett. He returned to baseball that season after three years in the military.[55]

### "A Combination Baseball Club and Bookie Hangout"

IN the most celebrated gambling scandal since the Black Sox, five players in the Class D Evangeline League were banished after they were accused of throwing games in the 1946 post-season playoffs: manager-first baseman Paul Fugit, third baseman Alvin W. Kaiser, center fielder Leonard Pecou, and pitcher Bill Thomas of the Houma, Louisiana, Indians and catcher Don Vettorel of Abbeville, Louisiana.[56]

One sportswriter said the investigation painted the Houma team as "a combination baseball club and bookie hangout where the players did everything except stop in the middle of a double play to rush off and play the daily double. Bookies not only invaded club premises but wore Houma uniforms."[57]

Although Houma won both playoff series, the players were accused of throwing one game against Abbeville in the finals and two others in the previous round against Alexandria, Louisiana.

National Association President W. G. Bramham

NATIONAL BASEBALL LIBRARY, COOPERSTOWN, NY

said the players had been hanging out in gambling houses and betting heavily on horse races. Bramham found "circumstantial evidence" of thrown games, but his official ruling banned them for associating with gamblers. Testimony indicated that some of the Houma players were employed by bookies. Fugit said some players came to Houma after a crackdown on gambling in New Orleans left them unemployed.

Bramham, who was retiring, said his successor, George Trautman, would continue the investigation. He added, "The situation in the Evangeline League is very, very bad."[58]

A month later, Trautman declared the investigation closed and gave the league "a clean bill of health."[59] At the National Association's fall meeting in Minneapolis, he lamented, "This evil [gambling], like the poor, is always with us."[60]

All the players maintained their innocence. Pecou and Thomas were reinstated three years later.[61] *The Sporting News* reported the bans were lifted due to "circumstances beyond (Trautman's) control." The circumstances were not mentioned.[62]

Thomas won a minor league record 383 games without reaching the majors. In 1946, when he was 41 years old, he won 35 regular-season games for Houma and four more in the playoffs. After he returned from suspension, he won 23 in the Evangeline League in 1950 and pitched on for two more years.[63]

### "They Don't Care Anything About You"

CENTER fielder Al McElreath of Muskogee in the Class A Western Association was declared permanently ineligible for trying to persuade teammates to throw a 1947 game and committing intentional misplays in the game. McElreath said the charges were "a lie."

A teammate said he refused to be part of the fix, and McElreath told him, "I don't see why you won't do it because they don't care anything about you."

National Association President Trautman heard testimony that the usually reliable outfielder staggered under a fly ball and let it drop behind him. At bat he signaled for a hit-and-run but didn't swing, and the runner was thrown out.

Marion Allen McElreath was 32 and had played in the minors since 1931, rising as high as AA, then the top level.[64]

### "A Considerable Temptation"

IN 1948 Barney DeForge, pitcher-manager of Reidsville, North Carolina, in the Class C Carolina League, and Emanuel Weingarten, owner of two teams in other Southern minor leagues, were banned after DeForge admitted fixing a game in return for the big payoff of $300.

DeForge put himself in as a relief pitcher when Reidsville was trailing Winston-Salem, 2–0, and quickly gave up four walks and a wild pitch. The final score, 5–0, beat the spread being offered by a gambler in the stands. (Betting on run spreads was unusual in baseball because the scores are usually so low.)

North Carolina was one of the few states where fixing games was a felony. A Forsyth County grand jury indicted the 31-year-old DeForge along with Weingarten, the alleged go-between, and the alleged gambler, a South Carolina used-car dealer named W. C. McWaters. Another South Carolina car dealer, Tommy Phillips, was later added as a defendant.[65]

At trial in Winston-Salem, DeForge testified as a prosecution witness, admitting guilt and implicating his co-defendants. He was convicted on the basis of his own testimony, but the jury acquitted McWaters and Phillips. *The Sporting News* account gives no explanation for that verdict. Weingarten had died, apparently of natural causes, before the trial.

DeForge appears to be the only player ever convicted on a criminal charge of throwing a game.

The prosecutor and the Forsyth County sheriff, former big league pitcher Ernie Shore, urged leniency for DeForge because he "came clean." He received a suspended sentence.[66]

Ed McAuley of the *Cleveland News*, commenting on the case, pointed to the pitifully small salaries in the low minors: "Three hundred dollars would represent a considerable temptation to a fellow in such circumstances."[67]

McAuley and Robert L. Burnes, sports editor of the *St. Louis Globe-Democrat*, saw a common thread in the betting scandals of 1946–1948: poor pay and the large number of veteran players who hung on in the expanding low minors after World War II.

"Are the players in the depths of the minor leagues, in the B, C and D classes, being paid a living wage?" Burnes asked. "The answer . . . is a definite no." He said Class C players were averaging about $10 a game, those in Class D $5 to $10—good enough for a young man with high hopes, not so good for a veteran who had to be resigned to earning $150 or $200 a month for the rest of his career.[68]

With 58 minor leagues in operation in 1948,[69] McAuley estimated 15,000 men were playing professional baseball. Many lost the prime of their careers to the war. "There are scores of veterans who long ago abandoned hope of reaching the majors," he said.[70]

Burnes's and McAuley's analysis is supported by later events. As the minors shrank dramatically in the 1950s, small-town independent leagues like the Evangeline disappeared. The surviving teams came under increasingly tight control by their big league parents. Shrunken farm systems had fewer slots for minor league lifers, while a growing American economy offered more and better job opportunities for poorly educated men.

Except for the Southern Association scandal in 1959, no minor leaguer has since been banned for involvement in gambling or game-fixing.

Another common theme connects the minor league scandals, from Babe Borton in 1920 to Jess Levan 39 years later: the accusations against one player, or a handful, usually led to reports of much wider gambling problems. League presidents promised crackdowns on betting in the stands; they vowed to enforce rules against players on the field talking to fans. But none of the investigations of widespread gambling ever went anywhere.

### Notes

1. *The Sporting News*, December 30, 1959, 5.
2. *Chattanooga Times*, July 31, 1959, 31. *The Times* printed the Associated Press transcript of National Association President George Trautman's July 30 ruling in the case, hereinafter cited as "Trautman ruling."
3. *Ibid.* and *Chattanooga Times*, August 1, 1959, 12.
4. Trautman ruling.
5. *Chattanooga Times*, July 6, 1959, 11. The author queried the present-day governing body of the minors and the Baseball Hall of Fame library, but no trace of the stenographic record has been found.
6. Trautman ruling.
7. Ibid.
8. Documents in Levan's file at the Hall of Fame library.
9. www.sportplanet.com.
10. *SABR Minor League Stars*, Vol. 3, 22.
11. *Washington Post*, March 30, 1955, 29.
12. *The Sporting News*, April 20, 1955, 22.
13. Retrosheet player page; Macmillan *Baseball Encyclopedia*, 8th ed.
14. *Washington Post and Times Herald*, July 5, 1959, C4.
15. *SABR's Minor League Stars* Vol. III, 95.
16. Trautman ruling.
17. *Chattanooga Times*, July 4, 1959, p. 1.
18. *Atlanta Journal*, July 28, 1959, p. 10.
19. *The Sporting News*, September 16, 1959, 31.
20. *Atlanta Journal*, September 2, 1959, 40.
21. Quoted in an Associated Press story, *Washington Post and Times-Herald*, August 19, 1959, C4.
22. Quoted in *Atlanta Journal*, November 14, 1959, 6. Bud Shrake, a famous Texas character, is the co-author of *Harvey Penick's Little Red Book*. *Austin Chronicle*, November 2, 2001.
23. Associated Press story in *Washington Post and Times Herald*, August 19, 1959, C4.
24. *Chattanooga Times*, August 4, 1959, 11.
25. Trautman ruling.
26. UPI story in the *New York Times*, July 31, 1959, 15. DeForge: *The Sporting News*, July 9, 1948, 5.
27. Trautman ruling. Gonzalez sat out the 1960 season, then played briefly for two minor league teams in 1961. (Old-Time Data, Shawnee Mission, KS.)
28. *The Sporting News*, August 5, 1959, 23. The Associated Press text of Trautman's ruling, published in the July 31 *Chattanooga Times*, reads, ". . . both Levan and Gonzalez testified that he actually did pass signs to certain Mobile batsmen." I accept *The Sporting News* version because it is consistent with the statements quoted in the rest of the ruling and because, if Gonzalez admitted "that he actually did pass signs," leniency would not have been justified. In all other respects, the AP text conforms to excerpts quoted elsewhere.
29. Trautman ruling.
30. *Chattanooga Times*, August 2, 1959, D1.
31. Trautman ruling.
32. UPI story in *New York Times*, July 31, 1959, 15.
33. *Chattanooga Times*, August 1, 1959, p. 11.
34. *Ibid.*, July 31, 1959, 31
35. *The Sporting News*, November 25, 1959, 6.
36. *Atlanta Journal*, August 2, 1959, D1. Bo's father probably wrote the story, since newspaper writers commonly picked up extra money by contributing to the wire services.
37. *Chattanooga Times*, July 7, 1959, 11.
38. *The Sporting News*, September 2, 1959, 22.
39. Associated Press story in *Atlanta Journal*, August 1, 1959, 11.
40. Associated Press story in *Chattanooga Times*, July 31, 1959, 31.
41. Associated Press story in *Washington Post and Times Herald*, August 19, 1959, C4.
42. *The Sporting News*, November 25, 1959, 6. Tipton was a backup catcher in the majors from 1948 through 1954. His only claim to fame is that he was traded from the White Sox to the Athletics for Nellie Fox. He died in 1994.
43. *The Sporting News*, December 30, 1959, 5.
44. *Ibid.*, Nov. 17, 1959, 7.
45. *Ibid.*, Aug. 3, 1960, 28.
46. Curiously, stories on that topic vanished from TSN after 1960. Whether the paper decided to stop reporting them, or whether police decided they had better things to do, cannot be determined.
47. The author was the young broadcaster.
48. *The Sporting News*, August 19, 1920, 3.
49. *Los Angeles Times*, August 12, 1920, III1; December 11, 1920, III1; December 25, 1920, 6.
50. *Ibid.*, October 21, 1920, III1.
51. Daniel Ginsburg, author of *The Fix Is In* (McFarland, 1995) in an e-mail exchange with the author, January 31, 2004.
52. *Sabermetric Baseball Encyclopedia*.
53. *L.A. Times*, July 3, 1941, 1.
54. *Ibid.*, October 22, 1942, 19.
55. *The Sporting News*, August 21, 1946, 17 and September 4, 1946, 12.
56. *Ibid.*, February 5, 1947, 1.
57. United Press story in the *New York Times*, January 30, 1947, 28.
58. *The Sporting News*, February 5, 1947, 1.
59. *Ibid.*, March 12, 1947, 18.
60. *Ibid.*, December 8, 1948.
61. George W. Hilton, "The Evangeline League Scandal of 1946," SABR's *Baseball Research Journal*, 1982, 102.
62. *The Sporting News*, September 14, 1949, 8.
63. SABR's *Minor League Stars*, vol. I, rev. ed. 1984, 122.
64. *The Sporting News*, June 11, 1947, 11.
65. *Ibid.*, July 9, 1948, 5.
66. *Ibid.*, November 3, 1948, p. 11; Weingarten's death: *Ibid.*, July 14, 1948, p. 42.
67. *Ibid.* June 16, 1948, p. 9.
68. *Ibid.*, p. 10.
69. *Total Baseball*, 5th ed., 460. Fifty or more minor leagues started each season from 1947 to 1951, the highest number in history.
70. *The Sporting News*, June 16, 1948, 9.

# Clemente's Entry into Organized Baseball
## Hidden in Montreal?

### by Stew Thornley

**A** lie can travel halfway round the world while the truth is putting on its shoes." Although this quote is often attributed to Mark Twain, at least one Twain researcher claims a different source.[1] Beyond the content of the quote, its disputed derivation highlights the need to resist the urge to assume something to be true just because it is repeated often enough or is viewed as "common knowledge."

So it is with Roberto Clemente's sole season in the minor leagues, with the Montreal Royals of the International League in 1954. This saga provides a striking example of a story retold so many times that it takes on a life of its own, eventually becoming so accepted as factual that even a careful researcher may fall into the trap of assuming the claims to be true and not feeling the need to verify them.

Although Clemente spent his entire major league career with the Pittsburgh Pirates, he was originally part of the Brooklyn Dodgers organization. He signed with the Dodgers in February 1954 for a reported salary of $5,000 as well as a bonus of $10,000.[2] Rules of the time required a team signing a player for a bonus, including salary, of more than $4,000 to keep him on the major league roster for two years or risk losing him in an off-season draft. Thus, the Dodgers' choice to have Clemente spend 1954 in the minors meant that they might lose him to another team at the end of the season.[3]

What has been written about Clemente in Montreal contains an assertion that the Dodgers and Royals tried to hide him—that is, play him very little so that other teams wouldn't notice him. The claim was expressed by Clemente at least as early as 1962

*A SABR member since 1979,* STEW THORNLEY *received the SABR-Macmillan Baseball Research Award in 1988 and the USA Today Baseball Weekly Award for the best research presentation at the 1998 SABR convention in San Mateo, California.*

in an article by Howard Cohn in *Sport* magazine. "Clemente, on the other hand, felt—and still does—that the Royals kept him out of the regular lineup so big-league teams would think him a weak prospect and ignore him in the post-season draft for which he'd be available as a bonus player if he weren't elevated to the Brooklyn roster," wrote Cohn.[4]

Since then, this claim has been trumpeted in much that has been written about Clemente's entry into organized baseball, including several biographies; one of them, by Arnold Hano, was written during Clemente's career, in 1968, and revised following Clemente's death in 1972; two biographies, by Kal Wagenheim and Phil Musick, were written shortly after Clemente's death while another, by Bruce Markusen, came out a quarter century later. In early 2006, noted biographer David Maraniss, whose works include Vince Lombardi and Bill Clinton, had a biography of Clemente published.[5]

The biographers and others who maintain that Clemente was hidden—and beyond that, that the organization may have tried to frustrate Clemente to the point that he would jump the team, making him ineligible to be drafted by another team[6]—offer numerous supporting examples. The examples, with few exceptions, turn out to be false.

### Decision on Clemente's Destination

THE first question, however, concerns not what happened in Montreal but why the Dodgers did not keep Clemente in Brooklyn in 1954. Many bonus players of this period were kept at the major league level, even though it meant pining on the bench for two years rather than developing in the minors.

As vice president of the Dodgers, Emil "Buzzie" Bavasi had the power to determine Clemente's fate. In 1955, Bavasi told Pittsburgh writer Les Biederman that the team's only purpose in signing Clemente had

CANADIAN BASEBALL HALL OF FAME

*The 1954 Montreal Royals. Clemente is in the front row, far left. Manager Max Macon is in the middle row, fourth from the left.*

been to keep him away from the New York Giants, even though they knew they would eventually lose him to another team.[7]

Other explanations offered center around an often cited but never documented informal quota system said to be in effect in the years following the breaking of the color barrier in organized baseball.[8] The Dodgers already had five blacks who would play at least semi-regularly on their parent roster in 1954, presumably leaving no room for another player of color. (The claim of an informal quota is another possible myth that has become widely accepted over time. A check of a specific claim made in Wagenheim's biography—that the Dodgers would never start all five blacks at the same time—is false, and there are other reasons to question the general claim of a quota system, but it is beyond the realm of this article to fully explore the issue.[9])

Although Bavasi had claimed at the time that they signed Clemente only to keep him from the Giants, in 2005 he offered a different reason. "I know your sources are not idiots," he wrote in e-mail correspondence with the author, "but not one of those things you mentioned are [sic] accurate. Let's start from the beginning." Bavasi then wrote that while there was not a quota in effect, race was the factor in their decision to have Clemente play in Montreal rather than Brooklyn:

"[Dodgers owner] Walter O'Malley had two partners who were concerned about the number of minorities we would be bringing to the Dodgers. . . . The concern had nothing to do with quotas, but the thought was too many minorities might be a problem with the white players. Not so, I said. Winning was the important thing. I agreed with the board that we should get a player's opinion and I would be guided by the player's opinion. The board called in Jackie Robinson. Hell, now I felt great. Jackie was told the problem, and, after thinking about it awhile, he asked me who would be sent out if Clemente took one of the spots. I said George Shuba. Jackie agreed that Shuba would be the one to go. Then he said Shuba was not among the best players on the club, but he was the most popular. With that he shocked me by saying, and I quote: 'If I were the GM [general manager], I would not bring Clemente to the club and send Shuba or any other white player down. If I did this, I would be setting our program back five years.'"[10]

### Clemente in Montreal

So Clemente was headed for Montreal to play for manager Max Macon. According to statements attributed to Clemente in a 1966 *Sports Illustrated* article by Myron Cope, and later picked up by the biographers, the treatment he faced went beyond an attempt to hide him: "The idea was to make me look bad. If I struck out, I stayed in there; if I played well, I was benched."[11]

Musick, in *Who Was Roberto?*, added, "A free swinger, Clemente suffered through stretches when he was not making contact with the ball. Fighting those slumps, he was showcased to disadvantage and stayed in the lineup days at a time."[12]

However, box scores from *The Sporting News* reveal that Macon started Clemente in five straight games early in the season, a strange strategy if a team was trying to hide a player. Clemente had one hit in the first of those games, started again, had three hits, and started the next three games, coming out of the starting lineup only after going hitless in those final three games. This would seem to belie the claims that the organization was trying to make him look bad by rewarding a good performance with a benching and vice versa.

After those five starts Clemente played sparingly over the next few months. Clemente may have, in part, been a victim of a crowded outfield situation in Montreal, which included Jack Cassini, Dick Whitman, and Don Thompson as well as Sandy Amoros, who was sent down from Brooklyn in mid-May and recalled by the Dodgers in mid-July, and Gino Cimoli, who was transferred to Montreal from the Dodgers' other Triple-A farm team, the St. Paul Saints, in early May. (Clemente's opportunities to play may not have been any greater had he been assigned to St. Paul rather than Montreal. With Bud Hutson, John Golich, Bert Hamric, Ed Moore, and Walt Moryn, the Saints, like the Royals, were also heavy on outfielders.)

When Clemente did play, he struggled with his hitting. In early July, his batting average was barely above .200. Part of that may be attributed to his infrequent playing time; it's hard for a batter to get in a groove and hit well when he doesn't play regularly. On the other hand, it's hard for a player to get regular playing time if he's not hitting well.

Macon said the reason he didn't use him much at that time was that he "swung wildly," especially at pitches that were outside of the strike zone. "If you had been in Montreal that year, you wouldn't have believed how ridiculous some pitchers made him look," Macon said of Clemente.[13]

Macon was known around the league for platooning his hitters,[14] and that is what happened with Clemente over the latter part of the season. In the first game of a doubleheader against Havana on July 25, Clemente entered the game in the ninth inning, came to the plate in the bottom of the 10th, and hit a game-ending home run.

He started the second game of the doubleheader, against left hander Clarence "Hooks" Iotts; for the rest of the regular season and through the playoffs, the right-handed–hitting Clemente started every game in which the opposing starter was left-handed and did not start any games against right-handed starters. After July 25, Clemente's usage was determined by the status of the opposing starting pitcher.

Other claims made to support the notion of Clemente being hidden:

- Clemente hit a long home run in the first week of the season and was benched in the next game.[15] (Clemente did not homer until July 25, and he started the next game. His only other home run came on September 5, and, like his earlier homer, was a game-ending shot. Clemente did not start the next game as a right hander, Bob Trice, was the starting pitcher for Ottawa.)

- Clemente was benched after a game in which he had three triples.[16] (Clemente did not have three triples in any game in 1954.)

- Clemente was often used only in the second game of a doubleheader, after the scouts had left.[17] (No such pattern of usage is indicated.)

The errors noted above were made by Wagenheim, Musick, and Markusen in their biographies. Maraniss, who went through Montreal newspapers for the 1954 season, avoided many of the inaccurate supporting examples made by the others. However, Maraniss parroted the claim that Clemente was being set up to fail, writing, "It seemed that whenever he got a chance to play and played well, Macon benched him."[18] Maraniss also wrote, "After the first four games, Clemente was leading the team in batting, going four for eight. Then he disappeared again."[19] However, Clemente's disappearance after getting three hits in the team's fifth (not fourth) game was not that abrupt; he started and went hitless in the next three games before going back to the bench.

Overall, Maraniss stuck to the standard story of Clemente being hidden and did not perform any real analysis of the claim. He also did not pick up on the pattern of usage that eventually developed, in which Clemente started regularly against left-handed pitching. As a result, Maraniss cites instances of Clemente not playing over the final seven weeks as evidence of attempts to hide him, rather than the fact that a right-handed pitcher was starting for the opposing team.[20]

One claim made by biographers that is true regards Clemente being pulled for a pinch-hitter in the top of the first inning of a game. It occurred June 7 at Havana. The Royals had two runs in and the bases loaded with two out when Havana changed pitchers—right-hander Raul Sanchez coming in for left-hander Hooks Iotts. Left-handed Dick Whitman then hit for Clemente. Although the story is presented as more evidence of how poorly Clemente was treated by Max Macon, it appears clear from the circumstances that it had more to do with Macon's affinity for platooning and a desire to try and break the game open.

An essentially opposite situation occurred two months later as Toronto manager Luke Sewell, trying to counteract Macon's platooning, employed a decoy starter. In the first game of an August 3 doubleheader, Sewell started right hander Arnie Landeck against the Royals and then relieved him with left hander Vic Lombardi in the second inning. As a result, Dick Whitman started for Montreal and was pinch-hit for by Clemente before Whitman could bat even once. Conveniently, this counterpoint to the June 7 story is never mentioned.

Also, the details of Clemente getting pulled in the first inning get botched by the biographers. Markusen says the incident happened against Richmond in the second week of the season.[21] Musick also says it occurred in a game against Richmond.[22] However, a few pages later, Musick contradicts himself and says the game was in Rochester (wrong in both cases), that it was the last game of the season (not true), and it was against Rochester's Jackie Collum (strike three).[23]

The name of Jackie Collum comes up again in an unrelated story by Wagenheim, who wrote that Clemente had two doubles and a triple off Collum and then was pulled for a pinch-hitter his next time up.[24] Nothing like this happened—regardless of the pitcher.

And one has to wonder about references to Collum by two different biographers. Collum did not even pitch for Rochester, or in the International League at all in 1954.

Clemente's first professional team was the Santurce Cangrejeros of the Puerto Rican Winter League.

SABR member and Montreal Royals historian Neil Raymond cross-checked the summary compiled by the author from *The Sporting News* box scores with game accounts and box scores from Montreal newspapers. (See Clemente's game-by-game compilation at the end of the article.) "What becomes apparent going through the Montreal papers daily (*La Presse, The Gazette, The Star*) is that this team was not perceived as a player-development exercise," maintained Raymond. "They were expected to win. Translation: Sandy Amoros's at-bats were deemed a lot more valuable than learning what Clemente could do, building his confidence, or training him by exposing him to opportunities to fail by being overmatched.

"I feel safe in saying that Clemente made very little impression on those who wrote about him during the 1954 campaign. These were iconoclastic writers. Their copy was eagerly sought-after breakfast or dinner fodder. If Clemente was being 'hidden' to the detriment of the team's ability to perform, they would have peeped up. Not once in my newspaper research is there an allusion to this possibility, or a subtle wink at the canniness of the 'brain trust.' As difficult as it may be to accept to those who, like me, marveled at Clemente's multifarious skills and dynamism throughout the 1960s (the bad-ball hitting, the cannon-like arm, the heady base running, etc.), it's abundantly clear that he was almost an invisible man in Montreal in 1954."[25]

TRANSCENDENTAL GRAPHICS

### A More Plausible Argument?

IT'S possible that the strongest argument for a theory of hiding could revolve around the timing of the Pittsburgh Pirates' discovery of Clemente and when Clemente began starting regularly against left-handed pitching.

The accounts surrounding the discovery are consistent in some ways, albeit consistently inaccurate on some details: Clyde Sukeforth, then a Pirates coach, was dispatched on a scouting mission by Branch Rickey, then the Pirates executive vice president-general manager, to check out Montreal pitcher Joe Black. All accounts say this occurred during a Royals series against Richmond in July. Almost every story says this series was in Richmond, with some of the accounts specifically mentioning Richmond's Parker Field, although the only series between the two teams that month was in Montreal.

Sukeforth said Black did not pitch that series (not true; he did) and that Clemente's only appearance was as a pinch-hitter (also not true; his only appearance in the series was as a pinch-runner). Even though Clemente barely appeared in the series, Sukeforth said he noticed, and was impressed by, Clemente while watching him bat and throw in pregame practice. On the basis of Sukeforth's report, Rickey sent scout Howie Haak for a follow-up visit.

The accounts vary to a much greater degree as to when the Pirates informed the Dodgers and/or Royals that they had discovered Clemente and planned on drafting him. Some reports contend that Sukeforth immediately told Macon of the Pirates' interest in Clemente.[26]

The key is when the Dodgers organization found out that the Pirates were planning to draft Clemente. *If* Clemente was first discovered in the Richmond series in July (meaning that the essence of the story of Sukeforth's scouting trip is correct even if the specific details are not), and *if* Sukeforth immediately informed Macon, it raises an interesting possibility. The Richmond series was immediately before the Havana series in which Clemente began starting regularly against left handers.

*If* the Royals began playing Clemente more after being informed of the Pirates' interest, then *perhaps* it could be argued that the Royals had been hiding Clemente up to that point; however, informed that their gambit had failed, they then decided to play Clemente more.

Even if all these *ifs* line up, the argument is still a stretch and nothing more than conjecture; however, it is still the most plausible one.

Interestingly, however, this is not the argument advanced by the biographers or anyone else claiming that Clemente was being hidden. In fact, most go in the other direction, saying that the Royals used Clemente even less after being informed of Pittsburgh's interest. Wagenheim and Markusen even make the outrageous and totally incorrect claim that Clemente did not play in any of the Royals' final 25 games. [27] Although Musick does not make the claim of Clemente not playing in the last 25 games, he writes that Macon restricted Clemente's playing time even more after Sukeforth's scouting trip and alleged revelation to Macon.[28]

### Treatment of Max Macon

MARKUSEN at least provided some balance with quotes from Macon in which the manager denied being under orders to hide Clemente.[29] Musick also provided some of Macon's denials as well as Macon's contention that pitchers were making Clemente look ridiculous. However, Musick offered these explanations on Macon's part in a patronizing manner as he wrote, "Macon pleads innocence for his former employer twenty years after the fact, but his pleas bring bemused grins to the faces of his contemporaries. And he is part of a baseball establishment that is superprotective of its leaders. There are no skeletons in baseball's closet: They are quickly ground to dust and scattered to the four winds, lest men of stature be embarrassed." Musick also refers to Macon's "southern drawl" becoming "increasingly less reassuring to the player's Puerto Rican ears."[30]

### Drafted by Pittsburgh

BY the end of the 1954 season, it had become clear to Bavasi and the rest of the Brooklyn brass that other teams were interested in Clemente. However, Bavasi said he still wasn't ready to give up. The Pirates, by having the worst record in the majors in 1954, had the first pick in the November draft.

If Bavasi could get the Pirates to draft a different player off the Montreal Royals roster, Clemente would remain with the Dodgers organization. (Each team could lose only one player, so if a different Montreal player was taken, then no other team could draft Clemente or any other Royals player.)

Bavasi said he went to Branch Rickey, who had run the Brooklyn Dodgers before going to Pittsburgh. Bavasi had declined Rickey's offer at that time to follow him to the Pirates, but, according to Bavasi, Rickey then told him, "Should I [Bavasi] need help at anytime, all I had to do was pick up the phone."

Bavasi said he used this offer of help in 1954 to get Rickey to agree to draft a different player, pitcher John Rutherford, off the Royals roster. However, Bavasi was dismayed to learn two days later that the deal was off and that the Pirates were going to draft Clemente. "It seemed that Walter O'Malley and Mr. Rickey got in another argument, and it seems Walter called Mr. Rickey every name in the book," Bavasi explained. "Thus, we lost Roberto."[31]

## Summary

SOME stories and claims may be difficult to fully verify or refute, and it's possible that the contention that Clemente was being hidden and/or mistreated in Montreal is one of them. While this analysis may not provide a definitive answer one way or another, it is telling that the examples used to support the hiding claim are so consistently incorrect.

In a rather supercilious manner, Phil Musick wrote, "Whether or not the Dodgers consciously tried to hide Clemente from the prying eyes of scouts from other major league clubs is questionable—barely. The evidence insists that the Dodgers ordered him into virtual seclusion in Montreal; Macon insists otherwise. The evidence does not support his claim."[32]

In reality, the claims not supported by the evidence are those made by Musick and the other biographers.

### Notes

1. Barbara Schmidt's web site on Mark Twain (www.twainquotes.com/Lies.html) says this quote has never been verified as originating with Twain and that a related quote may have originated with British preacher Charles Haddon Spurgeon, who attributed it to a proverb that he once used in a sermon.
2. *The Sporting News*, March 3, 1954, 26.
3. The bonus rule in effect at that time is chronicled in *Baseball's Biggest Blunder: The Bonus Rule of 1953-1957* by Brent Kelley, Lanham, MD: Scarecrow Press, 1997. The rule is also discussed in a *Baseball America* article ("Despite Baseball's Best Efforts, Bonuses Just Keep Growing" by Allan Simpson, June 20-July 3, 2005, 10-12). This article says, "Players with less than 90 days of pro experience were designated as bonus players if they signed multi-year contracts or were promised more than $4,000 from a major league team. Bonus players kept their tag for two years. They had to be placed on major league rosters immediately and could not be optioned to the minors unless they cleared waivers."
4. "Roberto Clemente's Problem" by Howard Cohn, *Sport*, May 1962, 56.
5. *Roberto Clemente: Batting King* by Arnold Hano, New York: G. P. Putnam's Sons, 1973 (update of 1968 edition); *Clemente!* by Kal Wagenheim, New York: Praeger, 1973; *Who Was Roberto? A Biography of Roberto Clemente* by Phil Musick, Garden City, NY: Doubleday, 1974; *Roberto Clemente: The Great One* by Bruce Markusen, Champaign, IL: Sports Publishing, 1998; *Clemente: The Passion and Grace of Baseball's Last Hero* by David Maraniss, NY: Simon & Schuster, 2006.
6. Musick, 80, 87; Markusen, 26.
7. "Dodgers Signed Clemente Just to Balk Giants" by Les Biederman, *The Sporting News*, May 25, 1955, 11.
8. Wagenheim, p. 35; Markusen, 33–34.
9. The claim that the Dodgers would not start five blacks in the same game was made by Wagenheim on page 35 of *Clemente!* Box scores of Brooklyn Dodgers games in 1954 from *The Sporting News* indicate four instances in which Jim Gilliam, Jackie Robinson, Don Newcombe, Sandy Amoros, and Roy Campanella were all in the starting lineup: July 17, August 24, September 6 (second game), and September 15. (The Dodgers had one other black player, pitcher Joe Black, briefly on their roster in 1954, but Black did not start any of the five games in which he pitched.)
10. E-mail correspondence with Buzzie Bavasi, June 3, 2005.
11. A quote from Clemente that contains these claims is in "Aches and Pains and Three Batting Titles" by Myron Cope, *Sports Illustrated*, March 7, 1966, 34. One or both of the sentences in the Clemente quote listed in this article are from Wagenheim, 40; Musick, 81; and Markusen, 26.
12. Musick, 81.
13. Musick, 89.
14. *The Sporting News*, August 18, 1954, 34.
15. Musick, 80–81; Markusen, 18–19.
16. This claim is made in the quote attributed to Clemente in Cope's 1966 *Sports Illustrated* article and also picked up by Hano, 27; Wagenheim, 40; Musick, 81; Markusen, 19.
17. Markusen, 27.
18. Maraniss, 46.
19. Maraniss, 43.
20. On page 51, Maraniss tells of a visit by Dodgers front-office personnel but that "it was back to the bench" upon their departure. He also does the same thing on pages 51-53 with stories of the trips by Pittsburgh Pirates scouts to see Clemente, claiming that Macon refused to play Clemente when scout Howie Haak visited. In reality, from the time that Clemente began platooning regularly, there were never more than two consecutive games in which he did not play, and, of course, these were games in which the opposing starting pitcher was right handed.
21. Markusen, 19.
22. Musick, 81.
23. Musick, 87.
24. Wagenheim, 42.
25. E-mail correspondence with Neil Raymond, July 2005.
26. The discovery of Clemente is described in Cope's 1966 *Sports Illustrated* article, 34; also by Hano, 29–30; Wagenheim, 41–42; Musick, 84-87; and Markusen, 22–24; Maraniss, 51–53, and it is also covered in *Branch Rickey in Pittsburgh: Baseball's Trailblazing General Manager for the Pirates, 1950-1955* by Andrew O'Toole, Jefferson, NC: McFarland, 2000, 140-143.
27. Wagenheim, 42; Markusen, 26–27.
28. Musick, 84, 86.
29. Markusen, 26–27.
30. Musick, 86, 88–89.
31. E-mail correspondence with Buzzie Bavasi, June 3, 2005.
32. Musick, 80.

## APPENDIX: Statistical Summary of Roberto Clemente's 1954 Season with the Montreal Royals

Compiled by Stew Thornley from 1954 box scores in *The Sporting News*. Assistance provided by Neil Raymond, who double-checked box scores from the *Montreal Gazette*, as well as the *Montreal Star* and *La Presse*. Games in which the position is in **bold** indicate games started by Clemente; ***bold italic*** indicates he played the entire game.

| DAY | DATE | OPPONENT | SCORE | AB | R | H | RBI | PO | A | Pos | OPPOSING STARTER |
|---|---|---|---|---|---|---|---|---|---|---|---|
| W | 4/21 | at Syracuse | L 6-7 | 0 | 0 | 0 | 0 | 1 | 0 | LF | Harry "Duke" Markell-R |
| Sa | 4/24 | at Syracuse | W 4-2 | 1 | 0 | 0 | 0 | 1 | 0 | LF | Jim Owens-R |
| Su | 4/25-1 | at Buffalo | L 3-4 | | Did not play* | | | | | | Hal Erickson-R |
| Su | 4/25-2 | at Buffalo | L 1-8 (7 inn.) | 3 | 0 | 1 | 0 | 2 | 0 | *CF* | *Ken Johnson-L* |
| M | 4/26 | at Buffalo, rain | | | | | | | | | |
| Tu | 4/27 | at Buffalo, rain | | | | | | | | | |
| Th | 4/29 | Syracuse | W 8-7 (10) | 4 | 2 | 3 | 1 | 3 | 0 | *CF* | *Kent Peterson-L* |

Also had a sacrifice before 11,089 in the Royals home opener.

| DAY | DATE | OPPONENT | SCORE | AB | R | H | RBI | PO | A | Pos | OPPOSING STARTER |
|---|---|---|---|---|---|---|---|---|---|---|---|
| F | 4/30 | Syracuse | W 2-1 | 3 | 0 | 0 | 0 | 1 | 0 | *CF-LF* | *Jack Spring-L* |
| Sa | 5/1 | Syracuse | L 3-5 | 2 | 1 | 0 | 0 | 0 | 0 | **LF** | Lynn Lovenguth-R |
| Su | 5/2-1 | Ottawa | L 3-5 | 3 | 0 | 0 | 0 | 3 | 0 | **CF** | *Vince Gohl-L* |
| Su | 5/2-2 | Ottawa | W 3-2 (7) | 0 | 0 | 0 | 0 | 0 | 0 | LF | Charlie Bishop-R |
| W | 5/5 | Rochester | L 1-12 | 1 | 0 | 0 | 0 | | | PH | Preacher Jack Faszholz-R |
| Th | 5/6 | Rochester | W 4-2 | 0 | 0 | 0 | 0 | 2 | 0 | PH-LF | Gary Blaylock-R |
| F | 5/7 | Rochester | W 4-2 | 0 | 0 | 0 | 0 | 0 | 0 | PR-LF | Harry Hoitsma-R |
| Sa | 5/8 | at Toronto | L 1-9 | 1 | 0 | 0 | 0 | | | PH | Frank Barnes-R |

OF Gino Cimoli joined Montreal from St. Paul and played his first game for the Royals.

| DAY | DATE | OPPONENT | SCORE | AB | R | H | RBI | PO | A | Pos | OPPOSING STARTER |
|---|---|---|---|---|---|---|---|---|---|---|---|
| Su | 5/9-1 | at Toronto | L 9-12 | | Did not play | | | | | | *Vic Lombardi-L* |
| Su | 5/9-2 | at Toronto | 0-0 (7) | | | | | | | | |

Game suspended by curfew with two out in the last of the seventh inning. Clemente did not start but entered the game in left field for Jack Cassini. He had one at bat before the game was suspended. Right hander Eddie Blake started for Toronto. The game would be resumed on July 30.

| DAY | DATE | OPPONENT | SCORE | AB | R | H | RBI | PO | A | Pos | OPPOSING STARTER |
|---|---|---|---|---|---|---|---|---|---|---|---|
| Tu | 5/11 | at Ottawa, rain | | | | | | | | | |
| W | 5/12-1 | at Ottawa | W 2-1 (7) | 0 | 0 | 0 | 0 | 0 | 0 | LF | *Bob Cain-L* |
| W | 5/12-2 | at Ottawa | W 4-2 | 0 | 0 | 0 | 0 | 0 | 0 | PR-LF | Walt Kellner-R |
| Th | 5/13 | at Ottawa | L 1-5 | | Did not play | | | | | | *Vince Gohl-L* |

OF Sandy Amoros joined Montreal from Brooklyn and played his first game for the Royals.

| DAY | DATE | OPPONENT | SCORE | AB | R | H | RBI | PO | A | Pos | OPPOSING STARTER |
|---|---|---|---|---|---|---|---|---|---|---|---|
| F | 5/14 | at Rochester | W 5-2 | 0 | 1 | 0 | 0 | 0 | 0 | LF | Harry Hoitsma-R |
| Sa | 5/15 | at Rochester | L 4-10 | 2 | 0 | 0 | 0 | 0 | 0 | RF | *Niles Jordan-L* |
| Su | 5/16 | at Rochester | L 1-3 | | Did not play | | | | | | *Guillermo "Memo" Luna-L* |
| Tu | 5/18 | Buffalo | W 5-4 | 1 | 0 | 0 | 0 | 0 | 0 | RF | Hal Erickson-R |
| W | 5/19 | Buffalo | L 4-19 | | Did not play | | | | | | *Bill Froats-L* |
| Th | 5/20 | Buffalo | W 4-3 | 0 | 0 | 0 | 0 | 1 | 0 | RF | Paul Foytack-R |
| F | 5/21 | Richmond, rain | | | | | | | | | |
| Sa | 5/22 | Richmond, rain | | | | | | | | | |
| Su | 5/23-1 | Richmond | W 3-2 | 0 | 0 | 0 | 0 | 2 | 0 | PR-RF | Bob Habenicht-R |
| Su | 5/23-2 | Richmond | W 2-1 (10) | 1 | 0 | 1 | 0 | 2 | 0 | RF-3B | *Frank Fanovich-L* |
| M | 5/24-1 | Havana | W 6-5 (7) | | Did not play | | | | | | Jim Melton-R |
| M | 5/24-2 | Havana | W 6-4 | | Did not play | | | | | | *Clarence "Hooks" Iott-L* |
| Tu | 5/25 | Havana | L 5-6 | 1 | 0 | 0 | 0 | | | PH | Emilio Cueche-R |

Struck out as a pinch-hitter in the eighth against right hander Charlie Harris Jr.

| DAY | DATE | OPPONENT | SCORE | AB | R | H | RBI | PO | A | Pos | OPPOSING STARTER |
|---|---|---|---|---|---|---|---|---|---|---|---|
| W | 5/26 | Havana | L 2-4 (10) | | Did not play | | | | | | Saul Rogovin-R |
| Th | 5/27 | Havana | W 8-2 | | Did not play | | | | | | Eusebio Perez-R |
| F | 5/28 | Toronto, rain | | | | | | | | | |
| Sa | 5/29 | Toronto, rain | | | | | | | | | |
| Su | 5/30-1 | Toronto | W 1-0 | 0 | 0 | 0 | 0 | 0 | 0 | RF | Clifford "Connie" Johnson-R |
| Su | 5/30-2 | Toronto | L 4-11 (7) | | Did not play | | | | | | Eddie Blake-R |
| M | 5/31-1 | at Rochester | W 6-5 (7) | 0 | 0 | 0 | 0 | 0 | 0 | RF | Harry Hoitsma-R |
| M | 5/31-2 | at Rochester | L 8-9 | | Did not play | | | | | | Cloyd Boyer-R |
| Tu | 6/1 | at Richmond | W 12-11 | 1 | 0 | 1 | 1 | 0 | 0 | RF | *Frank Fanovich-L* |
| W | 6/2 | at Richmond | L 2-7 | | Did not play | | | | | | Tom Fine-R |
| Th | 6/3 | at Richmond | L 2-7 | | Did not play | | | | | | Angelo "Wimpy" Nardella-R |
| F | 6/4-1 | at Richmond | L 0-5 (7) | 3 | 0 | 0 | 0 | 0 | 0 | *RF* | *John "Jocko" Thompson-L* |
| F | 6/4-2 | at Richmond | L 9-13 | 2 | 0 | 1 | 0 | 0 | 0 | LF | Bob Habenicht-R |
| Sa | 6/5 | at Richmond | W 12-7 | 5 | 1 | 0 | 0 | 0 | 0 | *RF* | *Frank Fanovich-L* |
| Su | 6/6-1 | at Havana | L 1-2 | | Did not play | | | | | | Emilio Cueche-R |
| Su | 6/6-2 | at Havana | W 4-1 (7) | | Did not play | | | | | | Maurice Fisher-R |

Joe Black, who joined the Royals in Richmond on June 2, pitches a two-hitter.

| Day | Date | Opponent | Score | AB | R | H | RBI | PO | A | Pos | Opposing Starter |
|---|---|---|---|---|---|---|---|---|---|---|---|
| M | 6/7 | at Havana | W 7-3 | 0 | 0 | 0 | 0 | 0 | 0 | RF | Clarence "Hooks" Iott-L |

Clemente batted eighth. The Royals had two runs in and the bases loaded in the top of the first. Havana relieved Iotts with right-hander Raul Sanchez, and Dick Whitman pinch-hit for Clemente.

| Day | Date | Opponent | Score | AB | R | H | RBI | PO | A | Pos | Opposing Starter |
|---|---|---|---|---|---|---|---|---|---|---|---|
| Tu | 6/8 | at Havana | W 3-1 | Did not play | | | | | | | Saul Rogovin-R |
| W | 6/9 | at Havana | L 0-2 | Did not play | | | | | | | Jim Melton-R |
| Th | 6/10 | at Havana | 0-0 (10) | 0 | 0 | 0 | 0 | 0 | 0 | PR-RF | Emilio Cueche-R |

Game called after 10 innings to allow Montreal to catch its plane. This game apparently was not resumed but instead was replayed when Montreal went back to Havana in August.

| Day | Date | Opponent | Score | AB | R | H | RBI | PO | A | Pos | Opposing Starter |
|---|---|---|---|---|---|---|---|---|---|---|---|
| Sa | 6/12 | Ottawa | W 3-2 | Did not play | | | | | | | Lee Wheat-R |
| Su | 6/13-1 | Ottawa | W 4-2 | Did not play | | | | | | | Vince Gohl-L |
| Su | 6/13-2 | Ottawa | W 4-3 (7) | Did not play | | | | | | | Charlie Haag-R |
| M | 6/14 | at Ottawa, rain | | | | | | | | | |
| Tu | 6/15-1 | at Ottawa | L 1-4 (7) | Did not play | | | | | | | Walt Kellner-R |
| Tu | 6/15-2 | at Ottawa | L 3-8 | Did not play | | | | | | | Charlie Bishop-R |
| W | 6/16-1 | at Ottawa | W 6-3 (7) | 1 | 1 | 1 | 0 | 1 | 0 | RF | Art Ditmar-R |

Stolen base.

| Day | Date | Opponent | Score | AB | R | H | RBI | PO | A | Pos | Opposing Starter |
|---|---|---|---|---|---|---|---|---|---|---|---|
| W | 6/16-2 | at Ottawa | W 7-5 | Did not play | | | | | | | Lee Wheat-R |
| Th | 6/17 | Rochester | W 11-4 | Did not play | | | | | | | Niles Jordan-L |
| F | 6/18 | Rochester | L 3-10 | Did not play | | | | | | | Preacher Jack Faszholz-R |
| Sa | 6/19 | Rochester | L 2-5 | 0 | 0 | 0 | 0 | 0 | 0 | RF | Bill Connelly-R |
| Su | 6/20-1 | Rochester | L 8-11 | Did not play | | | | | | | Guillermo "Memo" Luna-L |
| Su | 6/20-2 | Rochester | L 3-8 (7) | Did not play | | | | | | | Larry Jackson-R |
| M | 6/21 | Syracuse | W 11-1 | 5 | 2 | 1 | 0 | 1 | 0 | RF | Jack Spring-L |

Double (1).

| Day | Date | Opponent | Score | AB | R | H | RBI | PO | A | Pos | Opposing Starter |
|---|---|---|---|---|---|---|---|---|---|---|---|
| Tu | 6/22 | Syracuse | W 13-9 | Did not play | | | | | | | Jim Owens-R |
| W | 6/23 | Syracuse, rain | | | | | | | | | |
| Th | 6/24 | Syracuse | W 3-2 | 0 | 0 | 0 | 0 | 0 | 0 | RF | Marv Williams-L |
| F | 6/25-1 | Toronto | L 7-10 | Did not play | | | | | | | Eddie Blake-R |
| F | 6/25-2 | Toronto | W 17-7 | Did not play | | | | | | | Vic Lombardi-L |
| Sa | 6/26 | Toronto, rain | | | | | | | | | |
| Su | 6/27-1 | Toronto | L 8-10 | Did not play | | | | | | | Clifford "Connie" Johnson-R |
| Su | 6/27-2 | Toronto | W 6-1 (7) | Did not play | | | | | | | Arnie Landeck-R |
| M | 6/28 | Buffalo | W 7-0 | Did not play | | | | | | | Paul Foytack-R |
| Tu | 6/29 | Buffalo | W 3-0 | Did not play | | | | | | | Ken Johnson-L |
| W | 6/30 | Buffalo | W 4-3 | 0 | 0 | 0 | 0 | 0 | 0 | RF | Hal Hudson-L |
| Th | 7/1-1 | Buffalo | L 2-3 | Did not play | | | | | | | Hal Erickson-R |
| Th | 7/1-2 | Buffalo | L 0-1 (7) | Did not play | | | | | | | Bill Froats-L |
| F | 7/2 | at Ottawa | W 12-1 | 2 | 1 | 1 | 1 | 0 | 0 | LF | Vince Gohl-L |
| Sa | 7/3 | at Ottawa | L 6-16 | 2 | 0 | 0 | 1 | 0 | 0 | CF | John Gray-R |
| Su | 7/4-1 | Ottawa | W 5-0 | Did not play | | | | | | | Lee Wheat-R |
| Su | 7/4-2 | Ottawa | L 2-7 (7) | Did not play | | | | | | | Art Ditmar-R |
| M | 7/5-1 | at Buffalo | W 6-0 | Did not play | | | | | | | Hal Erickson-R |
| M | 7/5-2 | at Buffalo | L 4-5 (7) | 3 | 1 | 0 | 0 | 1 | 0 | RF | Hal Hudson-L |
| Tu | 7/6 | at Buffalo | W 8-6 | 3 | 0 | 0 | 0 | 2 | 0 | RF | Bill Froats-L |
| W | 7/7-1 | at Buffalo | W 7-6 (7) | 2 | 1 | 2 | 0 | 3 | 0 | LF | Paul Foytack-R |
| W | 7/7-2 | at Buffalo | W 7-1 | 4 | 0 | 0 | 0 | 3 | 0 | LF | Ken Johnson-L |
| Th | 7/8 | at Syracuse | W 12-8 | 1 | 1 | 0 | 0 | 1 | 0 | PR-LF | Kent Peterson-L |
| F | 7/9 | at Syracuse | W 5-2 | 1 | 1 | 0 | 0 | 0 | 0 | LF | Marv Williams-L |
| Sa | 7/10 | at Syracuse | W 4-0 | Did not play | | | | | | | Jack Sanford-R |
| Su | 7/11-1 | at Syracuse | L 8-10 | 0 | 0 | 0 | | | | PH | Jack Meyer-R |

Announced as pinch-hitter in the ninth with right hander Lynn Lovenguth pitching. When left hander Kent Peterson relieved Lovenguth, Tom Lasorda hit for Clemente.

| Day | Date | Opponent | Score | AB | R | H | RBI | PO | A | Pos | Opposing Starter |
|---|---|---|---|---|---|---|---|---|---|---|---|
| Su | 7/11-2 | at Syracuse | L 0-2 (7) | Did not play | | | | | | | Jim Owens-L |

Last game for Sandy Amoros with Montreal. Amoros, who set a new team record with a 27-game hitting streak, was recalled by Brooklyn.

| Day | Date | Opponent | Score | AB | R | H | RBI | PO | A | Pos | Opposing Starter |
|---|---|---|---|---|---|---|---|---|---|---|---|
| Tu | 7/13 | at Ottawa | W 4-2 | Did not play | | | | | | | Art Ditmar-R |
| W | 7/14 | at Ottawa | L 7-21 | Did not play | | | | | | | Bob Trice-R |
| Th | 7/15 | at Ottawa | L 1-2 | Did not play | | | | | | | Lee Wheat-R |
| F | 7/16 | at Rochester | W 5-0 | Did not play | | | | | | | Ed Ludwig-L |
| Sa | 7/17 | at Rochester | W 6-2 | Did not play | | | | | | | Gary Blaylock-R |
| Su | 7/18 | at Rochester | L 3-4 | Did not play | | | | | | | Preacher Jack Faszholz-R |
| M | 7/19-1 | Richmond | W 2-1 (8) | Did not play | | | | | | | Frank Fanovich-L |
| M | 7/19-2 | Richmond | L 4-9 | Did not play | | | | | | | Angelo "Wimpy" Nardella-R |
| Tu | 7/20 | Richmond | L 1-2 | Did not play | | | | | | | Ken Heintzelman-L |

| Day | Date | Opponent | Score | AB | R | H | RBI | PO | A | Pos | Opposing Starter |
|-----|------|----------|-------|----|----|----|----|----|----|----|----|
| W | 7/21-1 | Richmond | W 1-0 (7) | 0 | 1 | 0 | 0 | | | PR | *Irv Medlinger-L* |

Clemente ran for Dixie Howell in the last of the seventh and scored the winning run, coming home from second on Gino Cimoli's two-out single.

| Day | Date | Opponent | Score | AB | R | H | RBI | PO | A | Pos | Opposing Starter |
|-----|------|----------|-------|----|----|----|----|----|----|----|----|
| W | 7/21-2 | Richmond | W 2-1 | | Did not play | | | | | | Bob Habenicht-R |
| Th | 7/22 | Havana | W 4-2 | | Did not play | | | | | | *Ken Raffensberger-L* |
| Sa | 7/24 | Havana | L 2-9 | | Did not play | | | | | | Jim Melton-R |
| Su | 7/25-1 | Havana | W 7-6 (10) | 1 | 1 | 1 | 1 | 1 | 0 | LF | Saul Rogovin-R |

Home run (1). After Gino Cimoli was pinch-hit for in the bottom of the eighth inning, Clemente entered the game in left field in the top of the ninth. With one out in the bottom of the 10th, he homered off right hander Charlie Harris, Jr.

| Day | Date | Opponent | Score | AB | R | H | RBI | PO | A | Pos | Opposing Starter |
|-----|------|----------|-------|----|----|----|----|----|----|----|----|
| Su | 7/25-2 | Havana | W 4-1 | 2 | 0 | 1 | 1 | 1 | 0 | *LF* | *Clarence "Hooks" Iott-L* |

Double (2). Starting with this game, Clemente was in the starting lineup for each game when the opposing starter was left-handed. He did not start any games against a right-handed starter.

| Day | Date | Opponent | Score | AB | R | H | RBI | PO | A | Pos | Opposing Starter |
|-----|------|----------|-------|----|----|----|----|----|----|----|----|
| M | 7/26 | at Syracuse | W 6-3 | | Did not play | | | | | | Jack Sanford-R |
| Tu | 7/27-1 | at Syracuse | L 5-9 (7) | 2 | 0 | 1 | 0 | 3 | 0 | *LF* | *Marv Williams-L* |

Double (3).

| Day | Date | Opponent | Score | AB | R | H | RBI | PO | A | Pos | Opposing Starter |
|-----|------|----------|-------|----|----|----|----|----|----|----|----|
| Tu | 7/27-2 | at Syracuse | L 0-1 | 0 | 0 | 0 | 0 | | | PR | Jim Owens-R |
| W | 7/28 | at Syracuse | L 1-3 | 4 | 1 | 2 | 0 | 4 | 0 | *LF* | *Kent Peterson-L* |
| F | 7/30 | at Toronto | W 2-0 (9) | 2 | 1 | 1 | 0 | 0 | 0 | LF-RF | Eddie Blake-R |

Completion of a suspended seven-inning game May 9. In the top of the ninth, Clemente doubled (Double 4) and scored the go-ahead run.

| Day | Date | Opponent | Score | AB | R | H | RBI | PO | A | Pos | Opposing Starter |
|-----|------|----------|-------|----|----|----|----|----|----|----|----|
| F | 7/30 | at Toronto | W 7-1 | 2 | 0 | 0 | 0 | 0 | 0 | *LF* | *Vic Lombardi-L* |
| Sa | 7/31 | at Toronto | L 6-7 | 1 | 0 | 0 | 0 | 0 | 0 | *LF* | *Fred Hahn-L* |
| Su | 8/1-1 | at Toronto | W 4-2 (10) | 0 | 0 | 0 | 0 | 0 | 0 | RF | Clifford "Connie" Johnson-R |
| Su | 8/1-2 | at Toronto | 8-1 (6) | | | | | | | | |

Game was suspended by curfew with one out in the last of the sixth. Clemente did not play as right hander Frank Barnes started for Toronto.

| Day | Date | Opponent | Score | AB | R | H | RBI | PO | A | Pos | Opposing Starter |
|-----|------|----------|-------|----|----|----|----|----|----|----|----|
| M | 8/2-1 | at Toronto | W 5-3 | 0 | 0 | 0 | 0 | 0 | 0 | RF | Eddie Blake-R |
| M | 8/2-2 | at Toronto | W 4-2 (7) | 1 | 0 | 0 | 0 | 0 | 0 | PH-RF | Bill Powell-R |
| Tu | 8/3-1 | Toronto | L 4-22 (7) | 3 | 0 | 2 | 0 | 1 | 1 | PH-LF | Arnie Landeck-R |

Toronto manager Luke Sewell, in an attempt to counter Max Macon's platoon strategy, started right hander Arnie Landeck and removed him for a pinch-hitter in the top of the second inning. When left hander Vic Lombardi took the mound in the bottom of the second, Clemente hit for Dick Whitman and singled.

| Day | Date | Opponent | Score | AB | R | H | RBI | PO | A | Pos | Opposing Starter |
|-----|------|----------|-------|----|----|----|----|----|----|----|----|
| Tu | 8/3-2 | Toronto | W 10-3 | 0 | 0 | 0 | 0 | 0 | 0 | PR-RF | Rudy Minarcin-R |
| W | 8/4-1 | Toronto | W 3-2 (7) | 0 | 0 | 0 | 0 | 1 | 0 | RF | Clifford "Connie" Johnson-R |
| W | 8/4-2 | Toronto | L 4-10 | 2 | 1 | 0 | 0 | 0 | 0 | PH-RF | Clifford "Connie" Johnson-R |

Luke Sewell had Connie Johnson start the second game and then relieved him with left hander Fred Hahn with one out in the first inning. Clemente pinch-hit for Whitman against Hahn in the seventh. Montreal: 63-49, third place, seven games behind first-place Toronto (owned by Jack Kent Cooke) and six games behind second-place Rochester.

| Day | Date | Opponent | Score | AB | R | H | RBI | PO | A | Pos | Opposing Starter |
|-----|------|----------|-------|----|----|----|----|----|----|----|----|
| Th | 8/5 | Toronto | L 1-10 | 1 | 0 | 0 | 0 | | | PH | Frank Barnes-R |
| Sa | 8/7 | Rochester | W 6-3 | 4 | 0 | 0 | 1 | 0 | | *LF-RF* | *Guillermo "Memo" Luna-L* |
| Su | 8/8-1 | Rochester | L 2-3 (11) | | Did not play | | | | | | Preacher Jack Faszholz-R |
| Su | 8/8-2 | Rochester | W 9-0 (7) | | Did not play | | | | | | Mario Picone-R |
| M | 8/9 | Ottawa | L 4-7 | 4 | 1 | 1 | 2 | 5 | 0 | *LF* | *Vince Gohl-L* |

Triple (1).

| Day | Date | Opponent | Score | AB | R | H | RBI | PO | A | Pos | Opposing Starter |
|-----|------|----------|-------|----|----|----|----|----|----|----|----|
| Tu | 8/10 | Havana | W 5-3 | 1 | 0 | 0 | 0 | 0 | 0 | RF | Jim Melton-R |
| W | 8/11 | Havana, rain | | | | | | | | | |

Montreal: 66-52, third place, seven games behind Toronto and five behind Rochester.

| Day | Date | Opponent | Score | AB | R | H | RBI | PO | A | Pos | Opposing Starter |
|-----|------|----------|-------|----|----|----|----|----|----|----|----|
| Th | 8/12 | Havana | L 5-10 | 2 | 0 | 0 | 2 | 0 | 0 | *LF* | *Ken Raffensberger-L* |

Running in from left field at the end of the top of the sixth, Clemente fell crossing the mound and turned his ankle. It was thought he would be out a week, but he was back two nights later.

| Day | Date | Opponent | Score | AB | R | H | RBI | PO | A | Pos | Opposing Starter |
|-----|------|----------|-------|----|----|----|----|----|----|----|----|
| F | 8/13 | Richmond | W 5-3 | | Did not play | | | | | | Angelo "Wimpy" Nardella-R |
| Sa | 8/14 | Richmond | W 6-0 | 4 | 1 | 3 | 0 | 3 | 0 | *LF* | *Frank Fanovich-L* |
| Su | 8/15-1 | Richmond | W 8-0 | 4 | 0 | 1 | 0 | 4 | 0 | *LF* | *John "Jocko" Thompson-L* |
| Su | 8/15-2 | Richmond | L 1-5 (7) | 3 | 0 | 0 | 1 | 1 | 0 | *LF* | *Ken Heintzelman-L* |

Error (1).

| Day | Date | Opponent | Score | AB | R | H | RBI | PO | A | Pos | Opposing Starter |
|-----|------|----------|-------|----|----|----|----|----|----|----|----|
| Tu | 8/17 | at Toronto | W 10-1 (7) | | Did not play | | | | | | Frank Barnes-R |

Completion of suspended game from August 1.

| Day | Date | Opponent | Score | AB | R | H | RBI | PO | A | Pos | Opposing Starter |
|-----|------|----------|-------|----|----|----|----|----|----|----|----|
| Tu | 8/17 | at Toronto | W 5-3 | | Did not play | | | | | | Bill Powell-R |
| W | 8/18 | at Toronto | W 8-7 | 4 | 0 | 2 | 0 | 2 | 1 | *LF-RF* | *Vic Lombardi-L* |

Triple (2). Clemente threw out the potential tying run at the plate from right field to end the game. Canadian Press report: "A crowd of 6,706 saw Clemente throw a perfect peg from right field to the plate to nail Leaf runner Connie Johnson. With two outs Johnson attempted to score the tying run from second on first baseman Ed Steven's single." Montreal: 72-54, third place, 6½ games behind Toronto and 3½ games behind Rochester.

| Day | Date | Opponent | Score | AB | R | H | RBI | PO | A | Pos | Opposing Starter |
|-----|------|----------|-------|----|----|----|----|----|----|----|----|
| F | 8/20 | at Havana | W 8-5 | 5 | 1 | 1 | 0 | 1 | 0 | *LF* | *Ken Raffensberger-L* |
| Sa | 8/21 | at Havana | L 1-4 | | Did not play | | | | | | Bill Powell-R |

| Day | Date | Opponent | Score | AB | R | H | RBI | PO | A | Pos | Opposing Starter |
|-----|------|----------|-------|----|----|----|-----|----|----|-----|------------------|
| Su | 8/22-1 | at Havana | W 2-0 | | | Did not play | | | | | Jim Melton-R |
| Su | 8/22-2 | at Havana, rain | | | | | | | | | |
| M | 8/23-1 | at Havana | W 5-2 (7) | 0 | 1 | 0 | 0 | 0 | 0 | PR–RF | Emilio Cueche-R |
| M | 8/23-2 | at Havana | L 6-7 | 1 | 0 | 0 | 0 | | | PH | Julio Moreno-R |
| Tu | 8/24 | at Havana | W 2-0 | 3 | 0 | 0 | 1 | 1 | 0 | *RF* | *Ken Raffensberger-L* |
| W | 8/25 | at Richmond | L 4-7 | 4 | 0 | 0 | 0 | 2 | 0 | *LF* | *Frank Fanovich-L* |

Montreal: 76-57, third place, 8 games behind Toronto and 1 game behind Rochester.

| Day | Date | Opponent | Score | AB | R | H | RBI | PO | A | Pos | Opposing Starter |
|-----|------|----------|-------|----|----|----|-----|----|----|-----|------------------|
| Th | 8/26 | at Richmond | W 6-5 | | | Did not play | | | | | Bob Habenicht-R |
| F | 8/27 | at Richmond | W 9-0 | | | Did not play | | | | | Tom Fine-R |
| Sa | 8/28 | at Richmond | W 3-2 (10) | 3 | 0 | 0 | 0 | 1 | 0 | *RF* | *Ken Heintzelman-L* |
| Su | 8/29 | at Richmond | L 7-8 | 3 | 2 | 3 | 1 | 1 | 0 | *RF* | *John "Jocko" Thompson-L* |

2 triples (4).

| Day | Date | Opponent | Score | AB | R | H | RBI | PO | A | Pos | Opposing Starter |
|-----|------|----------|-------|----|----|----|-----|----|----|-----|------------------|
| M | 8/30 | at Buffalo, rain | | | | | | | | | |
| Tu | 8/31 | at Buffalo, rain | | | | | | | | | |
| W | 9/1-1 | at Buffalo | L 2-4 (7) | | | Did not play | | | | | Frank Lary-R |
| W | 9/1-2 | at Buffalo | L 3-5 | 4 | 0 | 1 | 0 | 2 | 0 | *RF* | *Ken Johnson-L* |

Montreal: 79-60, third place, 9 games behind Toronto and 1 game behind Rochester.

| Day | Date | Opponent | Score | AB | R | H | RBI | PO | A | Pos | Opposing Starter |
|-----|------|----------|-------|----|----|----|-----|----|----|-----|------------------|
| Th | 9/2 | Syracuse | W 6-4 | 0 | 0 | 0 | 0 | 0 | 0 | RF | Jim Owens-R |
| F | 9/3 | Syracuse | L 4-5 (10) | 2 | 1 | 1 | 0 | 3 | 0 | **LF-RF** | *Kent Peterson-L* |
| Sa | 9/4 | Syracuse | W 5-0 | | | Did not play | | | | | Jack Sanford-R |
| Su | 9/5-1 | Syracuse | W 3-2 | 3 | 0 | 1 | 1 | 4 | 0 | **LF-RF** | *Marv Williams-L* |
| Su | 9/5-2 | Syracuse | W 4-3 (8) | 1 | 1 | 1 | 1 | 0 | 0 | RF | Jack Meyer-R |

Home run (2). Homered off righthander Lynn Lovenguth to lead off last of the eighth and win the game (scheduled seven-inning game).

| Day | Date | Opponent | Score | AB | R | H | RBI | PO | A | Pos | Opposing Starter |
|-----|------|----------|-------|----|----|----|-----|----|----|-----|------------------|
| M | 9/6-1 | Ottawa | L 4-5 (10) | 0 | 0 | 0 | 0 | 1 | 0 | RF | Bob Trice-R |
| M | 9/6-2 | Ottawa | W 2-0 (7) | 2 | 0 | 0 | 0 | 3 | 0 | **LF** | *Vince Gohl-L* |
| Tu | 9/7 | at Rochester | W 8-5 | | | Did not play | | | | | Larry Jackson-R |
| W | 9/8 | at Rochester | L 2-3 (10) | 4 | 0 | 1 | 0 | 1 | 0 | *RF* | *Ed Ludwig-L* |

Montreal: 85-63, second place, 8 games behind Toronto.

| Day | Date | Opponent | Score | AB | R | H | RBI | PO | A | Pos | Opposing Starter |
|-----|------|----------|-------|----|----|----|-----|----|----|-----|------------------|
| Th | 9/9 | at Rochester | L 0-1 | 3 | 0 | 1 | 0 | 1 | 0 | *RF* | *Guillermo "Memo" Luna-L* |
| F | 9/10-1 | Buffalo | W 6-3 (7) | 3 | 0 | 0 | 0 | 0 | 0 | *LF* | *Hal Hudson-L* |
| F | 9/10-2 | Buffalo | W 10-4 | | | Did not play. | | | | | Duke Maas-R |
| Sa | 9/11 | Buffalo | L 6-7 | 2 | 2 | 1 | 2 | 2 | 0 | **LF-RF** | *Bill Froats-L* |
| Su | 9/12 | Buffalo | L 0-3 | | | Did not play | | | | | Frank Lary-R |
| Su | 9/12 | Buffalo | W 13-10 (7) | | | Did not play | | | | | Jim Harper-R |

Montreal finishes in second place with a record of 88-66-1, 7 games behind Toronto.

| COMPILATION | | AB | R | H | RBI | PO | A | |
|-------------|--|----|----|----|-----|----|----|-|
| 86 games (38 started) | | 148 | 28 | 38 | 14 | 83 | 2 | 1 error, 4 doubles, 4 triples, 2 home runs |

REGULAR-SEASON TOTALS FROM
THE 1955 OFFICIAL BASEBALL GUIDE

| | | AB | R | H | RBI | PO | A | |
|--|--|----|----|----|-----|----|----|-|
| 87 games (77 in outfield) | | 148 | 27 | 38 | 12 | 81 | 1 | 1 error, 5 doubles, 3 triples, 2 home runs. (Also 1 sacrifice, 1 sacrifice fly, 6 walks, 0 hit by pitch, 17 strikeouts) |

GAMES PLAYED BY OTHER MONTREAL OUTFIELDERS

Sandy Amoros 68 games, Gino Cimoli 114, Jack Cassini 126, Dick Whitman 82, Don Thompson 61, Ken Wood 15 (also played for Richmond).

| DAY | DATE | OPPONENT | SCORE | AB | R | H | RBI | PO | A | POS | OPPOSING STARTER |
|-----|------|----------|-------|----|---|---|-----|----|---|-----|------------------|
| Tu | 9/14 | Rochester | L 0-2 | | Did not play | | | | | | Preacher Jack Faszholz-R |
| W | 9/15 | Rochester | W 5-0 | 2 | 1 | 1 | 0 | 1 | 0 | *LF* | *Guillermo "Memo" Luna-L* |
| F | 9/17 | at Rochester | W 6-2 | | Did not play | | | | | | Larry Jackson-R |
| Sa | 9/18 | at Rochester, rain | | | | | | | | | |
| Su | 9/19 | at Rochester | L 4-5 | 0 | 1 | 0 | 0 | | | PR | Preacher Jack Faszholz-R |
| M | 9/20 | at Rochester | W 3-2 | 1 | 0 | 0 | 0 | 0 | 0 | *RF* | *Guillermo "Memo" Luna-L* |
| Tu | 9/21 | Rochester, rain | | | | | | | | | |
| W | 9/22 | Rochester, rain | | | | | | | | | |
| Th | 9/23 | Rochester | W 4-3 | 0 | 0 | 0 | 0 | 0 | 0 | RF | Preacher Jack Faszholz-R |
| TOTALS | | | | 3 | 2 | 1 | 1 | 0 | 0 | | |

| DAY | DATE | OPPONENT | SCORE | AB | R | H | RBI | PO | A | POS | OPPOSING STARTER |
|-----|------|----------|-------|----|---|---|-----|----|---|-----|------------------|
| Sa | 9/25 | Syracuse | W 5-0 | 2 | 2 | 1 | 1 | 1 | 0 | *RF* | *Kent Peterson-L* |
| | | Sacrifice fly | | | | | | | | | |
| Su | 9/26 | Syracuse | L 2-3 | | Did not play | | | | | | Jack Meyer-R |
| M | 9/27 | at Syracuse | L 1-2 | | Did not play | | | | | | Jim Owens-R |
| Tu | 9/28 | at Syracuse | L 1-15 | | Did not play | | | | | | Jack Sanford-R |
| W | 9/29 | at Syracuse | W 7-0 | 1 | 0 | 1 | 0 | 0 | 0 | RF | Jack Meyer-R |
| Th | 9/30 | Syracuse, rain | | | | | | | | | |

**October**

| DAY | DATE | OPPONENT | SCORE | AB | R | H | RBI | PO | A | POS | OPPOSING STARTER |
|-----|------|----------|-------|----|---|---|-----|----|---|-----|------------------|
| Fr | 10/1 | Syracuse | W 6-5 | 1 | 0 | 0 | 0 | 0 | 0 | *RF* | *Jim Owens-R* |
| Sa | 10/2 | Syracuse | L 6-7 | | Did not play | | | | | | Jack Meyer-R |
| TOTAL | | | | 4 | 2 | 2 | 1 | 3 | 0 | | |

## Discrepancies

*Neil Raymond reports that statistics up to May 3, 1954 (incorporating games through May 2) in the *Montreal Gazette* show that Clemente had played in all nine of Montreal's games to date; however, like *The Sporting News*, the *Gazette* box score for the first game of the April 25 doubleheader (the Royals' third game of the season) does not list Clemente as having played.

July 5, second game, *The Sporting News* shows Clemente with 1 putout. The *Montreal Gazette* shows no putouts.

July 30, completion of suspended game, *The Sporting News* shows Clemente with 1 run. The *Montreal Gazette* shows him with no runs; the *Gazette* indicates only a run scored by Dan Thompson (*The Sporting News* shows runs by Clemente and Thompson) in a 2-0 game, so this is almost certainly a typo on the part of the *Gazette*.

# The Winning Team
## Fact and Fiction in Celluloid Biographies

### by Rob Edelman

NARRATIVE films are not factual films—even when they purport to divulge the true-life stories of real people. Whether their subjects are sports figures, show business personalities, or world leaders, such movies often are rife with misinformation. But unless their function is to propagandize, they are not purposefully fashioned to toss the viewer curveballs and spitballs. They exist as entertainments, not as historical records.

*The Winning Team* (1952), a Hollywood biography of Hall of Fame pitcher Grover Cleveland Alexander, is a case study in skewing the facts in a baseball biography. In the film, which was produced by Warner Bros. and released two years after Alexander's death, Ronald Reagan is cast as Alex the Great and Doris Day plays his wife, Aimee.

In 1952, Reagan was 41 years old. His career as a big-screen leading man was on the downside. By far his best roles came during the previous decade; two years later, he began hosting the dramatic anthology series *General Electric Theater* on television. Day, meanwhile, was a rising actress and singing star. At the time she was earning notoriety for playing cheery, idealized all-American girls: the type of young woman a clear-minded male would fall for, and proudly bring home to mother. This precisely is her role in *The Winning Team*.

Reagan's and Day's respective status within the Hollywood star hierarchy explains why, even though the scenario ostensibly centers on the plight and fate of Grover Cleveland Alexander, Day is billed above Reagan. In fact, in a review of the film published in the May 28, 1952, *Variety*, the motion picture trade publication, it is noted that "Doris Day, on whose name rests the film's chief marquee draw, contributes a sincere, moving portrayal of Alexander's wife." Even though *The Winning Team* is not a musical, and Aimee Alexander was not known for her singing ability, Day's vocal talents are worked into the script; in a Doris Day film, viewers anticipated hearing her sing. And so her Aimee performs a perky Christmas tune, "Ol' Saint Nicholas," and absentmindedly vocalizes a few bars of "Take Me Out to the Ball Game" while doing household chores.

Moreover, the title *The Winning Team*—the film was called *The Big League* and *Alexander, The Big Leaguer* while in production—does not refer to the Philadelphia Phillies, Chicago Cubs, or St. Louis Cardinals, Alexander's major league affiliations. It represents the union of Grover and Aimee Alexander. In its advertising the following blurbs were employed to market the film: "When all America called him Alex the Great, they were really throwing kisses at her!"; and "They'll win your heart too! This hero who won fame the second time—this blue-eyed girl whose love helped turn jeers to cheers! The true story and truly wonderful story of Grover Cleveland Alexander." In its re-release trailer, *The Winning Team* was heralded as "the warmest, most wonderful, most human story ever told—the true story of Grover Cleveland Alexander and the woman who shared all the adventures of his fabulous career." Aimee Alexander was described as "the strength behind (Alex's) every pitch. She was the light in his darkest hours. Hers was the love that gave him the courage to win his greatest victories."

As the film opens, a point that was emphasized in its marketing campaign is reaffirmed as the viewer is informed that *The Winning Team* is "the True Story of Grover Cleveland Alexander." A number of real-life individuals are worked into the script: Bill Killifer (James Millican), Alexander's catcher with

ROB EDELMAN *is the author of* Great Baseball Films *and* Baseball on the Web. *He teaches film history at the University at Albany (SUNY) and offers film commentary on WAMC (Northeast) Public Radio.*

The Winning Team: *Ronald Reagan (left) as Grover Alexander, Frank Lovejoy as Rogers Hornsby; at right, Alex passes out on the mound.*

the Philadelphia Phillies; Phillies catcher-manager Red Dooin (Billy Wayne); famed umpire Bill Klem (Pat Flaherty); and a pair of Hall of Famers, Rogers Hornsby (Frank Lovejoy) and Joe McCarthy (Hugh Sanders). Several then-current major leaguers appear in the film: Bob Lemon (who plays St. Louis Cardinals hurler Jesse Haines); Gerry Priddy; Peanuts Lowrey; Catfish Metkovich; Irv Noren; Hank Sauer; Al Zarilla; and Gene Mauch. Yet ultimately, the film's content and thrust are reflections of the input of one of the film's technical advisors: Mrs. Grover Cleveland Alexander (who earns screen credit in this capacity with Priddy and Arnold "Jigger" Statz).

In the film (whose screenplay is credited to Merwin Gerard, Seeleg Lester, and Ted Sherdeman), Aimee is the girlfriend and eventual wife of Alex, a small-town Nebraska telephone linesman-turned-big league pitching star. Initially, Aimee does not support Alex's love of sports. He yearns to toss baseballs, but she wants him to pitch hay instead, preferring that he remain home and become a farmer. Even after Alex makes the majors, Aimee admits that she is jealous of her husband's love of the sport, but she supports him when she realizes he will be devastated if he does not play ball. While serving in World War I, Alex is knocked dizzy after an explosion. Upon returning to the majors, he falls ill in the locker room and then, in a Hollywood touch, passes out on the mound. A doctor implores him to give up baseball; he informs no one about his unnamed illness (which actually was epilepsy), and begins drinking to escape his troubles. He eventually becomes an alcoholic, at which point he is abandoned by Aimee. Alex, now out of professional baseball, becomes a disheveled drifter and "stumbling has-been" who pitches for a semi-pro House of David team and pathetically recounts his heroics in amusement hall sideshows. Aimee rescues him upon learning the details of Alex's illness. He signs with the St. Louis Cardinals and regains his stardom. The story concludes with Alex pitching triumphantly in the 1926 World Series, striking out New York Yankee second sacker Tony Lazzeri at a key juncture.

Beyond its plot, *The Winning Team* is not so much a story of baseball in the 1910s and '20s as a reflection of the era in which it was made: the America of post–World War II, the America of 1952. At its core, it is the tale of a talented but flawed hero and his noble, pre-feminist, girl-next-door wife. Perhaps within the framework of the story Aimee does not support her beloved's desire to play baseball because, as a woman, she is oblivious to the appeal of athletics. (In *On Moonlight Bay* [1951], Day plays an adolescent tomboy who disregards her passion for baseball once she dons her first party dress and goes on her first date.) As the scenario develops, Aimee may go through several transformations, but she ultimately is supportive of Alex: the stereotypical good woman behind the respectable but imperfect man. She is the type of woman who would be thanked by her husband at a testimonial. He might conclude his remarks with a heartfelt sentiment such as "If it wasn't for her love and support, I would not be standing here tonight."

In *The Winning Team*, the viewer accesses the facts of Alexander's life as presented on-screen. As he faces his obstacles and crises, several questions arise. How accurately does the scenario mirror the reality of Grover Cleveland Alexander? How much is exaggerated? What has been omitted?

One of the unwritten laws in Hollywood is that movies must have smiley-face endings. A romantic but uneventful courtship does not translate into good drama or comedy, so a young man and woman will squabble and face assorted obstacles throughout a scenario. Even though the chances of their enjoying a happy union are almost nil, given the differences in their personalities, they lovingly embrace at the finale. Such is the case in *The Winning Team*. Aimee joins Alex after his World Series heroics, and the implication is that the pair lived happily ever after.

Such is the Hollywood biopic fantasy. The facts of Aimee's and Alex's life are something else altogether.

Grover Cleveland Alexander lived for 20 years after his 1930 major league swan song. He was elected to the Baseball Hall of Fame in 1938. But as Jan Finkel notes in his SABR Baseball Biography Project article on Alexander, "The last two decades of Alexander's life are the picture of a man spinning out of control with nobody able to stop the free-fall."

Aimee and Alex were no "winning team." They did not enjoy marital bliss, as they divorced in 1929, remarried two years later and divorced again in 1941. Alexander spent much of those final two decades in solitude, grappling with poverty, ill health, and other assorted sorrows.

After being released by the Phillies early in the 1930 season, the 43-year-old hurler was signed by the Dallas Steers of the Texas League. Almost immediately, he was suspended for breaking training. "Maybe

I've had enough," he told the Associated Press on July 16. "One thing I can say, I've given more to baseball than it's given me. I've never been a 'goody-goody' boy, but I stayed in there and pitched." But he did not stay in and pitch for the Steers. Following a brief reinstatement, he was released on July 21. After pitching a game for the Galesburg Independents, for whom he had played two decades earlier, Alex was signed and quickly cut loose by the American Association Toledo Mud Hens. Then in September he was jailed in Grand Island, Nebraska, for driving while drunk and leaving the scene of an auto accident.

In 1931, Alex the Great first became affiliated with the House of David team, for whom he managed and pitched. However, in February 1932, Grantland Rice reported that the 45-year-old hurler was "preparing for a comeback with the Chicago Cubs." This return to the majors did not materialize. That August, New York Times columnist John Kieran wrote of Alexander, "The old campaigner . . . was turned loose to wander hither and yon and the roads were not smooth. Picking up a few dollars for pitching wherever he could, he probably got up dreaming of other days and fell asleep in some tank town bullpen and woke up to find his chin covered with whiskers and his arm covered with moss." Kieran also reported that Alex could not recall the details of his 1926 World Series heroics.

In 1940, Alexander was hired as gatekeeper at a Detroit racetrack. His new employer was Clarence E. Lehr, president of the Detroit Racing Association. Back in 1911, Alexander and Lehr were Philadelphia Phillies rookies. Alex made the club. Lehr, an infielder, did not. After quitting baseball, he attended the University of Michigan and became a lawyer. A report of the hiring, released by the Associated Press, ended with the observation that "a modest job perhaps means more today to the 53 year old Alexander than memories of glory."

Alex's racetrack career was short-lived. The Associated Press reported that, in February 1941, he placed an ad in "a national baseball paper" seeking a job "as manager, coach or in any other capacity in which my experience and knowledge of the game will prove valuable." His fondness for alcohol had long been acknowledged throughout the baseball world, and no offers were forthcoming. By the following month he had begun a three-week stay in a Bronx, New York, veterans hospital. Then on July 26, a small item in the New York Times reported that Alexander, "once one of the star pitchers of organized baseball," had been discovered by one of New York's Finest "on the sidewalk at Sixth Avenue and Thirty-ninth Street, cut about the left eye." He was rushed to Bellevue Hospital, where he remained for six days. The Times noted that Alex "recently has been appearing in a sideshow in a West Forty-second Street amusement hall. A New York morning paper has been raising a fund for his benefit." According to the United Press, the Hall of Famer was "suffering from alcoholism" and also had "been found on the street in bad condition" twice before: in Evanston, Indiana, in August 1936, and in early 1937 in Springfield, Illinois.

In April 1943, Alex was interviewed in Cincinnati, at a game between the Reds and Cardinals. He was just another fan in the stands—and he was unemployed. "Right now I'm looking for a job, of course," he declared. "I'd like to hook up with some team as a coach, but if I can't land that I want to get some war work. I've tried several places around Cincinnati, but my age is against me."

It was not without irony that in October 1946—20 years after starring in the World Series—Alexander was stricken with a mild heart attack after leaving St. Louis's Sportsman's Park, where the Cardinals had just won the fall classic.

Such was the tenor of his life after his major league heroics.

Alex's cheerless presence at one final World Series was noted in the media. The Philadelphia Phillies played the New York Yankees in the 1950 fall classic and, in the October 7, 1950, New York Times, sportswriter Louis Effrat reported Alex in attendance at Yankee Stadium. After describing his on-field accomplishments in the 1926 Series, Effrat wrote that the ex-hero "was lost in the crowd . . . [and] stood by obscurely in the back of the mezzanine." The scribe noted that an old-time sportswriter recognized Alexander and invited him into the press box, where he spent the rest of the game reminiscing about the "old days." Effrat concluded by noting, "Baseball may have forgotten Grover Cleveland Alexander, but he had not forgotten baseball."

About a month later, the newspapers were filled with reports of Alexander's death. He had returned to his home in St. Paul, Nebraska, where he died of a heart attack. The extensive press coverage reported that the Hall of Famer was living in a rooming house and that he was divorced from his wife.

When *The Winning Team* went into production, Grover Cleveland Alexander no longer was living; the events and relationships in the film were filtered through the perceptions and agendas of wife Aimee. In his review of the film, published in the June 21, 1952 *New York Times*, critic Bosley Crowther questioned the veracity of the screenplay and concluded, with a note of sarcasm, "Most reassuring, however, is the fact that a technical advisor on this film was Mrs. Grover Cleveland Alexander. After all, she should know." In a second piece, published the following day, Crowther added, "And the story here is that his salvation—his ascendance to pitching heights, such as his great feat in the 1926 World Series—was to be credited entirely to his wife. A likely story!"

Prior to the film's release, Aimee Alexander insisted that the screenwriters "stuck quite close to the truth, juggling facts only for story and dramatic effects." Her observation applies to the depiction of Alexander toiling for the House of David team and in amusement hall sideshows *before* his exploits in the 1926 World Series. Such episodes are fashioned to represent "problems" to be overcome before the happy-ever-after finale, rather than as manifestations of the troubles that plagued Alex until his death.

Aimee's comment also fits the triumphant manner in which the film ends. It is implied that Alex's celebrated strikeout of Tony Lazzeri was the final play in the deciding series game—when in fact it ended the seventh inning. Additionally, while promoting *The Winning Team*, Aimee admitted that she was not present during her husband's heroics. She figured that the game would be called because of rain, and remained in her hotel room. Yet on screen, she breathlessly arrives at Yankee Stadium. As he winds up, Alex looks in her direction and Aimee blows him a kiss.

Another example of artistic license involves a sequence in which Alex sympathizes with a struggling rookie who will be sent to the minors if he fails in his next at-bat. The pitcher grooves a pitch, and the batter's subsequent hit keeps him in the majors. The rookie is none other than Rogers Hornsby, and the implication is that Hornsby owed his Hall of Fame career to Alex's generosity. *Total Baseball* describes Hornsby as having "a royal disdain for the opinions and feelings of everybody he ever met," yet this "brusque, blunt, hypercritical, dictatorial, moody, and argumentative" baseball legend is portrayed in *The Winning Team* as an all-around nice guy.

A baseball fan who wishes to learn the true story of Grover Cleveland Alexander might peruse his clipping file in the National Baseball Hall of Fame library or read about him in a well-researched history book. *The Winning Team* is nothing more than an entertainment, the story of a famous ballplayer told from the perspective of his wife. It may be placed within the context of the popular culture of the early 1950s, from a point of view of the manner in which men, women, and American ball-playing heroes are portrayed on screen.

It is not the definitive word on its subject.

## Sources

BOOKS
Edelman, Rob. *Great Baseball Films.* Secaucus, NJ: Citadel Press, 1994.

ARTICLES
"Alex Named Pilot of House of David." *Washington Post*, April 5, 1931.
"Alexander, Found Here, Fired by Toledo Club." *Chicago Daily Tribune*, August 6, 1930.
"Alexander Found in Bronx Hospital after Job Appeal." *Washington Post*, March 21, 1941.
"Alexander Gets Release: Veteran Pitcher Let Go by Dallas Steers for Failing to Keep in Shape." *Los Angeles Times*, July 22, 1930.
"Alexander Held on Rum Charge after Accident." *Chicago Daily Tribune*, September 25, 1930.
"Alexander Is Stricken: Cards' 1926 Series Hero Suffers Heart Attack after Game." *New York Times*, October 16, 1946.
"Alexander Is Dead; Noted Pitcher, 63." *New York Times*, November 5, 1950.
"Alexander, Once The Great, Waits Decision on Fate: Yearns for Glory of Past, Careless of Future." *Chicago Daily Tribune*, July 17, 1930.
"Alexander Seeking Job: Former Pitching Star Wants to Return to Baseball as Coach." *New York Times*, April 22, 1943.
"Alexander Signed to Pitch for Dallas." *New York Times*, June 20, 1930.
Brog. "The Winning Team." *Variety*, May 28, 1952.
Crowther, Bosley. "Ladies and Sports: Two New Films Elevate the Fairer Sex." *New York Times*, June 22, 1952.
——. "'The Winning Team,' Story about Grover Cleveland Alexander, Arrives at the Mayfair." *New York Times.* June 21, 1952.
Effrat, Louis. "Old Pete Standee; Sic Transit Gloria: Alexander, Unrecognized by Fans, Finally Gets Seat, Recalls Days as Phil." *New York Times*, October 7, 1950.
"Forgotten Phil Buddy Gives Alexander Job." *Chicago Daily Tribune*, May 15, 1940.
Kieran, John. "Sports of the Times: The Old Age of Alexander the Great." *New York Times*, August 27, 1932.
"Old Pitcher Is Injured: Grover Cleveland Alexander Is Sent to Bellevue." *New York Times*, July 26, 1941.
Rice, Grantland. "The Sportlight." *Los Angeles Times*, February 7, 1932.
Walsh, Jack. "Alexander's Wife Missed Big Moment." *Washington Post*, April 15, 1952.

# Fascinating Aspects About the Retired Uniform Numbers of the Detroit Tigers

## by Herm Krabbenhoft

**W**HAT makes these Detroit Tigers uniform numbers—2, 5, 6, 16, and 23—special?

Nearly every Tigers fan knows the answer to this question—each of those uniform numbers has been retired, in honor of Charlie Gehringer (2), Hank Greenberg (5), Al Kaline (6), Hal Newhouser (16), and Willie Horton (23).

Each of these five former Tigers greats was a top performer on the baseball diamond. Indeed, four of them have been enshrined at the Baseball Hall of Fame in Cooperstown, New York.

Appropriately, the official retirements of these five uniform numbers provided that no other Tiger players would ever wear them again. However, quite a few players have, in fact, worn those numbers—between the date the honored player last played for the Tigers and the actual date that the uniform number was officially retired. In addition, four of these honored Tigers also wore numbers other than their retired numbers.

Here are the fascinating histories of the retired uniform numbers of the Detroit Tigers.

### Number 2

THE first year that the Detroit Tigers used uniform numbers was 1931 with the season-opening game on April 14, at Sportman's Park in St. Louis. Charlie Gehringer had been with Detroit since he made his major league debut on September 22, 1924. He became the regular second baseman in 1926. In 1931, he wore uniform number 3 (while Gee Walker, a rookie outfielder, wore #2). That Gehringer wore number 3 was consistent with his slot in the batting order—at

least at the beginning of the campaign. However, he missed much action during May, June, and July, and when he returned to the lineup, Charlie was stationed in the number 2 hole, which he kept for the remainder of the season. [It is noted that for virtually the entire 1931 campaign, Dale Alexander and Marty McManus, wearing numbers 4 and 5, respectively, were Detroit's number four and five hitters. Also, the opening day lineup featured Frank Doljack (#6), Billy Akers (#7), and Wally Schang (#8) batting in those slots, respectively.] For the 1932 season, during spring training, manager Bucky Harris scheduled Charlie to bat second. So, appropriately, Gehringer wore uniform #2 (while Gee switched to #27). Gehringer kept number 2 for the rest of his career, playing his last game on September 27, 1942. Gehringer was primarily a coach for the Tigers during the 1942 campaign with only 45 at-bats in 45 games, mostly as a pinch-hitter before entering the armed forces for World War II service.

Following his stint in the military, the 43-year-old Gehringer retired from the diamond. Gehringer, having twice turned down offers to be Detroit's field manager, later served as a vice president for the Tigers (1951–1959). On the strength of his significant diamond accomplishments (including a career batting average of .320 with 2,839 hits, six All-Star games, and the American League's MVP Award in 1937), "The Mechanical Man" was elected to the Hall of Fame in 1949.

However, it was not until 1983 that the Tigers retired his number 2 uniform. So, as it turned out, from 1943 through 1982, a total of 19 players wore uniform #2 for the Tigers. They are listed in Table 1.

The Tiger who wore #2 the longest during the 1943–1982 period was Jake Wood—seven years from 1961 through 1967. In the field, Wood played primarily at second base; he was Detroit's regular keystoner

HERM KRABBENHOFT *is the author of* Leadoff Batters of Major League Baseball—Complete Statistics, 1900–2005 *(McFarland, 2006), and has been a loyal Tigers fan since the day he was born in Detroit on July 15, 1945. Zeb Eaton (#17) hit a pinch grand slam homer that day.*

in 1961, when he led the AL in triples (14). Next in line, in terms of most seasons wearing uniform #2, was catcher Frank House (four years, 1954–1957).

### Table 1. Tigers who wore #2 in 1943–1982

| Year(s) | Player |
|---|---|
| 1943–1944 | Dick Wakefield |
| 1944 | Chief Hogsett |
| 1945 | Don Ross |
| 1945 | Ed Mierkowicz |
| 1946–1947 | Roy Cullenbine |
| 1948 | Paul Campbell |
| 1949–1952 | Johnny Lipon |
| 1952 | Fred Hatfield |
| 1952–1953 | Joe Ginsberg |
| 1953 | Al Aber |
| 1953 | Reno Bertoia |
| 1954–1957 | Frank House |
| 1958–1960 | Frank Bolling |
| 1961–1967 | Jake Wood |
| 1968–1969 | Tom Matchick |
| 1970–1972 | Dalton Jones |
| 1973 | no one |
| 1974–1975 | John Knox |
| 1976–1979 | Phil Mankowski |
| 1980–1982 | Richie Hebner |

Perhaps the most interesting aspect of the players who wore uniform number 2 before it was retired is that three different players each wore #2 in both the 1952 and 1953 seasons. Shortstop Johnny Lipon (who had worn #2 since 1949) was traded (on June 3, 1952) to the Red Sox in a multi-player deal; infielder Fred Hatfield came to Detroit from Boston and took uniform number 2. Then, a couple of months later, Hatfield and catcher Joe Ginsberg (who had uniform number 1) switched uniform numbers. So, in 1952, Lipon, Hatfield, and Ginsberg all wore #2. Similarly, in 1953, Ginsberg, Al Aber (a pitcher), and Reno Bertoia (an infielder) all wore #2.

### Number 5

HANK Greenberg made his major league debut (in a pinch-hitting assignment) with the Tigers on September 14, 1930—i.e., with no number on his uniform. That was his only big league appearance until 1933, when he became Detroit's regular first baseman. In his first full season, Hank wore uniform number 7. (Two other players wore uniform #5—Billy Rhiel at the beginning of the campaign—his final Tigers game being on July 9, 1933—and Johnny Pasek (who made his major league debut on July 28, 1933.) In 1934, Greenberg took #5 and wore it exclusively every season through the 1941 campaign (during the middle of which he joined the armed forces). During his three-year absence from the Tigers because of military service, uniform number 5 was worn by four players—Rip Radcliff (in 1942 and 1943), Don Heffner and Jake Mooty (1944), and Billy Pierce (1945, until June 21, when Hank returned to the Tigers to begin his belated spring training). In his final season with Detroit (1946), Greenberg again wore #5.

After his contract was sold to the Pittsburgh Pirates in January 1947, Hank played but one more season in the Big Show. For Detroit, at the beginning of the 1947 campaign, George Vico "wore" uniform number 5—although he didn't participate in any of the six games played by the Tigers before he was sent down to the minors on April 24. In other words, he was a "phantom" Tiger in 1947. No other player wore uniform number 5 for the Bengals in 1947.

Vico did, however, play with the Tigers in 1948 and 1949, wearing #5 in each season. Interestingly, on April 20, 1948, in his first major league at-bat, he connected for a home run—on the very first pitch he saw! Certainly an impressive beginning for the player who inherited Hank Greenberg's uniform number.

And, as it turned out, a total of 14 Tigers would go on to wear uniform number 5 during the 1947–1982 period; they're listed in Table 2.

### Table 2. Tigers who wore #5 in 1947–1982

| Year(s) | Player |
|---|---|
| 1947–1949 | George Vico |
| 1950 | no one |
| 1951 | Vic Wertz |
| 1952 | Cliff Mapes |
| 1953–1954 | Bob Nieman |
| 1955–1956 | Bill Tuttle |
| 1957 | Jim Finigan |
| 1958–1960 | Gail Harris |
| 1960 | Sandy Amoros |
| 1960–1961 | Dick Gernert |
| 1961 | Frank House |
| 1962–1963 | Purnal Goldy |
| 1964–1966 | no one |
| 1967–1974 | Jim Northrup |
| 1975 | no one |
| 1976–1980 | Mark Wagner |
| 1981 | no one |
| 1982 | Howard Johnson |

The player who wore Greenberg's #5 the longest during the 1947–1982 period was outfielder Jim Northrup (eight years, 1967–1974). Next, in terms of having uniform number 5 the longest, was backup shortstop Mark Wagner—five years (1976–1980).

A particularly interesting story about the Table 2 players involves outfielder Bill Tuttle. He had worn uniform number 5 beginning with the 1955 campaign. However, in mid-July 1956, while mired in a batting slump, he changed uniform numbers with the hope of changing his luck—he took uniform #13.

As can be gleaned from Tables 1 and 2, Frank House wore both uniform number 2 (1954–1957) and uniform number 5 (1961).

Getting back to Greenberg, during his career with the Tigers, Hank smacked 306 home runs, topping the junior circuit four times (36 in 1935, 58 in 1938, 41 in 1940, and 44 in 1946) while carving out a .319 batting average. He was an All-Star in five seasons and earned the AL MVP Award twice. He was elected to the Hall of Fame in 1955. His #5 uniform was retired by the Tigers in 1983—in the same July 12 ceremony that Gehringer's #2 uniform was retired.

### Number 6

AL Kaline joined the Tigers in 1953, shortly after graduating from high school. He made his major league debut on June 25, wearing uniform number 25. (Eddie Kazak had #25 during spring training and was slated to be with the Tigers when they headed north to begin the regular season. But because of a broken finger, he was signed over to Buffalo—the Tigers AAA farm club; he ended up never making it back to the bigs.)

NATIONAL BASEBALL LIBRARY, COOPERSTOWN, NY

*Al Kaline*

During spring training in 1954, Kaline again wore uniform No. 25. But before the regular season began, Pat Mullin (who had worn #6 since 1947) announced his retirement. Al then switched to number 6, which he wore until he retired after the 1974 season. Since then only one Tigers player has ever worn uniform number 6 again—and then for just one game. Who was he? (Answer below.)

On August 17, 1980, the Detroit Tigers retired Al's number 6. Two weeks before that (on August 3), Kaline was enshrined in the National Baseball Hall of Fame in recognition of his numerous diamond accomplishments—including 3,007 hits, 18 All-Star game selections, 10 Gold Glove Awards, and two Sporting News American League Player-of-the-Year Awards (1955 and 1963). After his playing career, Al was a color commentator for 26 years (1976–2001) for the Tigers television broadcasts.

### Number 16

HAL Newhouser made his major league debut with the Tigers on September 29, 1939, wearing uniform number 16. Number 16 was available because George Gill (who had worn #16 since 1937) had been traded to the St. Louis Browns on May 13, 1939. It is also noted that, according to a number of 1939 Detroit Tigers scorecards covering the period from June 4 through September 10, a person with the surname Jackym (perhaps former minor league pitcher Joe Jachym?) wore uniform number 16 (perhaps while serving as a batting practice pitcher?). We have not yet been able to find out anything about "Jackym." Prince Hal continued to wear #16 for the rest of his career with the Tigers, through late July 1953, when he was released. Newhouser then completed his ML career hurling for the Cleveland Indians in 1954 and 1955.

Following Hal's departure for Cleveland, several players wore #16 during the 1954–1996 period; see Table 3. The player who wore uniform number 16 the longest during this period was third baseman Tom Brookens—10 years (1979–1988). Other players with five or more seasons of wearing No. 16 were infielder Reno Bertoia (1954–1958), pitcher Phil Regan (1960–1965), and hurler Earl Wilson (1966–1970). Note that Bertoia also wore Gehringer's #2 in 1953 (Table 1). The last player to wear Prince Hal's #16 before it was retired was pitcher David Wells (1993–1995).

### Table 3. Tigers who wore #16 in 1954–1996

| YEAR(S) | PLAYER |
| --- | --- |
| 1954–58 | Reno Bertoia |
| 1959 | Ray Narleski |
| 1960 | Ray Semproch |
| 1960–65 | Phil Regan |
| 1966–70 | Earl Wilson |
| 1971 | Jim Hannan |
| 1971–72 | Ron Perranoski |
| 1973–74 | no one |
| 1975 | Gene Michael |
| 1976–78 | no one |
| 1979–88 | Tom Brookens |
| 1989 | David Palmer |
| 1989–90 | Brian DuBois |
| 1991–92 | Dave Haas |
| 1993–95 | David Wells |
| 1996 | no one |

Prince Hal was elected to the Baseball Hall of Fame by the Veterans Committee in 1992—many people felt it was long overdue—he had back-to-back AL MVP Awards in 1944 and 1945, 207 lifetime victories (including four 20-win seasons), and two ERA titles. Five years later, on July 27, 1997, the Tigers retired #16 in honor of Hal Newhouser.

### Number 23

WILLIE Horton was a baseball star at Detroit's Northwestern High School. He joined the Tigers in 1963, making his ML debut with them on September 10; he wore uniform #48. [Relief pitcher Bob Anderson had uniform number 23 in 1963, his only season with the Tigers.] In 1964, Willie took No. 23 and wore it for the rest of his playing career with the Tigers, which came to a close on April 12, 1977, when he was traded to the Texas Rangers.

*Hal Newhouser*

NATIONAL BASEBALL LIBRARY, COOPERSTOWN, NY

NATIONAL BASEBALL LIBRARY, COOPERSTOWN, NY

*Willie Horton*

From 1978 through 1980, Willie played for Cleveland, Oakland, Toronto, and Seattle, after which he retired. Since January 2002, Horton has been a special assistant (along with former teammate Al Kaline) to Tigers president Mike Illitch.

In the all-time Detroit Tigers rankings in slugging percentage (for players with at least 5,000 plate appearances) Willie Horton's .472 places eighth and his 262 homers stand fourth; he was an All-Star four times (1965, 1968, 1970, and 1973). In recognition of his contributions to the Tigers as a player—and to the city of Detroit as an outstanding citizen—Willie was honored on July 15, 2001, by having a statue in his likeness placed at Comerica Park (joining the statues for Ty Cobb, Charlie Gehringer, Hank Greenberg, Al Kaline, and Hal Newhouser) and by having his uniform #23 retired.

*The 1934–1935 Tigers "Battalion of Death" (L to R): 1B Hank Greenberg (#5), 2B Charlie Gehringer (#2), SS Billy Rogell (#7), and 3B Marv Owen (#8).*

However, between 1978 and 2000, seven players wore uniform number 23 for the Tigers; see Table 4.

**Table 4: Tigers who wore #23 in 1978-2000**

| YEAR(S) | PLAYER |
|---------|--------|
| 1978 | no one |
| 1979–87 | Kirk Gibson |
| 1988–89 | Torey Lovullo |
| 1990 | Dan Petry |
| 1991–92 | Mark Leiter |
| 1993–95 | Kirk Gibson |
| 1996–98 | no one |
| 1999 | Gabe Kapler |
| 2000 | Hideo Nomo |

One player in particular stands out—Kirk Gibson. Kirk wore uniform #23 from 1979 through 1987 (nine years). Then, after playing with the Dodgers, Royals, and Pirates during the 1988–1992 seasons, he rejoined the Tigers in 1993 and reclaimed uniform #23. (Mark Leiter, who had worn #23 since 1991, took #13 for the 1993 season.) Gibson wore #23 through the 1995 season, after which he retired as a player.

Of course, Gibson later returned to the Tigers, serving as coach for manager Alan Trammell. Because "his" number 23 had been retired in honor of Willie Horton, Kirk chose #22 for his uniform number when he joined the coaching staff in 2003.

Another interesting aspect about Horton's uniform number came about in 1966 after the Tigers manager Charlie Dressen died during the season. In the August 27, 1966, issue of *The Sporting News*, the following was reported: "Heart-Broken Horton Asks To Wear Dressen's No. 7. When Dressen died, Willie Horton sobbed openly. 'I want to wear that man's number,' Horton announced, 'and do things on the field for him.' This would be a switch from uniform No. 23 to the 7 left behind by Dressen. 'You'll have to earn his number,' a friend told Horton. 'If you finish strong at the plate, maybe they'll give it to you next year.'" However, that switch in uniform numbers did not come to pass, as reported in the January 14, 1967, edition of *The Sporting News*: "Horton Changes His Mind, He'll Stick With Old 23. Willie Horton has changed his mind and he'll again be wearing No. 23 on his uniform next season. 'Some day I want to wear that man's number,' declared Horton following the death of manager Charlie Dressen. For a while it seemed likely that Horton would switch to Dressen's No. 7 in 1967. Willie thought it over a while and decided to stay with No. 23."

Those are the stories of the five uniform numbers retired by the Tigers—and the great players for whom they were retired. Of course, on April 15, 1997, the Tigers—along with every other major league team—retired #42 in honor of Jackie Robinson. However, because Jose Lima had been wearing that number prior to April 15, 1997, he was allowed to continue wearing it. Thus, in 2002, Lima was the last Tigers player to wear #42. The Tigers player who had #42 for the most seasons was Buddy Groom (four years, from 1992 to 1995).

While those uniform numbers will not be worn by any future Tigers players, each of these retired numbers was, in fact, subsequently worn *after* they were retired. For one game only—on September 27, 1999—to commemorate the final major league game at historic Tiger Stadium and to honor Gehringer, Greenberg, Kaline, Newhouser, and Horton, the following Tigers wore uniforms with the retired numbers—Damion Easley (2); Tony Clark (5); Karim Garcia (6); C. J. Nitkowski (16); and Juan Encarnacion (23). In addition, to honor Ty Cobb, Gabe Kapler wore a uniform with no number; see also the "Ahead of Their Times" section below.

### Procedure for Ascertaining the Tigers Uniform Numbers and the Reliability of the Uniform Numbers Reported

"HERM'S Detroit Tigers Uniform Numbers Project" commenced on January 21, 2001. The objective is to ascertain the uniform number(s) of each Tigers player for each season since 1931, when the Tigers first used numbers on their uniforms. While I was aware that a book on uniform numbers (*Baseball by the Numbers* by Mark Stang and Linda Harkness) for all major league teams had been published in 1996, I was cautioned that it contained numerous errors—both of omission and commission. So, I decided to do my research completely independently and not use the information in the book.

Also, I was forewarned that uniform numbers reported in yearbooks and media guides were frequently unreliable—since the numbers they report are spring training numbers, and because players often switched their spring training numbers for other, more desirable numbers when they made it to The Show. So, I decided to rely exclusively on "official" scorecards and programs as my sources of documentation for the uniform numbers. (Of course, I appreciate that there can be, and are, errors in the "official"

*Ty Cobb, "A Genius in Spikes."*

score books. However, I reasoned that such errors would be relatively rare and would likely be corrected in subsequently printed programs, the printings being done numerous times, for virtually every series, during the course of a season. Also, while my strong preference is for Detroit Tigers scorecards, I would also utilize out-of-town scorecards—until I could obtain a Tigers score book, if possible.

During these past five-plus years I've been very active in acquiring the relevant programs needed to document the Tigers uniform numbers. I have also benefited enormously from the graciousness of many people who have kindly provided to me photocopies of their scorecards.

At this point, I have proof-positive documentation of the uniform numbers for all but four Tigers players out of the 2,818 player-seasons in the 1931–2005 period. I have incontrovertible documentation of the uniform numbers for all of the Tigers managers (87 manager seasons) and all of the Tigers coaches (310 coach seasons). The four Tigers players for whom I do not yet have irrefutable documentation of their

uniform numbers are Frank Doljack (1932), Luke Hamlin (1933), Roxy Lawson (1933), and Bill Faul (1964).

With respect to the reliability of the Detroit Tigers uniform numbers ascertained in this project, they are 100% correct according to official scorecards. Moreover, in those relatively few instances where a player's scorecard number(s) seemed unusual or doubtful, I obtained additional information from relevant newspaper articles and action photographs to put the uniform number(s) on terra firma. In addition, whenever possible, I also contacted the players. Thus, the Tigers uniform numbers presented in this article are completely accurate.

### Ahead of Their Times

THREE Tigers players had long and glorious careers with Detroit, but played before 1931 when the club began using uniform numbers. Had these players—each a Hall of Famer—worn uniforms with numbers, it seems likely that their uniform numbers would have ultimately been retired: Sam Crawford (1903–1917), Ty Cobb (1905–1926), and Harry Heilmann (1914–1929). Indeed, because Ty Cobb—often referred to as "The Greatest Tiger of All"—did not have a uniform number to retire, Detroit's upper management long took the position that no Tigers uniform number should be retired. That position changed in 1980, when Al Kaline became the first Tigers player to be honored by having his uniform number retired. (It is noted that, since Cobb's diamond greatness could not be recognized by retiring his uniform number, the Tigers chose to place a "Cobb Memorial Plaque" near the office entrance to Tiger Stadium on Trumbull Avenue. On July 17, 1963, Detroit Tigers president John E. Fetzer unveiled the plaque, which included the inscription "Greatest Tiger of All, A Genius in Spikes."

The Detroit Tigers have recognized players whose uniform numbers have been retired by presenting their names on the brick wall in left-center field at Comerica Park. Ty Cobb is included in this display—from left to right are Horton, Cobb, Gehringer, Greenberg, Newhouser, and Kaline. Moreover, above each player's name is his retired uniform number—#23, blank, #2, #5, #16, and #6.

Placed on Comerica Park's brick wall in right-center field are two rows of names of other famous Tigers. The top row has Heilmann, (Hughie) Jennings (manager), (Mickey) Cochrane, and (Ernie) Harwell (broadcaster); at the extreme right is #42 for Jackie Robinson. The second row has (Heinie) Manush, Crawford, and (George) Kell. There are no numbers displayed with any of these players (each a Hall of Famer). Of these Tigers, only Cochrane and Kell were with the team during the uniform number era (i.e., since 1931)—Cochrane wore #3 and Kell wore #21, #15, #21 (again), and #7.

While Cochrane has not had his uniform number retired, in autumn 1962 the city of Detroit changed the name of the street adjacent to the west side of Tiger Stadium from National Avenue to Cochrane Avenue in memory of Black Mike (who had passed away a few months earlier). A similar honor was extended to Al Kaline a few years later: Cherry Street, the thorough-fare adjacent to the north side of Tiger Stadium, was renamed Al Kaline Drive at the Al Kaline Day festivities on August 2, 1970.

**Bonus #1:** In addition to the retired numbers for Hall of Famers Kaline, Gehringer, Greenberg, and Newhouser, several others wore the English D for Detroit during the 1931–2005 period and were subsequently elected to the Hall of Fame.

### Uniform numbers for Tigers players subsequently elected to the Hall of Fame

| Player | With Tigers | Uni#s | HOF |
| --- | --- | --- | --- |
| Charlie Gehringer | 1924–42 | 3, 2 | 1949 |
| Hank Greenberg | 1930; 1933–46 | 7, 5 | 1956 |
| Waite Hoyt | 1931 | 14 | 1969 |
| Mickey Cochrane | 1934–38 | 3 | 1947 |
| Goose Goslin | 1934–37 | 4 | 1968 |
| Al Simmons | 1936 | 6 | 1953 |
| Earl Averill | 1939–40 | 24, 27 | 1975 |
| Hal Newhouser | 1939–53 | 16 | 1992 |
| George Kell | 1946–52 | 21, 15, 21, 7 | 1983 |
| Al Kaline | 1953–74 | 25, 6 | 1980 |
| Jim Bunning | 1955–63 | 15, 14 | 1996 |
| Larry Doby | 1959 | 25 | 1998 |
| Eddie Mathews | 1967–68 | 7 | 1978 |

**Bonus #2:** Two Tigers managers and four coaches from the 1931–2005 period have been enshrined at Cooperstown.

### Uniform numbers for Tigers managers and coaches now in the Hall of Fame

| Manager/Coach | With Tigers | Uni #s | HOF |
| --- | --- | --- | --- |
| Bucky Harris (mgr) | 1931–33; 1955–56 | 34, 32 | 1975 |
| Roger Bresnahan (ch) | 1931 | 52 | 1945 |
| Ted Lyons (ch) | 1949–53 | 33 | 1955 |
| Rick Ferrell (ch) | 1950–53 | 36 | 1984 |
| Luke Appling (ch) | 1960 | 31 | 1964 |
| Sparky Anderson (mgr) | 1979–1995 | 7, 11 | 2000 |

**Bonus #3:** In addition to the five numbers officially retired by the Tigers, the uniform numbers worn by four Tigers seem to have been "unofficially" retired—no one has worn these numbers since they retired.

### Uniform numbers for Tigers "unofficially" retired

| Tiger | With Team | Number | Years Not Worn |
| --- | --- | --- | --- |
| Jack Morris | 1977–90 | 47 | 15 |
| Lou Whitaker | 1977–95 | 1 | 10 |
| Alan Trammell | 1977–96 | 3 | 9 |
| Sparky Anderson | 1979–95 | 11 | 10 |

In 1977, Lou Whitaker and Alan Trammell (both September call-ups) wore uniform numbers 43 and 42, respectively. Trammell wore "his" number 3 when he came back to manage the Tigers during the 2003–2005 period. Finally, Sparky Anderson began his managerial tenure with the Tigers (in 1979) wearing uniform number 7. However, he switched to number 11 after only a few games.

### Dedication

This article is dedicated to Walt Streuli, who wore numbers 19, 40, and 25 as a catcher for the Tigers (1954–1956).

### Acknowledgments

The author gratefully acknowledges the following people who provided photocopies of their score books/programs/score sheets—Ray Billbrough, Tom Broecker, Ed Budnick, Bob Crabill, Tom DeLisle, Dan Dickson, Steven DiNobile, Bill Dunstone, Patrick Gallagher, Doug Goodman, Liz Goodrich, Jon Greenberg (Milwaukee Brewers), David Holtzman (Kansas City Royals), Maxwell Kates, Doug Kath, Ted Kowalski, Jim Lannen, Jack Looney, Alan May, Kevin McGraw, Jeff Messens, Jerry Nechal, Art Neff, Jeff Ortiz, Larry Pilut, Rich Robinson, Eric Rosekrans, Dennis Sell, Kent Sheets, Dave Smith (Retrosheet), Mark Stang, Tom Sticha, Mike Swanson (Arizona Diamondbacks), Keith Thompson, Ronald Wilczak, Alan Willey, and Jim Wohlenhaus.

The author also heartily thanks the following people who have been very helpful in the project: Gary Gillette, Bob McConnell, Mark Pattison, Dave Raglin, Rick Schabowski, and Mario Ziino.

# Crossing Red River
## Spring Training in Texas

### by Frank Jackson

SEVERAL years ago when the Texas Rangers explored the idea of moving their spring training headquarters from Port Charlotte, Florida, one option they briefly considered was building a spring training complex in the Rio Grande Valley of Texas. Of course, for the move to be feasible, at least three other teams would have to be persuaded to go along to provide competition for exhibition games. The Houston Astros were a natural for the Rio Grande Valley, as they were the closest (about 350 miles) major league team to the area. But would anybody else be interested? As it turned out, nobody was, so the idea died a quick death. The Rangers (along with the Kansas City Royals) went to Surprise, Arizona; the Astros chose to renovate their existing complex in Kissimmee, Florida, and nobody came to the Rio Grande Valley for spring training. But in the early years of the 20th century, spring training in Texas was hardly an unusual proposition.

Spring training was not meticulously chronicled in early years of professional baseball, but preseason trips to warmer climes have a history almost as long as organized baseball itself. The first trip to Florida was made by the Washington Capitals, who set up shop in Jacksonville in 1888. In 1886, Cap Anson, a staunch believer in preseason preparation, took his Chicago White Stockings to Hot Springs, Arkansas, a popular locale for a number of teams well into the 20th century. The White Stockings and the Cincinnati Red Stockings took trips to New Orleans in 1870, the first time two teams were in the Crescent City. The powerful Reds defeated the local Pelicans, 51–1, on April 25 of that year.

FRANK JACKSON *is not a native Texan, but has lived in Dallas for 30 years. He grew up rooting for the Phillies in the late 1950s and early 1960s, something he considers excellent preparation for becoming a Rangers fan.*

The teams that headed south played themselves into shape not just against each other but also against local talent, including minor league teams[1] and college teams, thus presenting a great opportunity for young players to make an impression on major league managers. To a certain extent, the level of competition was determined by the other major league teams training nearby. In 1917, however, when the White Sox were training in Mineral Wells, Texas, Charles Comiskey decided his team's confidence could be enhanced by scheduling only minor league opponents, even though the Cardinals, Giants, Browns, and Tigers were then all training in Texas. That might not appear to be sound preparation for the regular season, but it obviously didn't hurt the White Sox, as they were World Series champions that year.

During its heyday in Texas, spring training had at least as much in common with barnstorming as it did with spring training as we know it today. Then, as now, it provided an opportunity to evaluate rookies and other unknowns (or "Yannigans") before the regular season rosters had to be drawn up. Perhaps most important, from a fan's point of view, it gave people in the hinterlands their only opportunity to see major league ballplayers plying their trade. Whatever the vagaries of springtime pilgrimages in the 19th century, by the early years of the 20th century, spring training in some form or fashion was an established fact of life for all major league ballplayers. From 1903 to the eve of World War II, Texas was a popular destination for major league teams in search of spring training facilities. Of the 16 major league teams in existence from 1903 to 1941, only two teams, the Brooklyn Dodgers and the Chicago Cubs, never trained in Texas.

The Rio Grande Valley, with its palm trees and citrus groves, embodies the subtropical ideal for spring training, yet aside from one season (1920 in Brownsville), it did not figure in major leaguers' plans.

In the early years of the 20th century, the Valley was largely undeveloped, except for Brownsville, which dates back to 1846 and the establishment of Fort Brown during the Mexican War. The city hosted minor league baseball (the Brownsville Brownies of the Southwest Texas League) as early as 1910. The rest of the Valley didn't begin to grow until midwestern farmers, attracted by the year-round growing season, headed south to see what crops their skills could coax from the south Texas soil. Harlingen and Edinburg, which have hosted independent minor league baseball in recent years, were not even on the map in the first decade of the 20th century. Harlingen was not incorporated till 1910, Edinburg a year later. Minor league baseball did not reach Edinburg till August 1926 (when the Victoria Rosebuds relocated there) and Harlingen till 1931 (Rio Grande Valley League), and by that time the golden age of spring training in Texas had passed. For the record, the Valley also hosted minor league teams in Mission, San Benito, and McAllen in the late 1920s and early 1930s.

If the Rio Grande Valley was too remote and undeveloped for spring training in the early years of the 20th century, the state of Texas offered many other options. Even with its wide-open spaces and wild reputation, Texas had no shortage of "civilized" locales for major league teams in search of sunshine and warm temperatures. The most popular host city was San Antonio, one of the oldest cities in Texas and, until the 1920s, the largest. The Alamo City hosted 29 seasons of spring training, including 10 of the 14 teams that ventured to Texas. Surprisingly, after San Antonio the most popular location was the small town of Marlin Springs (now known as merely Marlin), a resort town 26 miles southeast of Waco. The New York Giants were particularly fond of the town, as they trained there in 1908–1918. Like Mineral Wells, west of Fort Worth, and Hot Wells, southeast of San Antonio,[2] the town catered to tourists who came for the healing waters.

To anyone familiar with Texas history and geography, the lineup of towns and teams presents many tantalizing questions. For example, why was the established seaside city of Galveston given short shrift—a mere two seasons? Perhaps the answer lies with the weather. The Galveston hurricane of 1900— still the most deadly natural disaster in American history—had surely embedded itself in the national consciousness, but even lesser storms had made their

mark. One such storm on August 15, 1915, destroyed the ballparks in Galveston and Houston, and the Galveston Sandcrabs and Houston Buffaloes rerouted their "home" games to Brenham, Austin, and Corpus Christi. That was the end of spring training in Houston, and Galveston hosted but one more season (1921). Of course, tropical storms still present a major problem for spring training facilities in Florida, as the 2004 hurricane season proved, and have probably played a key role in the increasing popularity of Arizona.

Other Texas Gulf Coast towns fared poorly as spring training locations. Corpus Christi—a fairly large port city similar in atmosphere and climate to Florida—was never selected for a spring training site, even though the city had hosted minor league ball as early as 1910 (the Corpus Christi Pelicans of the Southwest Texas League). Orange was limited to two seasons (1921 and 1922) and Brownsville to one (1920). While the avoidance of coastal cities may be understandable, it is difficult to fathom the total absence of Austin and Fort Worth, inland Texas League cities that were certainly capable of hosting major league teams in the spring.[3] Perhaps the ultimate puzzler is the appearance of the Philadelphia A's in the remote border town of Eagle Pass in 1922. What was Connie Mack thinking?

It's easy to see why Texas was so popular with the Browns and Cardinals, as St. Louis was the closest major league city to the Lone Star State in the first four decades of the 20th century. Other teams based in the Midwest—the Cubs, White Sox, Tigers, and Reds—were not much farther away. But why were the Giants—who spent 18 springs in Texas, more than any other team—so fond of the state? Couldn't they have found something back east a little closer to home? Here we must introduce Giants manager John McGraw and the key role he played in spring training history.

As a member of the Baltimore Orioles in 1894, McGraw attended an intensive eight-week spring training camp in Macon, Georgia, under manager Ned Hanlon. The players were drilled endlessly on the hit-and-run play and the Baltimore chop, among other "small ball" tactics. The results were immediately apparent once the season began. After a mediocre 1893, when the Orioles finished with a 60–70 record, eighth in a field of 12 teams, they came out swinging (sometimes literally) in 1894. They won 34 of their

HERZOG: TRANSCENDENTAL GRAPHICS   COBB: NATIONAL BASEBALL LIBRARY, COOPERSTOWN, NY

*Buck Herzong (left) and Ty Cobb.*

first 47 games, but did not clinch the pennant until September 28. Other teams couldn't help but notice that the seeds for the Orioles' successful season had been planted in Macon in the spring. Without that fast start in April, the Orioles would not have won the pennant. The lesson was obvious: a leisurely spring training was no longer an option for a major league team seriously bent on contending.

When McGraw became manager of the New York Giants, he remained convinced that players should peak in the spring to be ready for the opening of the season. During his first spring training with McGraw at San Antonio in 1920, Frankie Frisch had one of his earliest tiffs with the Giant manager. "I woke at seven and walked four miles to the field," recalled Frisch. "At nine, I jogged five laps. I hit, fielded, threw, and slid until noon. Then I lunched, hit, fielded, threw, and slid until dusk. Then I walked four miles back to the hotel." A rigorous regimen, to be sure—and not subject to the slightest modification. One day when Frisch hitchhiked back to the hotel for lunch, his meal was interrupted by an irate McGraw, who fumed, "You rockhead. Next time I catch you riding anywhere I'll fine you five bucks a mile. You know what legs are for . . . baseball."

To that end, McGraw's first foray into Texas was to Marlin Springs in 1908. He returned every year through 1918. Today, a town of about 6,400, in those days it was home to about 4,000 people. While not exactly "the sticks," it was a long way from New York City in more ways than one. But McGraw was looking for a place where his men would find few distractions from their baseball discipline. Marlin Springs was big enough to provide good rail service to Dallas, Fort Worth, Waco, and other cities where the Giants could play exhibition games against Texas League teams. Since the town catered to tourists, it had hotels, a Hilton and the Arlington,[4] suitable for major league ballplayers. This was an important consideration for the status-conscious McGraw, who insisted his ballplayers were not second-class citizens, no matter what the more respectable elements of society said.

Considering the large quantities of alcohol imbibed by players of that era, the elimination of toxins might have been a key factor in the selection of a spring training venue. This would explain why Marlin Springs and other towns with spas were so popular. Since many Texas counties were (and still are) dry, the difficulty of buying liquor might have made some remote Texas towns particularly attractive as spring training sites before Prohibition. On the other hand, New Orleans was also a popular spring training locale, and a venue more conducive to boozing could hardly be found in the Deep South or anywhere else.

Then as now, a sweetheart deal with a municipality was a big inducement to a team in search of a spring home. In 1910, Marlin Springs deeded the local ballpark, Emerson Field, to the Giants for as long as they trained in Marlin, which turned out to be another nine years. The Giants actually controlled the property until the 1970s.

The annual presence of the Giants, the "glamour" team of major league baseball during McGraw's reign, was a big event in the social life of Marlin Springs, though some of the town's leading families would not allow their daughters to socialize with the ballplayers. Fish fries and community dances were recurring events, and the Giants frequently played intra-squad games to benefit local charities.

In small Texas towns, the annual springtime sojourn of major leaguers provided a publicity boost that similarly sized hamlets could only dream of. Today it taxes the imagination to envision Ty Cobb sitting in the lobby of the Rogers Hotel (still standing) in downtown Waxahachie,[5] Joe Jackson going out for a bite to eat in Mineral Wells, or Christy Mathewson playing checkers with the locals in Marlin Springs. But these legendary figures and many other major leaguers of lesser repute were regular seasonal visitors to small towns in the Lone Star State.

The figures that dominated the headlines during the regular season also did so during spring training. Since the outcome of the games was of little importance, many of the more entertaining anecdotes from Texas spring training history are not from the games themselves but from game-related events.

During the Giants' final spring (1918) in Marlin, the Giants played a team from the Waco Air Service Pilot Training Center. Doubtless more entertaining than the game itself were the pilots performing stunts in biplanes above the field. John McGraw himself donned helmet and goggles for a 20-minute flight to Waco. This was possibly the first time a major league manager rode in an airplane.

One historic first took place when the Giants played their first night game during spring training in San Antonio in 1931. After witnessing a rookie outfielder undergo a coughing spasm due to inhaling insects attracted by the artificial lighting, McGraw, ever the canny strategist, advised his troops, "One thing to remember. You must keep your mouth shut when you play these night games."

Sometimes the games were eclipsed by off-the-field activities, such as Rube Marquard firing a pistol at a billboard outside his Marlin Springs hotel room—an act frowned upon even in Texas and necessitating a visit from the local peace officer. The Falls County sheriff attempted to arrest Marquard, but he backed down after McGraw intimidated him by asserting, "The Giants put this town on the map, and the Giants can just as quickly wipe it off by leaving."[6]

The best chronicled event in Texas spring training history was probably Ty Cobb's set-to with Giants second baseman Buck Herzog. The rhubarb happened during spring training

NATIONAL BASEBALL LIBRARY, COOPERSTOWN, NY

*Giants manager
John McGraw*

in 1917, when training camps in Texas, as well as other locales, were the scene of ballplayers engaging in military drills, supposedly to prepare them for America's anticipated entry into the Great War. The Giants and Tigers had set a string of exhibition games to be played in Texas and points north as the two teams made their way home after their training camps closed. Herzog ragged Cobb about showing up at the last minute for an exhibition game at Gardner Park in the Oak Cliff section of Dallas. Cobb took offense and spiked Herzog at the first opportunity. A brawl broke out, the dugouts emptied, and the cops stormed the field. That evening at a banquet at the Oriental Hotel, Herzog challenged Cobb to fisticuffs and was soundly trounced by him in the latter's hotel room. A confrontation between Cobb and McGraw took place the next day in the hotel lobby. Realizing he could be a marked man for the rest of the exhibition series, Cobb refused to play in any more games till the regular season began. While he trained with the Cincinnati Reds, the Tigers and Giants continued the exhibition series, punctuated by occasional scraps. Though the teams played in different leagues, the bad blood remained. Four years later, when both teams were training in San Antonio, the teams were still not on speaking terms, even though they were headquartered just blocks apart downtown and civic leaders were imploring them to stage exhibition contests. McGraw said he would not play unless Cobb, who had just been named the manager of the Tigers,

### Spring Training in Texas, 1903–1941

| Year | Locale | Teams |
|---|---|---|
| 1903 | Dallas | St. Louis Cardinals |
| 1904 | Corsicana | St. Louis Browns |
|  | Dallas | Cincinnati Reds |
|  | Houston | St. Louis Cardinals |
|  | Marlin Springs | Chicago White Sox |
|  | San Antonio | Cleveland Indians* |
| 1905 | Dallas | St. Louis Browns |
|  | Marlin Springs | St. Louis Cardinals |
| 1906 | Dallas | St. Louis Browns |
|  | Houston | St. Louis Cardinals |
|  | San Antonio | Cincinnati Reds |
| 1907 | Dallas | Philadelphia A's |
|  | Galveston | Washington Senators |
|  | Houston | St. Louis Cardinals |
|  | Marlin Springs | Cincinnati Reds |
|  | San Antonio | St. Louis Browns |
| 1908 | Houston | St. Louis Cardinals |
|  | Marlin Springs | New York Giants |
| 1909 | Houston | St. Louis Browns |
|  | Marlin Springs | New York Giants |
|  | San Antonio | Detroit Tigers |
| 1910 | Houston | St. Louis Browns |
|  | Marlin Springs | New York Giants |
|  | San Antonio | Detroit Tigers |
| 1911 | Marlin Springs | New York Giants |
|  | Mineral Wells | Chicago White Sox |
| 1912 | Marlin Springs | New York Giants |
|  | San Antonio | Philadelphia A's |
|  | Waco | Chicago White Sox |
| 1913 | Marlin Springs | New York Giants |
|  | San Antonio | Philadelphia A's |
|  | Waco | St. Louis Browns |
| 1914 | Houston | New York Yankees |
|  | Marlin Springs | New York Giants |
| 1915 | Hot Wells | St. Louis Cardinals |
|  | Houston | St. Louis Browns |
|  | Marlin Springs | New York Giants |
|  | San Antonio | Cleveland Indians |
| 1916 | Hot Wells | St. Louis Cardinals |
|  | Marlin Springs | New York Giants |
|  | Mineral Wells | Chicago White Sox |
|  | Palestine | St. Louis Browns |
|  | Waxahachie | Detroit Tigers |
| 1917 | Hot Wells | St. Louis Cardinals |
|  | Marlin Springs | New York Giants |
|  | Mineral Wells | Chicago White Sox |
|  | Palestine | St. Louis Browns |
|  | Waxahachie | Detroit Tigers |
| 1918 | Marlin Springs | New York Giants |
|  | Mineral Wells | Chicago White Sox |
|  | San Antonio | St. Louis Cardinals |
|  | Waxahachie | Detroit Tigers |
| 1919 | Mineral Wells | Chicago White Sox |
|  | San Antonio | St. Louis Browns |
|  | Waxahachie | Cincinnati Reds |
| 1920 | Brownsville | St. Louis Cardinals |
|  | San Antonio | New York Giants |
|  | Waco | Chicago White Sox |
| 1921 | Cisco | Cincinnati Reds |
|  | Dallas | Cleveland Indians |
|  | Galveston | Boston Braves |
|  | Orange | St. Louis Cardinals |
|  | San Antonio | Detroit Tigers |
|  |  | New York Giants |
|  | Waxahachie | Chicago White Sox |
| 1922 | Dallas | Cleveland Indians |
|  | Eagle Pass | Philadelphia A's |
|  | Mineral Wells | Cincinnati Reds |
|  | Orange | St. Louis Cardinals |
|  | San Antonio | New York Giants |
|  | Seguin | Chicago White Sox |
| 1923 | San Antonio | New York Giants |
|  | Seguin | Chicago White Sox |
| 1924 | San Antonio | Boston Red Sox |
| 1925 | NONE | NONE |
| 1926 | San Antonio | St. Louis Cardinals |
| 1927 | San Antonio | Detroit Tigers |
| 1928 | San Antonio | Detroit Tigers |
| 1929 | Dallas | Chicago White Sox |
|  | San Antonio | New York Giants |
| 1930 | San Antonio | New York Giants |
|  |  | Chicago White Sox |
| 1931 | San Antonio | New York Giants |
|  |  | Chicago White Sox |
| 1932 | San Antonio | Chicago White Sox |
| 1933 | San Antonio | Detroit Tigers |
| 1934 | NONE | NONE |
| 1935 | NONE | NONE |
| 1936 | San Antonio | Pittsburgh Pirates |
| 1937 | San Antonio | St. Louis Browns |
| 1938 | San Antonio | St. Louis Browns |
| 1939 | New Braunfels | Philadelphia Phillies |
|  | San Antonio | St. Louis Browns |
| 1940 | San Antonio | St. Louis Browns |
| 1941 | San Antonio | Boston Braves† |
|  |  | St. Louis Browns |

*Then known as the Cleveland Blues.    †Name changed to the Boston Bees that season.

came to him in person and requested the matchup. Cobb refused, so that was that. This was despite the fact that Hughie Jennings, the former Detroit manager who had joined the Giants coaching staff, could have served as a go-between. Ironically, it was not until the death of Jennings in 1928 that Cobb and McGraw spoke to each other again.

Since World War I had cut into baseball revenues in 1918, owners decided to cut costs and play a truncated schedule in 1919, preceded by a shortened spring training. In mid-March McGraw moved the Giants to the college town of Gainesville, Florida, for one spring. As in Marlin, however, he had secured a sweetheart deal: free use of the university facilities. When fan interest returned during the 1919 season, the owners went back to business as usual, and McGraw returned to Texas for four years. This time, however, the Giants trained in San Antonio, which offered far more in the way of distractions than Marlin Springs.[7] The team stayed at the Crockett Hotel—just a long fly ball from the Alamo and still a popular downtown destination. It might be that McGraw felt that San Antonio was now a "safe" location, given that Prohibition was in force. Actually, the city of 162,000 provided more opportunities for procuring illegal brew. In 1923, McGraw levied an unprecedented number of fines. Most of the players could afford it, however, as McGraw boasted that he had 12 of the 14 highest paid players (the exceptions were Rogers Hornsby and Edd Roush) in the National League.

During the early 1920s, it looked as though Texas had the potential to develop into a permanent site for spring training. Seven teams trained in Texas in 1921 and six in 1922. But in 1923 only two teams chose Texas, in 1924 only one, and in 1925 none.

Why did spring training drop off so drastically after 1922? In a word: Florida. With the help of boosters, notably Al Lang (for whom the waterfront ballpark in St. Petersburg was named), Florida and spring training quickly became synonymous. Thanks largely to two railroad magnates, John Plant on the Florida peninsula's west coast and Henry Flagler on the east coast, rail service to Florida had improved greatly since the turn of the century. The increasing popularity of motorcars and the building of highways also played a major role in transforming Florida from an inaccessible wilderness to a tourist destination. As a result, Florida underwent a real estate boom in the 1920s and the rest of the nation—including major

### Cities Ranked by Number of Teams Hosted

| | | |
|---|---|---|
| 11 | San Antonio . . . . . . . | Boston Braves, Boston Red Sox, Chicago White Sox, Cincinnati Reds, Cleveland Indians, Detroit Tigers, New York Giants, Pittsburgh Pirates, St. Louis Browns, St. Louis Cardinals, Philadelphia A's |
| 5 | Dallas . . . . . . . . . . . | Chicago White Sox, Cincinnati Reds, Cleveland Indians, St. Louis Cardinals, Philadelphia A's |
| 3 | Houston . . . . . . . . . | New York Yankees, St. Louis Browns, St. Louis Cardinals |
| | Marlin Springs. . . . . | Cincinnati Reds, Chicago White Sox, New York Giants |
| | Waxahachie . . . . . . . | Chicago White Sox, Cincinnati Reds, Detroit Tigers |
| 2 | Galveston . . . . . . . . | Boston Braves, Washington Senators |
| | Mineral Wells. . . . . . | Cincinnati Reds, Chicago White Sox |
| | Waco . . . . . . . . . . . | Chicago White Sox, St. Louis Browns |
| 1 | Brownsville. . . . . . . | St. Louis Cardinals |
| | Cisco . . . . . . . . . . . | Cincinnati Reds |
| | Corsicana . . . . . . . . | St. Louis Browns |
| | Eagle Pass. . . . . . . . | Philadelphia A's |
| | Hot Wells . . . . . . . . | St. Louis Cardinals |
| | New Braunfels . . . . | Philadelphia Phillies |
| | Orange . . . . . . . . . . | St. Louis Cardinals |
| | Palestine . . . . . . . . . | St. Louis Browns |
| | Seguin . . . . . . . . . . . | Chicago White Sox |

### Cities Ranked by Number of Seasons

| | |
|---|---|
| 29 | San Antonio |
| 14 | Marlin Springs |
| 8 | Dallas |
| | Houston |
| 6 | Mineral Wells |
| 5 | Waxahachie |
| 3 | Hot Wells |
| | Waco |
| 2 | Galveston |
| | Orange |
| | Palestine |
| | Seguin |
| 1 | Brownsville |
| | Cisco |
| | Corsicana |
| | Eagle Pass |
| | New Braunfels |

### Teams Ranked by Number of Seasons

| | |
|---|---|
| 18 | New York Giants |
| 16 | St. Louis Browns |
| 14 | Chicago White Sox |
| | St. Louis Cardinals |
| 9 | Detroit Tigers |
| 6 | Cincinnati Reds |
| 4 | Cleveland Indians |
| | Philadelphia A's |
| 2 | Boston Braves |
| 1 | Boston Red Sox |
| | New York Yankees |
| | Philadelphia Phillies |
| | Pittsburgh Pirates |
| | Washington Senators |

league club owners—couldn't help but pay attention.[8] Also, teams knew that those cold fronts that periodically swept over southern states (Texans call them "blue northers" or sometimes just "northers") usually petered out before they got too far down the Florida peninsula, thus minimizing the games and practice time lost to bad weather in late winter and early spring.

By 1924, nine teams were training in Florida. The Grapefruit League that we know today was starting to take shape. Spring training in Texas and other Southern states wasn't entirely dead, but the pulse was weak. Between 1926 and 1941, Texas had no more than one spring training city per year (and hosted no teams in 1934–1935), with the exception of 1939, when the Browns returned to San Antonio and the Phillies made their lone appearance (at New Braunfels) in the Lone Star State.

World War II finished off spring training in Texas. Travel restrictions forced teams to choose northern spring training sites close to their homes, but the annual Florida migration resumed after the war. Arizona also beckoned, as the Cleveland Indians and the New York Giants trained there for the first time in 1947. But spring training in Texas was history.[9]

If Texas was a popular destination for baseball teams during the early years of the previous century, could it make a comeback during the current century?

Doubtless the smart money folks would never bet on the return of major league spring training camps to the Lone Star State. But stranger things have happened in baseball history.

## Sources

Alexander, Charles C. *John McGraw*. New York: Viking, 1988.

Cataneo, David. *Peanuts and Crackerjack*. Nashville: Rutledge Hill Press, 1991.

Evans, Wilbur and Bill Little. *Texas Longhorn Baseball—Kings of the Diamond*. Huntsville, AL: Strode Publishing, 1983.

Falkner, David. *The Short Season: The Hard Work and High Times of Baseball in the Spring*, New York: Penguin, 1986.

Fehrenbach, T. R. *Lone Star*. New York: Wings Books, 1991.

Frommer, Harvey. *Baseball's Greatest Managers*. New York: Franklin Watts, 1985.

Graham, Frank. *The New York Giants: An Informal History of a Great Baseball Club*. Carbondale, IL: Southern Illinois University Press, 2002; originally published in 1952.

Holaday, Chris and Mark Presswood. *Baseball in Dallas*. Mount Pleasant, SC: Arcadia Press, 2004.

Holaday, Chris and Mark Presswood. *Baseball in Fort Worth*. Mount Pleasant, SC: Arcadia Press, 2004.

O'Neal, Bill. *The Texas League, 1888–1987: A Century of Baseball*. Austin, TX: Eakin Press, 1987.

Torres, Noe. *Ghost Leagues: A History of Minor League Baseball in South Texas*. Tamarac, FL: Llumina Press, 2005.

Valenza, Janet Mace. *Taking the Waters in Texas; Springs, Spas and Fountains of Youth*, Austin, TX: University of Texas Press, 2000.

Wilbert, Warren N. and William C. Hageman. *The 1917 White Sox; Their World Championship Season*, Jefferson, NC: McFarland, 2004.

Texas 2005 State Travel Guide (Austin, 2005)

www.springtrainingonline.com

## Notes

1. In the days before major league affiliation and vast spring training complexes, Texas was also popular with minor league teams—and not just Texas League teams—in search of suitable springtime digs. The Milwaukee Brewers and the Buffalo Bisons, among others, trained in Texas.

2. Hot Wells no longer appears on Texas maps. When the Cardinals trained there (1915–1917), it was just southeast of the San Antonio city limits and has since been absorbed by the city.

3. Though no major league teams set up camp in Austin and Fort Worth, the two cities hosted numerous exhibition games. At various times, the University of Texas Longhorns hosted the Cardinals, Browns, White Sox, Tigers, Giants, and Yankees at Clark Field in Austin.

4. Named after the famed Arlington Hotel in Hot Springs, Arkansas, the Arlington in downtown Marlin has since been razed and a post office was erected on the site.

5. Surprisingly, it is still possible to see baseball played on the field where the Tigers, White Sox and Reds trained. Now known as Richards Field (after native son Paul Richards), it is currently the home of the local high school team.

6. A 2005 visit to the forlorn streets of Marlin bears out McGraw's prophecy. Aside from a faded mural on the outside wall of the town's modest history museum, there is nothing to commemorate the 11-year presence of John McGraw and the New York Giants.

7. San Antonio was also attractive to McGraw because Hot Wells was accessible by streetcar.

8. McGraw himself became embroiled in real estate speculation in the Sarasota area, the winter home of his friend, circus impresario John Ringling. This was one factor in relocating the Giants to Sarasota during the 1924 and 1925 spring training seasons.

9. Preseason exhibition games, however, were not. In 1946, for example, the Pirates and White Sox, who had been training in California, played a series of exhibition games in El Paso, Del Rio, Houston, Dallas, and Fort Worth on their way home before opening day. Even today, preseason exhibition games are common if not annual occurrences, not just in Houston and Arlington, but in minor league cities like Midland and Round Rock.

# The Windowbreakers
## The New York Giants in 1947

### by Steve Treder

NOBODY saw it coming. Nobody could have, because nothing quite like it had ever happened before.

It is true that they had led the league in home runs the previous season, 1946. In fact, they had done so by a huge margin: they had hit 40 more homers than any other team in the league. But their league-leading total that year had been just 121, which was an unremarkable figure for a league leader in that era. The fact that no other team in the league hit more than 81 was a more unusual fact than their hitting 121.

They had hit more than 121 home runs five times in the past; their franchise record for team homers was 143, set 17 years earlier. The league record for team homers was 171, so obviously a team hitting 121, while achieving a mark that might lead the league, wasn't remotely threatening league history. And the major league record was 182, a full 50 percent ahead of 121.

Moreover, the roster that had fashioned the 121 gave no indication of having much capacity to exceed it, and the team had made no significant acquisitions in the off-season. They began the new campaign with just three players on the roster who had ever hit more than 13 home runs in a big league season, and two of those three figured to ride the bench, given that one (Ernie Lombardi) was a 39-year-old backup catcher, and another (31-year-old Babe Young) was blocked on the depth chart at his first base position by the third guy who had hit that many.

That third guy, the lone accomplished power hitter who did figure to play regularly, was, to be sure, one of the very best sluggers of the period: The Big Cat, Johnny Mize. He had once hit as many as 43 homers

STEVE TREDER *writes a weekly column on baseball history for* The Hardball Times, *where a version of this article first appeared. A lifelong Giants fan, he has had numerous articles published in* Nine: A Journal of Baseball History and Culture.

in a season. But that had been seven years earlier. Mize was now 34, and was coming off a season in which a broken hand had limited him to 101 games and 22 home runs. At this point in his career, there was no reason to anticipate him ever hitting as many as 43 again; 30 to 35 was a realistic upside, and a decline could hardly be considered unlikely.

Little of the rest of the lineup looked to be imposing. Despite leading the league in homers the preceding season, they hadn't done much else well, ranking fifth in runs scored. This, in combination with a lackluster pitching staff, had resulted in a last-place finish. In addition to Mize, there were three regulars who figured to keep their starting roles: 32-year-old catcher Walker Cooper, 26-year-old right fielder Willard Marshall, and 24-year-old shortstop Buddy Kerr. Cooper and Marshall were established as good line-drive hitters, but neither had demonstrated outstanding home run capability. Kerr was a slick fielder with a meager bat.

One other veteran, Sid Gordon, figured to compete for a starting job, but at 29, he had never been a true regular, instead performing more as a "super sub," roving between the outfield and infield. He had demonstrated value, but his career high in home runs was nine, and he was coming off a season in which he had produced just five in 450 at-bats.

Various other journeymen, and several rookies, would compete for playing time at second base, third base, center field, and left field. While giving significant opportunities to new talent introduces an obvious element of unpredictability into forecasting a team's performance, in looking at this roster and envisioning all possible scenarios, no one could reasonably anticipate this ball club hitting significantly more than 121 home runs.

Nobody saw it coming. Nobody could have, because nothing quite like it had ever happened before.

## 221

THE 1947 New York Giants hit 221 home runs. This has been a fact for more than half a century now, and generally if we're aware of it at all, it's just an obscure notation buried deep in a long list: today that total is tied for 37th on the all-time list of major league team home run totals. Since 1996 alone, 33 different teams have hit more than 221 homers in a season, and the current record is 264, by the 1997 Seattle Mariners. Hitting as many as 221 homers has become a routine occurrence under modern-day baseball conditions.

Through 1946, only 14 ball clubs in history had managed to hit as many as 150, just six of them within the past 10 years, and none in the past five. The idea that a team could possibly hit 221 home runs in a season was entirely ludicrous. At any time prior to 1947–most certainly including 1946–the very phrase, "the 1947 New York Giants hit 221 home runs" would have reasonably been perceived as nonsense, complete gibberish.

It was a silly number, fantasy land. Two-twenty-one was the batting average of your utility infielder. It was nothing resembling how many home runs your team would hit, or even could hit.

### Dominance

IN the entire National League of 1947, a total of 886 home runs were hit—thus the Giants contributed almost exactly one-quarter of the league's output. The other seven NL teams averaged 95 homers apiece, making the Giants' 221 mark 2.3 times that of their typical opponent; in the 58 years since, no other league has demonstrated anything close to such single-team home run dominance.

One ball club in history did dominate its league in homers at greater proportional rates than the '47 Giants, and that was the New York Yankees of the 1920s, with Babe Ruth in particular playing a very different game than just about anyone else. But in terms of absolute magnitude, rather than percentage, the Giants outdid even those Yankee teams. The Yankees' greatest numerical margin over their competitors occurred in 1927, when, with Lou Gehrig bursting on the scene to join Ruth, the Yanks hit a new-record 158 homers while their average opposing team managed 40, for a differential of 118. The 1947 Giants produced 126 more home runs than the average of their competitors.

### Ballpark

THE Giants' home park was, of course, Harlem's Polo Grounds, with a long, narrow horseshoe configuration, yielding the most oddly shaped playing field in modern major league history. The foul lines were comically short–279 feet to left field, and 257 to right–and then the walls angled very sharply out to a cavernously deep center field, measured at 484 feet from home plate in 1947. It added up to an extremely good environment for home runs (though interestingly, the enormous expanse of foul territory meant it was a very poor ballpark for batting average, and on balance it played as a neutral to slightly above-average scoring environment).

So there's no question that the 1947 Giants' home run total was enhanced by playing half their games in the Polo Grounds: that year the ballpark yielded home runs (for the Giants and their opponents combined) at a rate 46% above the league-average yard, highest in the NL, and a mark typical of how the Polo Grounds played throughout the late 1940s and early 1950s.

But to think that their achievement was little more than a park-effect illusion would be to commit a serious miscalculation. The 1947 Giants hit 131 home runs at home, far and away the most in the league–but they also hit 90 away from the Polo Grounds, also far and away the most in the league. The total of 90 road home runs was easily a new league record (the previous mark was 78, by the 1930 Cubs). If the Giants had produced no more home runs at home than they did on the road, they still would have set a new league record for total homers. Their power production was completely genuine.

*Johnny Mize, one of the premier hitters of the 1930s and 1940s, blasted a career-high 51 home runs at age 34 for the '47 Giants.*

NATIONAL BASEBALL LIBRARY, COOPERSTOWN, NY

### Windowbreakers

DESPITE the constant stream of long balls, the 1947 Giants weren't an especially good ball club overall. They were briefly in first place in early and mid-June, but then fell back and never really challenged again, finishing at 81–73, in fourth place, 13 games behind Jackie Robinson's champion Dodgers. Their great hitting (best in the league with 142.1 batting Win Shares) wasn't matched by either their pitching (69.8 pitching Win Shares, sixth in the league) or fielding (31.1 fielding Win Shares, seventh in the league).

Their batting average was third best in the league. They were tied for fourth in triples, fifth in OBP, and sixth in walks, doubles, and stolen bases. It was pretty much an all-or-nothing attack.

Nonetheless, the home run barrage was dramatic and exciting, undoubtedly all the more so because it was so completely unexpected. Through 77 games, the season's halfway point, the Giants had blasted 118 homers, and it was obvious they were going to shatter every standard. On August 2, they broke their franchise record; on August 24 the league mark went down, and on the first of September—with a full month to go—they became the major league record holders.

The fans loved it, and along with home-run benchmarks, the 1947 Giants surpassed their franchise attendance record by a mile, drawing 1.6 million, 25 percent over their previous best. Longtime club secretary Eddie Brannick, as he merrily toted up gate receipts, affectionately nicknamed the long-balling crew "The Windowbreakers," and the apt and colorful moniker stuck.

### Aftermath

ESSENTIALLY the same roster was retained for 1948, and the Giants remained the NL's premier slugging ball club, leading the league in runs and homers (yet, with their other weaknesses still intact, finished fifth at 78–76). But their major league–best home run total in 1948 was 164, falling short of the '47 output by 57. None of their big four boppers of 1947 was able to sustain his production, as Mize went from 51 homers to 40, Marshall from 36 to 14, Cooper from 35 to 16, and '47 rookie sensation Bobby Thomson from 29 to

*Catcher Walker Cooper had never hit more than 13 homers until exploding for 35 in 1947. He would never again hit more than 20.*

16. Following 1948, the New York Giants would lead the league in home runs only one more time, and that season (1954), they tied for the most, with 186. The Windowbreakers' moment was as brief as it was intense.

Playing in a National League that produced 38% more homers than the 1947 version, the 1956 Cincinnati Redlegs would match the record of 221. The mark was then broken by the storied 1961 Maris–Mantle Yankees, who thumped 240. No National League team would hit more than 221 homers in a season until 1997, fully half a century after the Giants set the standard.

### References and Resources

A delightful, informative read about the Giants of this era is Fred Stein's *Under Coogan's Bluff: A Fan's Recollections of the New York Giants Under Terry and Ott* (Alexandria, VA: Automated Graphic Systems, 1979). The chapter "The Windowbreakers" is on pp. 123–130.

# Marathon Men

## Rube and Cy Go the Distance

### by Dan O'Brien

Cy Young didn't have a problem when asked to choose his biggest thrill in baseball. Old Cy quickly picked his 1904 perfect game against Rube Waddell and the Philadelphia Athletics. Young's perfecto was the first in modern major league baseball history.

Also rating high on Young's list of personal favorites was another masterpiece against Waddell and the A's, a game which marks its 101st anniversary this Independence Day. The game was not, however, another of Cy's 511 career victories. It was a loss to Waddell in one of the most storied games of early American League history.

On July 4, 1905, Young and Waddell got the starting nods for the second game of a doubleheader at Boston's Huntington Avenue Grounds. The game lasted 20 innings, and so did both pitchers.

With the possible exception of a pennant- or World Series-clinching victory, a Hollywood screenwriter couldn't have created a more dramatic scenario: a pair of future Hall of Fame hurlers for two of the young league's best teams (the A's and Americans won four of the first five AL pennants) squaring off on our nation's birthday.

Granted, complete games were hardly unusual then. From 1900 to 1909 major league pitchers completed nearly 80% of their starts. Young and Waddell were in the upper echelon; Young competed 96 percent of his starts from 1902 through 1905, and Waddell went the distance nearly 87 % of the time.

Twenty innings, though, was almost unknown territory for both (Waddell pitched 22 innings in one

DAN O'BRIEN *lives in Indiana and is a former Emmy award-winning television sportscaster and producer. He is the co-author of two books:* Mark May's Tales from the Washington Redskins *(with Dan O'Brien) and* MizzouRah! Memorable Moments in Missouri Tiger Football History. *O'Brien is a founding board member of the Pittsburgh Pandas of the Tri-State Summer Collegiate Baseball League.*

day in the minors). Waddell, who relieved in the last inning of the morning game, shut out Boston batters over the last 19 innings of the afternoon contest. The eccentric southpaw also drove in the winning run in the Athletics' 4–2 victory.

Young didn't allow a walk and tossed 13 consecutive scoreless frames from the seventh through the 19th inning. "For my part, I think it was the greatest game of ball I ever took part in," Young later wrote.

Despite the long scoring drought, the game was packed with drama. "[T]he two teams kept at it with the excitement at fever beat until three hours and a half had been consumed, suppers forgotten, engagements neglected, trains and boats missed," reported the *Philadelphia Inquirer*, "for very few would allow anything to interfere with their presence at the finish of such a game."

This Boston marathon represented the longest completed game in major league history to that point. That in itself was enough to create a stir, but the presence and performances of Waddell and Young added to the mystique—as did the date.

"The fact that it was the 4th of July kept me going," Waddell noted. "I guess the shooting of revolvers and the fireworks and the yelling made me pitch better."

Waddell guessed he "must've pitched about 250 balls" during the game. Young rather generously estimated his own workload at four pitched balls per batter (the A's recorded 74 official at-bats). Neither seemed the worse for wear.

Waddell, according to legend, used the game's notoriety to quench his notorious thirst. "Often he'd go into saloons, triumphantly flourishing a baseball as the one which he had used in defeating Cy Young," Athletics' manager Connie Mack remembered. "It was a different ball every occasion, but it always was good for few drinks."

The game didn't begin in classic fashion. Waddell

gave up two runs in the bottom of the first. Young blanked Philadelphia over the first five innings but the A's pulled even in the sixth on a two-run homer by first baseman Harry Davis.

Boston threatened when shortstop Freddie Parent opened the bottom of the eighth inning with a triple. But Rube struck out the following two batters and retired the next hitter on a routine fly ball. Boston runners reached second and third in the 10th inning but Waddell again pitched himself out of the jam. "[W]henever danger threatened he put on the speed and the Boston batsmen might just as well been trying to hit his curves with toothpicks," wrote the *Philadelphia North American* reporter. Only three Bostonians reached base in the last six innings.

The game wasn't without controversy, albeit a mild one. In the bottom of the 12th, Boston manager–third baseman Jimmy Collins reached second base. Catcher Lou Criger followed with a sinking fly ball to right field. A charging Socks Seybold made a shoe-top catch and then doubled Collins off second.

The Boston fans weren't convinced Seybold made the catch. Young wasn't so sure, either. "I couldn't tell whether he caught the ball or not," Young wrote. "But he said the next day that he did and he is one of those kind you believe when he makes a statement."

The defensive support behind Young, characterized as "superb" for most of the game, finally broke down in the 20th inning.

After Collins booted Danny Murphy's ground ball, Young followed with one of his few errant pitches of the day, hitting A's shortstop John Knight in the head. Athletics catcher Ossee Schreckengost lofted a floater between Young and second baseman Hobe Ferris which neither could field. The A's had the bases loaded with no outs.

With a chance to win his own game, Waddell sent a slow roller to shortstop. When Parent fumbled the ball, Murphy scored the go-ahead run. A single by Hoffman drove home Schreckengost to give Waddell a two-run cushion.

Boston didn't go down without a fight. With one out, first baseman Bob Unglaub doubled off Waddell, who remained unfazed.

"I felt that two-bagger was a flash in the pan," recounted Waddell. "I knew, too, the Bostons would be easier, as they would be too anxious, so I didn't get nervous." Waddell retired the next two batters on easy pop-ups to finally put an end to it. The flaky Rube, none the worse for wear, celebrated with a few cartwheels across the diamond.

"It didn't take a feather out of me," claimed Waddell. "I felt just as good after the game was over as I did during the game."

Schreckengost, Waddell's catcher, was probably less energetic at the conclusion. He not only caught every inning of the afternoon tilt, but the entire morning game as well. His major league record for innings caught in a single day remains unequaled.

Waddell's 1905 season was his best full season in the big leagues. Waddell topped the American League in wins (27), strikeouts (287), and ERA (1.48), even though he pitched just one inning in the final month due to an injury.

The marathon was indicative of Young's hard-luck season. He finished among the league leaders in ERA (1.82), complete games (31), and strikeouts (210), but struggled to an 18–19 record, his first losing season in the majors.

Boston, the defending AL champions, finished in fourth place, 16 games behind the A's. Waddell's injury also kept him out of the World Series, which the Giants won in five games behind three shutouts by Christy Mathewson.

The Waddell–Young single-game record for combined innings pitched lasted only a year. On September 1, 1906, Philadelphia's Jack Coombs and Boston's Joe Harris each pitched every out of the A's 24-inning, 4–1 victory at—where else?—Boston's Huntington Avenue Grounds.

Waddell and Young seemed to bring out the best in each other. They started against each other 14 times. Six of those games ended in shutouts. In their first matchup in 1900—their only NL confrontation—Young's St. Louis squad blanked Waddell and Pittsburgh, 1–0. Their final dual in 1907—another Huntington Avenue Grounds classic—ended in a scoreless tie after 13 innings.

"I'd like to say that beating Rube anytime was a big job," Young recalled years later. "I never saw many who were better pitchers."

Even Waddell reflected on the 1905 epic with uncharacteristic modesty: "I can't claim that I did better work than Young. Cy Young is the best pitcher in the business, even now, and to have won over him is credit enough."

# I'm a Faster Man Than You Are, Heinie Zim

### by Richard A. Smiley

ALTHOUGH not now as legendary as Fred Merkle's base-running blunder or Fred Snodgrass's muffed fly ball, Heinie Zimmerman's failed pursuit of Eddie Collins in the final game of the 1917 World Series was quite notorious in its time. Most present-day descriptions of the play originate from the account given by Frank Graham in his team history of the New York Giants:

> Felsch slapped a high bounder to Benton, who threw to Zimmerman and there was Collins, flat-footed, yards off third base. Rariden, instead of remaining at the plate, moved up the line, thinking to close in on Collins for a run-down. Benton in the box and Holke at first base merely looked on, and Collins, seeing in a flash that the plate was uncovered, dug for it, brushing past the bewildered Rariden, and easily running away from Zimmerman. It was a blow from which the Giants could not recover.
>
> McGraw defended Zimmerman and blamed Holke for not covering the plate. It was Zim, however, who entered the best defense when he answered his critics with the question, "Who the hell was I going to throw the ball to, Klem?"[1]

But how accurate is Graham's account? What actually happened during the play? How did the media report the events? Why did Zimmerman get the blame? What was Zim's reaction? This paper will make use of an extensive review of the media of the time to answer these questions and reveal that part of Graham's version is a myth.

RICHARD A. SMILEY *lives in Chicago where he works as a statistician and demographer. He has contributed biographies of Reb Russell and Matty McIntyre to* Deadball Stars of the American League *and is currently researching Chicago's Twenty-third Street Grounds. He is a longtime fan of the Chicago White Sox.*

### 1917 World Series: Game One to Game Five

THE New York Giants, with stellar years from Heinie Zimmerman, Bennie Kauff, and George Burns, entered the 1917 World Series as slight betting favorites over the Chicago White Sox, which were led by Eddie Collins, Joe Jackson, and Happy Felsch. Newspaper prognosticators were evenly split over who would capture the title, but all were in agreement that the end result would come down to which of the equally fine pitching staffs would shine. The Series opened in Chicago, where the White Sox won the first two games behind the solid pitching of Eddie Cicotte and Red Faber and the hitting of Shano Collins and Happy Felsch. In New York, back-to-back shutouts by Rube Benton and Ferdie Schupp and a two-homer game from Bennie Kauff enabled the Giants to even the Series. The teams returned to Chicago for game five and staged one of the sloppiest games in World Series history.[2] The White Sox overcame an early Giant lead and six errors (three by Buck Weaver) to win the game and retake the Series lead.

### 1917 World Series: Game Six

PRIOR to the start of the sixth game on October 15, a coin flip to determine the site of a possible game seven went in favor of the Giants. That was the only break they would get on the day. Starters Rube Benton and Red Faber staged a tight pitchers duel for three innings as neither side threatened to score. In the top of the fourth, the roof caved in on the Giants and the White Sox plated three runs.

The first White Sox batter in the fourth inning was Eddie Collins. He hit a ground ball to third baseman Heinie Zimmerman which should have resulted in the first out of the inning. Instead, Eddie reached second as Zimmerman's throw was low in dirt and wide of first baseman Walt Holke. The next White Sox batter

*Third baseman Heinie Zimmerman*

was Joe Jackson, who lifted a lazy fly ball to short right center. Right fielder Dave Robertson came in under the ball to make the easy play, but he muffed the catch. As a result of the drop, Collins advanced to third base and Jackson landed on first base.[3] Thus the stage was set for one of the most memorable plays in World Series history.

With runners on first and third and nobody out, Happy Felsch hit a sharp bounder back to the pitcher Benton. After snaring the ball, Benton moved toward Collins, who had taken too large of a lead off third. Collins waved the other base runners forward and jockeyed along the third base line in hopes of extending the rundown play as long as possible. Eyewitness accounts of the play vary after this point. Many observers (including Frank Graham) claimed that after forcing Collins back toward third base, Benton threw the ball to Zimmerman, who immediately began a futile chase of Collins, which ended with the latter crossing an unguarded home plate to score the first run of the game. A somewhat lesser number claimed that after Benton threw the ball to Zimmerman, he tossed the ball to the catcher Bill Rariden, who chased Collins back toward third before returning the ball to Zimmerman, who then began his chase. An even smaller number of observers claimed that Benton's initial throw did not go to Zimmerman, but instead

was delivered to Rariden, who then chased Collins back toward third and threw the ball to Zimmerman, who started the chase.[4] Finally, *The Sporting News* reviewed the play at length and tracked the ball as going from Benton to Rariden to Zimmerman to Rariden (again) to Zimmerman (again), who then started the chase.[5]

We may never know which of the versions of the play was correct, but it does seem likely that Rariden did have the ball at some point and ran Collins back to third, as he was halfway up the third base line at the end of the play.

One point that almost all of the firsthand accounts agreed on was that the sight of Heinie Zimmerman chasing Eddie Collins across an unguarded home plate produced great laughter and mockery in the Polo Grounds crowd.

After the play was over, the demoralized Giants were down by a run with still nobody out and White Sox runners on second and third.[6] Chick Gandil quickly lashed a single down the first-base line to bring home both runners and up the White Sox lead to 3–0. Those runs were all that Red Faber needed and the White Sox held on to win the game and the Series by a 4–2 score.

### The Blame

INITIAL newspaper accounts of the game reveal that almost all members of the New York press community thought that the chase was the key play of the game and that Zimmerman should get the blame for it. Many writers and cartoonists used the play as a launching pad of mockery and lambasted Zimmerman with wicked humor. The best example of this could be found on the front page of the *New York Times*, where Harry Cross began his write-up this way:

> While 34,000 fans frantically implored the Giants at the Polo Grounds yesterday to produce a hero on whose classic brow they could nestle a wreath of laurel, the New York club went down to an ignoble 4 to 2 defeat before the Chicago White Sox in the deciding game of the world's series and instead of crowning a new baseball king, Manhattan placed a clown's cap on the head of Heinie Zimmerman of the Bronx.
>
> The once great Zim played the dunce's role in the fourth inning, when he made a weird heave to first which permitted Eddie Collins to race

around as far as second and a moment later he had a foot race down the third base line desperately trying to tag Collins as Eddie sped on over the plate two jumps ahead of him and started the Sox on their way to the world's championship. Heinie could just as well have thrown the ball to Bill Rariden and squelched Collins, but Zim thought it was a track meet instead of a ball game and wanted to match his lumber wagon gait against the fleetest sprinter in the game.

The great crowd shook with laughter and filled the air with cries of derision at one of the stupidest plays that has ever been seen in a world's series. It was a tough finish for poor Heinie after playing great ball all season, and Zim had been expected to be one of the sensations of the big classic against Chicago. Groans and more of them rumbled through the stands, and the Chicago players who have been predicting all the time that Heinie would sooner or later stage the marble top play of all time, were so happy that they hopped around like jumping jacks. The crowd called Heinie a "bonehead" and he took his place in baseball history along with Bonehead Barry, the mythical player who is supposed to have made all the foolish, rattle-brained plays of the game.

"Throw the ball!" yelled the crowd. "Throw the ball!" yelled the Giant players, but all the thousands of supplications fell on tin ears. Heinie refused to throw the ball—he wanted to catch Eddie Collins and put him out all by himself. Collins outsprinted Heinie and won the race by yards.[7]

Conversely, initial accounts written by press outside of New York tended to include Holke and Rariden (and sometimes Benton) in the blame along with Zimmerman. The vehemence with which the New York press focused on Heinie as the lone culprit may have been in response to hearing a verdict of guilt from the fans in the Polo Grounds who were their readers. And the fans may have been responding to the culmination of events that they had witnessed in the inning. In some sense, Heinie was certainly to blame for the run scoring, as he was the one who put Collins on base.

### Photographic Evidence

A look at photographs of the play provides a little clarity about what actually happened. The most commonly seen photograph of the play, which appeared in a number of newspapers, was shot from a location approximately where a modern third base dugout would be and focused on home plate. It shows four figures: the catcher Rariden, who had gotten out of the way of the base runner; the umpire Bill Klem; Eddie Collins *sliding* across home plate; and Heinie Zimmerman leaping over Eddie. That Zimmmerman was close enough to Collins at the end of the play to need to jump over him dispels any notions that Eddie

TRANSCENDENTAL GRAPHICS

*Program cover from the 1917 Series. Eddie Collins scores in the third inning of the first game.*

had an easy time outrunning Zim. In fact, Collins later expressed his belief that he gained no ground on Zim during the chase.[8] *The Sporting News* made use of this photo and an extensive diagnosis of the events to absolve Zimmerman of the blame and place it on Rariden.[9]

Another photo taken from a somewhat similar angle, but starting from a spot nearer to home plate and aimed down the first base line appeared in the *New York Tribune*.[10] It also was snapped at the moment that Collins slid across home, but with one additional detail—in the background, New York Giant first baseman Walt Holke is visible with his foot planted on first base. Giant manager John McGraw placed the blame for the play on Holke because he did not come down to help out in the rundown.[11]

### A Life of Its Own

THE play began to take on a life of its own after the series ended. The day after it occurred, the White Sox and Giants participated in a benefit game for the troops overseas in which Fred McMullin and Germany Schaefer elaborately mimicked the play. Members of the audience recognized the play from press accounts and roared their approval of the skit.[12]

Prior to the Zimmerman-Collins chase, similar plays were given little notice. In a midsummer 1917 game against the Tigers, Eddie Collins was chased across an unoccupied home plate, but the play was barely mentioned in the papers.[13] The year after the chase happened, writers began to pay more attention to such events. When Giant shortstop Art Fletcher unsuccessfully chased a runner home in a 1918 regular season game, the headline included the phrase FLETCHER EMULATES ZIM.[14] Likewise, headlines were made when Zim *successfully* chased down Rogers Hornsby in a 1919 regular season game.[15]

References to the play while describing base running blunders were common in the 1920s and 1930s.

### Heinie's Comments

OVER time the most notable feature about the play has shifted from being the comical chase of a base runner over an unguarded home plate by the third baseman to being the fielder's clever retort upon cross-examination that the only person he could have thrown the ball to was the umpire. But where did that quote come from? For two days after the play occurred, not one sign of a quote or comment from Zimmerman could

be found in any of the newspapers. He finally appears in print on October 18, when *New York Evening Sun* columnist Joe Vila mentions bumping into him:

> Heinie Zimmerman, who has been boiled in oil since Monday, when he vainly tried to outrun Eddie Collins in the final game of the world's series, came down from the Bronx yesterday to see the New York Club officials on a matter of business. When I ran across Zim at the Fifth Avenue Building he was hobnobbing with Ferdinand Schupp, the Giants' young southpaw, who whitewashed the Chicago White Sox in the fourth combat at the Polo Grounds last Thursday.
>
> "I'll take all the blame!" said Zim manfully. "When I started after Collins I thought I could outrun him. That was why I didn't throw the ball to Rariden, who stood on the base line. After I had passed Rariden I suddenly realized that Collins was too fast for me, but I kept on chasing him because the plate was uncovered.
>
> "I made a big mistake when I didn't throw to Rariden in the first place, but I didn't believe that Collins could run so fast. It was bad judgment on my part and I intend to take my medicine without grumbling."[16]

So given the opportunity in 1917, Zimmerman made no reference to throwing the ball to the umpire when discussing the play. After McGraw became suspicious of Zim's gambling activities during the 1919 season, he removed Zim from the Giants. Zim again made no reference to the umpire in 1921:

> Since McGraw banished me from baseball he has accused me of throwing the 1917 World's Series to the White Sox. He has declared that I deliberately chased Eddie Collins across the plate with the winning run in the final game.
>
> However, in the clubhouse, after that game, McGraw said that he did not blame me for that play. He gave both Bill Rariden and Walt Holke a terrible panning for not covering the plate. He absolutely cleared me of all blame.[17]

Heinie's version of where McGraw placed the blame in the clubhouse was later backed up by other accounts. Zimmerman's claim that he did not throw the series was backed by Dave Robertson:

Zimmerman was a much faster man than Collins and under ordinary conditions he could have caught him. He simply misjudged Collins' start. I don't think McGraw ever said a word to Zimmerman about the play because Heinie was more sorry than anybody. He came to the club-house crying.[18]

Despite the appearance of numerous newspaper descriptions of the play in the 1920s and 1930s, no use of the quote was made. The closest any piece came to mentioning the quote was a 1927 *New York Times* "Sports of the Times" column written by John Kieran in which he stated, "It was discovered some time later that Heinie had no one to throw the ball to except the umpire."[19] But this was still not a quote being attributed to Heinie Zimmerman. So where did it come from?

### Ring Lardner

IN his October 16, 1917, "Wake of the News" column in the *Chicago Tribune*, Ring Lardner mentioned that he had not gone to New York in person to cover game six of the series and that his reports of the game were coming from the wire-service stories:

On last Saturday, inst., the gentleman in charge called up and said I didn't have to go to New York if I didn't want to. So I said I didn't want to. He expressed the opinion that I could write as accurately about the game from Here as the other Dirty Rats from the field of play. And perhaps better, he said. I thanked him for the high compliment implied and below is the result. I know only that Faber and Benton were the opposing pitchers at the start; that the Sox scored three runs in the fourth inning; that the Giants got two in the fifth, and that the Sox got another in the ninth, and that Perritt was Benton's successor. Also [let's not cheat here] that Heinie Zimmerman made a wild throw that had a great deal to do with the result.[20]

As Lardner's "coverage" of the game was second-hand, he probably read many accounts of the game including one by G. W. Axelson in the *Chicago Herald* which contained this comment about the chase:

Zimmerman's only play was to throw the ball to McGraw or Bill Klem. Neither probably could

have held the pill, anyway, so he gave chase to Eddie on his own hook.

In his October 18 "Wake of the News" column, Lardner used what he had learned about the game to concoct an imaginary conversation in the Giants clubhouse after game six in which the players rip each other apart. The piece was entitled "The House of Glass" and it began this way:

(A rat's guess at the conversation in the New York club-house after Monday's game).
McGraw—Well, Heinie, you gave a great exhibition!
Kauff—I'll say he gave a great exhibition!
Zim—You're a fine lot o' yellow quitters!
McGraw—Who told you you could outrun Collins?
Zim—What the hell was I goin' to do, throw the ball to Klem? Where was Holke? Where was Benton?[21]

In addition to being syndicated in New York, this particular column made it into *The Sporting News* of October 25, 1917, alongside the paper's dissection of the play, which blamed Rariden. And for good measure, Lardner included the phrase "Who'll I throw it to? Klem?" in his "Follies of 1917" musical revue at the end of the year.[22]

In short, Heinie Zimmerman never said, "Who the hell was I going to throw the ball to, Klem?" Ring Lardner did.

### Frank P. Graham

THE first time that the quote was actually attributed to Zimmerman seems to have been when Frank Graham included the following passage in his 1944 book *McGraw of the Giants*:

Heinie answered his critics with an unforgettable question: "Who the hell was I going to throw the ball to? Klem?"[23]

One can only speculate that, writing 25 years after the fact, Graham had remembered Lardner's column but had forgotten that it was not a real conversation being reported! Graham would later go on to include a similar version of the play and quote in his Giants team history.

<h1 style="text-align:center">Articles about Game 6 of the 1917 World Series</h1>

## NEW YORK PAPERS

| # | Author | Publication | Pub. Date | Article | Benton's Action | Zim's Action | Blames |
|---|--------|-------------|-----------|---------|-----------------|--------------|--------|
| 1a | H. Cross | *New York Times* | October 16 | Page 1 Story | Chases Collins, throws to Zim | Starts chase | Zim |
| 1b | Uncredited | " | October 16 | Recap | Throws to Zim | Throws to Rariden | Zim |
| 1c | I. Cobb | " | October 16 | Column | Throws to Zim | Throws to Rariden | Zim |
| 2a | D. Runyon | *New York American* | October 16 | Column | Chases Collins, throws to Zim | Starts chase | Zim |
| 2b | Uncredited | " | October 16 | Recap | Chases Collins, throws to Zim | Starts chase | -- |
| 3a | R. Edgren | *Evening World* | October 15 | Column | Chases Collins, throws to Zim | Starts chase | Zim |
| 3b | A. Baer | " | October 15 | Column | -- | -- | Zim |
| 3c | Uncredited | " | October 15 | Recap/Lead | Throws to Zim | Starts chase | Zim |
| 4a | W. Trumbull | *World*/Syndicated | October 16 | Column | Chases Collins, throws to Zim | Starts chase | Zim |
| 5a | G. Rice | *Tribune*/Syndicated | October 16 | Page 1 Story | Chases Collins, throws to Zim | Starts chase | Zim |
| 5b | W. Macbeth | *New York Tribune* | October 16 | Second Story | Chases Collins, throws to Zim | Starts chase | Zim |
| 6a | J. Vila | *New York Evening Sun* | October 15 | Page 1 Story | Chases Collins, throws to Zim | Starts chase | Zim |
| 6b | F. Graham | " | October 16 | Lead Story | -- | -- | Zim |
| 6c | J. Vila | " | October 16 | Column | -- | -- | Zim |
| 6d | J. Vila | " | October 18 | Column | -- | -- | Zim* |
| 7a | S. Crane | *NY Evening Journal* | October 16 | Lead Story | -- | -- | Rariden |
| 7b | T. A. Dorgan | " | October 16 | Pg. 1 Cartoon | -- | | Zim |
| 7c | Uncredited | " | October 16 | Column | -- | -- | Zim |
| 8a | S. Mercer | *New York Globe* | October 16 | Lead Story | -- | -- | Zim, Rariden |
| 8b | R. Ripley | " | October 16 | Cartoon | -- | -- | Zim |
| 9a | L. Perry | *New York Evening Post* | October 15 | Recap/Page 1 | -- | Starts chase | Zim |
| 10a | Uncredited | *New York Herald* | October 16 | Recap/Page 1 | -- | -- | Zim |
| 10b | W. Hanna | " | October 16 | Lead Story | Throws to Rariden | Starts chase | Zim |
| 10c | Col. J. Ruppert | " | October 16 | Column | -- | -- | Zim |
| 10d | W. Hanna | " | October 17 | Column | -- | -- | Zim |
| 11a | Uncredited | *Brooklyn Daily Eagle* | October 15 | Recap/Page 1 | Throws to Zim | Starts chase | Zim |
| 11b | G. Rice | " | October 16 | Lead Story | Chases Collins, throws to Zim | Starts chase | Zim |

## CHICAGO PAPERS

| # | Author | Publication | Pub. Date | Article | Benton's Action | Zim's Action | Blames |
|---|--------|-------------|-----------|---------|-----------------|--------------|--------|
| 12a | H. Fullerton | Examiner/Syndicated | October 16 | Column | Throws to Rariden | Starts chase | Zim |
| 13a | I. E. Sanborn | Chicago Tribune | October 16 | Page 1 Story | Chases Collins, throws to Zim | Starts chase | Rariden, Holke, Zim |
| 13b | Uncredited | " | October 16 | Recap | Chases Collins, throws to Zim | Starts chase | -- |
| 13c | J. Crusinberry | " | October 16 | Sidebar | -- | -- | Zim |
| 14a | B. Bailey | Chicago American | October 15 | Lead Story | -- | -- | Zim |
| 14b | Uncredited | " | October 15 | Recap | Throws to Zim | Starts chase | -- |
| 15a | O. Reichow | Chicago Daily News | October 15 | Column | Chases Collins, throws to Zim | Starts chase | Zim |
| 15b | G. Robbins | " | October 15 | Recap | Chases Collins, throws to Zim | Starts chase | -- |
| 16a | G. W. Axelson | Chicago Herald | October 16 | Page 1 Story | Chases Collins, throws to Zim | Starts chase | Rariden, Holke |
| 16a | B. Birch | " | October 16 | Sidebar | Chases Collins, throws to Zim | Starts chase | Rariden, Holke |

## OTHER PAPERS

| # | Author | Publication | Pub. Date | Article | Benton's Action | Zim's Action | Blames |
|---|--------|-------------|-----------|---------|-----------------|--------------|--------|
| 17a | J. V. Fitzgerald | *Washington Post* | October 16 | Page 1 Story | Chases Collins, throws to Zim | Starts chase | All (incl Benton) |
| 18a | M. Webb Jr. | *Boston Globe* | October 16 | Page 1 Story | Chases Collins, throws to Zim | Starts chase | Zim |
| 19a | Uncredited | Associated Press | October 16 | Story | Chases Collins, throws to Zim | Starts chase | -- |

## SPORTING PRESS

| # | Author | Publication | Pub. Date | Article | Benton's Action | Zim's Action | Blames |
|---|--------|-------------|-----------|---------|-----------------|--------------|--------|
| 20a | Uncredited | *The Sporting News* | October 25 | Analysis | Chases Collins, throws to Rariden | Throws to Rariden | Rariden |
| 21a | W. Phelon | *Baseball Magazine* | Dec. 1917 | Story | Whirls with ball, traps Collins | -- | Zim |

*Heinie Zimmerman blamed himself in this interview with the *Evening Sun*'s Joe Vila.

## Arthur Daley and the Spread of the Quote

AMONG those who read and enjoyed Graham's book was Arthur Daley, who had taken over the *New York Times*' "Sports of the Times" column from John Kieran. Daley's 1944 review of the Graham book mentioned the Zimmerman–Collins chase, but did not use the quote.[24]

In 1946, Bob Broeg and Bob Burrill published an entertaining collection of sports boners and mishaps entitled *Don't Bring That Up!* The final pages of their collection included a description of the Zimmerman–Collins chase which closely paraphrased Graham's text.[25] Daley praised the book in his column and included the version of the quote that appeared in the book: "Who was I gonna throw the ball to? The umpire?"[26] Afterward, Daley became an "advocate" for this particular version of the quote, finding reasons to use it in his column at least 10 times over the next 15 years.[27]

Over time the quote became entrenched in baseball literature as writers such as Tom Meany[28] and Charles Alexander,[29] using the Graham books as reference, included it in their own texts. Other variations on the quote began to appear, such as replacing "Klem" with "myself."[30] Like the play itself, the quote had taken on a life of its own.

Like everything else about the play, the best thing written about it was somewhat unfair, slightly inaccurate, and tremendously funny. Grantland Rice, tipping his hat to Rudyard Kipling, closed his report of the game in the *New York Tribune* with:

The 1917 affair looked to be New York's and the National League's best chance after a long period in the wilderness, but the end came when Eddie Collins slid safely over the plate, softly humming, according to expert testimony, the following refrain:

> *Where do we go from here, Old Dog*
> *where do we go from here?*
> *Come on Heinie, run it out,*
> *the open way is clear,*
> *Altho you thought you had me hooked*
> *out safely on a limb,*
> *I'm a faster man than you are*
> *Heinie Zim, Heinie Zim.*[31]

## Notes

1. Frank P. Graham. *The New York Giants*. New York: Putnam, 1952.
2. *Baseball Digest*, October 2004.
3. Some accounts have Jackson reaching second base on the play.
4. Newspapers researched for accounts of the play: *Atlanta Constitution, Boston Globe, Brooklyn Daily Eagle, Chicago American, Chicago Daily News, Chicago Examiner, Chicago Herald, Chicago Tribune, New York American, New York Evening Journal, New York Evening Post, New York Evening Sun, New York Evening World, New York Globe, New York Herald, New York Times, New York Tribune, New York World, and Washington Post*.
5. *The Sporting News*, October 25, 1917.
6. Accounts vary as to whether or not Jackson reached third and Felsch reached second as a specific result of the chase. Many of the writers ignored the trailing runners entirely in their accounts and focused only on Collins.
7. *New York Times*, October 16, 1917.
8. *New York Tribune*, October 19, 1917, and *American Legion Weekly*, August 10, 1923.
9. *The Sporting News*, October 25, 1917.
10. *New York Tribune*, October 16, 1917.
11. McGraw also blamed Holke for another game six play in which an opportunity for the Giants to get a double play was botched by poor thinking. As a result, McGraw replaced Holke in 1919 with Hal Chase. See Donald Dewey and Nicholas Acocella, *The Black Prince of Baseball: Hal Chase and the Mythology of Baseball*. Toronto: Sportclassic Books, 2004.
12. *New York Times*, October 17, 1917.
13. *The 1917 White Sox: Their World Championship Season*. Warren N. Wilbert and William C. Hageman. Jefferson, NC: McFarland, 2003.
14. *New York Times*, June 7, 1918.
15. *New York Times*, May 24, 1919.
16. *New York Evening Sun*, October 18, 1917.
17. *New York Times*, March 4, 1921.
18. *Washington Post*, January 1, 1927.
19. *New York Times*, October 6, 1927.
20. *Chicago Tribune*, October 16, 1917.
21. *Chicago Tribune*, October 18, 1917.
22. *Chicago Tribune*, December 30, 1917.
23. Frank P. Graham. *McGraw of the Giants*. New York: Putnam, 1952.
24. *New York Times*, April 25, 1944.
25. Bob Broeg and Bob Burrill. *Don't Bring That Up!*. New York: A. S. Barnes, 1946.
26. *New York Times*, June 30, 1946.
27. See Daley's columns in the *New York Times* on October 11, 1946; October 3, 1947; August 14, 1949; October 7, 1950; March 27, 1951; April 5, 1953; September 25, 1955; June 3, 1958; October 6, 1960; and October 6, 1961.
28. Tom Meany. *Baseball's Greatest Teams*. New York: A. S. Barnes, 1949 and Tom Meany. *Baseball's Greatest Players*. New York: A. S. Barnes, 1953.
29. Charles C. Alexander. *McGraw*. New York: Viking, 1988.
30. John Devaney and Burt Goldblatt. *The World Series: A Complete Pictorial History*. New York: Dial, 1972 and *Baseball Digest*, October 2004.
31. *New York Tribune*, October 16, 1917.

# Twilight at Ebbets Field

## by Rory Costello

EBBETS Field has been gone for nearly half a century, but the place still has a remarkable grip on our consciousness. Two recent books have been devoted to the lovable old ballpark in Flatbush.[1] Yet even these in-depth works don't shine much light on what happened *after* the Dodgers left Brooklyn. They touch briefly on some teasing references to post-Dodger history, but there's more to this period than mere footnotes. It is a buried chapter of stadium lore—featuring two Hall of Fame stars.

This article does not reexamine whether club owner Walter O'Malley or New York City power broker Robert Moses could have kept the club from going west. By late 1957, it was a foregone conclusion. In major league terms, Brooklyn had been reduced to a bargaining chip or at best a fallback option in case O'Malley's negotiations with Los Angeles blew up. People like Abe Stark—the local tailor ("Hit Sign, Win Suit") turned City Council president—were hoping against hope.

What many don't recall is how long Ebbets clung to life. Even people who are Brooklyn to the bone, like journalist Pete Hamill, are prone to misty memory. On his web site, Hamill says, "Within a year after the Dodgers lammed to Los Angeles, Ebbets Field was smashed into rubble." Not true—the Bums played their last home game on September 24, 1957, but the wrecking ball did not swing until February 23, 1960.

To recap, the Dodgers played the '57 season on the first year of O'Malley's three-year lease-back deal with developer Marvin Kratter, who had bought the property for $3 million on October 30, 1956. Kratter hinted in October '57 that another club might relocate to Ebbets,[2] but that may have been just a PR red herring. In 1958, the new Dodger home was the Los Angeles Coliseum; meanwhile O'Malley was also paying for three other parks: Wrigley Field in L.A., Roosevelt Stadium in Jersey City (where the Dodgers had played seven "home" games in '56 and eight in '57), and Ebbets. The cagey Irishman estimated his carrying costs on the Brooklyn facility at $170,000 a year—$80K in rental, $40K in maintenance, and $50K in real estate taxes.[3] So in an effort to cut his losses, he subleased.

Enter Robert A. Durk, a local home builder who thought he saw an opportunity. Durk, aged 36 in early 1958, was the front man for Ebbets Field Productions. This venture had grand plans for various sporting attractions and other events; rent would be paid on a percentage basis. One such hope was to bring in the Yomiuri Giants, Japan's version of the Yankees, to play a Latin American team.[4]

The idea was years ahead of its time, but didn't pan out. Instead, a demolition derby paid a visit. Jack Kochman's Hell Drivers apparently were hell—on the Ebbets Field turf. The New Jersey-based troupe put on two performances a day from May 30 through June 1. Kochman's Auto Thrill Show survived through 2004, as did the man himself, who passed away at the age of 97. For better or worse, there are likely no other records of the "Smashing! Crashing! Racing!!" (as the spectacle was billed in a *New York Daily News* ad). Charlie Belknap, who took over the business in 1989, said, "Jack probably would have remembered those shows because they were in the metropolitan area. But he wouldn't have kept programs or anything like that. He'd have said, 'That's clutter—get rid of it.'"

The evidence shows that Ebbets Field Productions staged only one more event: the Hamid-Morton circus, also booked for two daily performances from June 29 through July 12. Robert A. Durk Associates, Inc. (liabilities: $86,828—assets: $9,110) declared bankruptcy in August 1958.[5] Durk, who later became an

RORY COSTELLO *is a longtime Brooklyn resident but was years too late to have the pleasure of seeing a game at Ebbets Field.*

ad man in Connecticut, then faded from the scene. He died in 1988.

The most popular post-Dodger activity at 55 Sullivan Place was soccer. On May 25, 1958, 20,606 spectators braved the rain to see Hearts of Midlothian (Scotland) beat Manchester City (England) 6–5 on a muddy pitch. Had the weather been better, the crowd might have approached capacity. One day short of a year later, Dundee and West Bromwich Albion drew 21,312—the best turnout of the twilight years. There were 15 programs in 1959, played both in the afternoon and under the lights. New York Hakoah, a Jewish-oriented team in the old American Soccer League (ASL), moved in from the Bronx. A strong array of international squads—from Italy, Spain, Poland, Sweden, and Austria, as well as the U.K.—built the audience for the ASL.

At first it might seem surprising to see what a drawing card this sport was—it did better than a lot of Dodgers games toward the end. But it is less remarkable in view of Brooklyn's historically large and varied immigrant population. Plus, there was an echo of when Dodger fans occasionally crossed the line from avid and boisterous to riotous. Hundreds of unruly Napoli partisans erupted on the field to attack the officials on June 28, 1959. A patrolman was also knocked out with a linesman's flag.[6]

Although Ebbets had hosted a good deal of boxing and American football in its past, neither sport was visible there during 1958–59. Brooklyn was considered a possibility for the AFL as that rival league was forming in 1959,[7] but the New York Titans (later the Jets) went with the Polo Grounds instead. Other ideas were merely fanciful. In July 1959, Abe Stark—briefly acting mayor in Robert Wagner's absence—injected himself into a racial debate over the West Side Tennis Club in Forest Hills. Dr. Ralph Bunche, the eminent statesman and civil rights leader, and his son ran into the club's color barrier. Stark postured against Forest Hills and announced that he had gained permission from Marvin Kratter to use Ebbets free of charge for Davis Cup matches and the National Championship.[8] But the flap died down within a week, and with it Stark's sentimental hope.

At its core, Ebbets Field was still a baseball venue. In the spring of 1958, Long Island University played six home games there and St. John's played four, under the auspices of the Dodgers. LIU coach William "Buck" Lai, a Dodgers scout and instructor at the Dodgertown Camp for Boys, was instrumental. Then in '59, LIU returned for one more, while St. John's played two. These matches

weren't much of a draw—especially the first year, most Dodger fans were still in shock or mourning. College ball was a pretty thin substitute.

However, the St. John's roster boasted two future big leaguers, even if they were "cup of coffee" guys. Brooklyn-born infielder Ted Schreiber hit a game-winning two-run homer at Ebbets on April 24, 1958; in 1963, he made 55 plate appearances for the New York Mets.[9] A further look at Redmen alumni in the majors shows Billy Ott, who enjoyed two brief stints in the outfield with the Chicago Cubs in 1962 and 1964 after signing as a free agent before the 1960 season. Larry Bearnarth, another early Met who later became a major league pitching coach, was probably just a little too late. He had a great collegiate career at St. John's, but he most likely did not play with the varsity as a freshman in 1959.

Even now, Ted Schreiber (who went to Ebbets three or four times a year growing up) has clear recall:

"I remember it almost like it was yesterday. I just got through basketball season and I was struggling for hits. Most of my career, I never saw the ball hit the bat. But a lefty was pitching, so the angle was good, and the ball was out in front of the plate. My concentration was so keen, I didn't look up, I was running hard to first base. Then I heard a rattle, and I knew it had to be the ball in the seats. The crowd was just a handful, people who loved college ball—that time of year wasn't conducive to real good baseball.

"And you know what was special? The field was so smooth! The regular places I played in Brooklyn, the Parade Grounds was good, but get in front of a ball in Marine Park, you deserve combat pay. I was impressed. As soon as you come out of the tunnel, you see the lights and it takes hold. It was very exciting to be on a major league field."

### College Baseball at Ebbets Field, 1958–59

| Date | Score |
| --- | --- |
| 4/5/58 | UConn 7, LIU 6 |
| 4/9/58 | LIU 11, Adelphi 4 |
| 4/10/58 | Rutgers 4, St. John's 3 |
| 4/24/58 | St. John's 2, Manhattan 1 |
| 4/30/58 | St. John's 4, Hofstra 0 |
| 5/1/58 | NYU 3, St. John's 0 |
| 5/2/58 | Fairfield 6, LIU 4 |
| 5/9/58 | LIU 7, Bridgeport 5 |
| 5/12/58 | LIU 3, NY Maritime 1 |
| 5/17/58 | LI Aggies 5, LIU 3 |
| 4/18/59 | Manhattan 5, St. John's 3 |
| 4/25/59 | St. John's 11, Manhattan 0 |
| 5/6/59 | LIU 7, Queens College 6 |

Source: *New York Times; Washington Post, Times Herald*

STEPPING down another level, high school players still had the pleasure of performing at Ebbets too, as the Dodgers also sponsored the Public School Athletic League finals. On June 23, 1958, Martin Van Buren High of Queens defeated Curtis High of Staten Island 5–3.[10] The next year, on June 5, Roosevelt High (Bronx) was the champ, and Curtis once more the runner-up, in a 6–5 battle before a crowd of 4,000.[11]

Going younger still, there is a nice anecdote about Babe Ruth ball. Paul Jurkoic was born in 1946 and grew up on Governor's Island when it was an Army post. He knows it must have been the summer of 1959 when his Fort Jay all-star squad came to Brooklyn—the base paths were 90 feet long, not the Little League distance. Jurkoic still has vivid memories of that special day:

> Our opponents were from somewhere in Brooklyn . . . Fort Hamilton, or maybe Gravesend. The game was attended only by the family and friends of the players—a very small crowd indeed—maybe a few hundred. I don't remember ever being in the locker room (disappointment!), so I suspect we traveled to and from the game in uniform. What I most remember was that the field was still very well kept, even though the Dodgers weren't there anymore.
>
> The infield grass was very green and healthy, and was mown short—like a golf fairway, and there were no pebbles or other obvious imperfections on the dirt part. This was like playing in heaven for us, because although the Army did a pretty good job of maintaining the field we played on (which was also used by the soldiers, I believe), it was not up to major league standards. I was struck by the Spartan appearance of the dugout. I had thought that a big league dugout would be somehow more fancy than it was. I also have an impression about the telephone that the managers used to call the bullpen—it was missing, but the wires were hanging out of the wall where it had been. It was definitely a thrill for all of us to play in a real big league stadium.

Yet the most intriguing baseball action during the "twilight era" had fallen into total obscurity until this research unearthed it. A team called the Brooklyn Stars played at Ebbets in 1959. Their sponsor was one of "The Boys of Summer"—Roy Campanella, about

18 months after the auto accident that made him a paraplegic.

The Stars first came to this author's attention in 1999 as a side note while writing the history of baseball in the Virgin Islands. One key source, a St. Croix native named Osee Edwards, also mentioned that he played for this semi-pro squad of black and Latin players. Osee worked as an X-ray technician in a Brooklyn hospital. He and his teammates advertised their games around the community, posting flyers in places like barbershops. He talked about Campy as well as facing another Dodger hero of the '50s, Joe Black. Two years after Joe's last major league appearance, the first black pitcher to win a World Series game was a schoolteacher in his hometown of Plainfield, NJ. But he still hurled on occasion for a local team called the Newark Eagles,[12] a namesake of the Negro League team of 1936–48, whose Brooklyn forerunner played one year at Ebbets in 1935.

A letter seeking confirmation went out to Mr. Black shortly thereafter, but his brief reply was a damper. He pooh-poohed the idea that his old battery mate could have been involved. However, the newspaper archives show that his memory was not as clear as Osee's. Looking back, Roy Campanella was a surprisingly busy man after he got out of the hospital in late 1958. His health was delicate, but he was still tending to his business ventures (and the misadventures of his wayward stepson David). He attended spring training at Vero Beach and went out to Los Angeles for the big night in his honor at the Coliseum on May 7. He appeared at Yonkers Raceway on July 1. In August, he even acted in an episode of the TV show *Lassie*. Among all these other activities he fit in the formation of a ball club at his old home field.[13]

Other Stars opponents included the Gloversville Merchants, who represented the leather-goods town on the southern fringe of Adirondack Park. They and the Newark Eagles met at old Hawkins Stadium in Albany, which by coincidence was also razed in 1960. Campy's club often played in doubleheaders with teams such as the Memphis Red Sox from the Negro American League. The Negro Leagues, another institution on its last legs, would limp on through one more season.

But Ebbets Field had one last baseball hurrah—built around a genuine icon. On August 23, 1959, none other than Satchel Paige was the main attraction in a doubleheader that drew 4,000 fans.

NATIONAL BASEBALL LIBRARY, COOPERSTOWN, NY

Barnstorming with the Havana Cubans, he gave his age as "somewhere between 40 and 60." The Kansas City Monarchs topped the Stars 3–1 in the opener. Then Satch—wearing a Chicago White Sox uniform lent to him by former employer Bill Veeck—came on to strike out four in a three-inning start. The master allowed three runs, but only one was earned. He gave up a homer when he got cute and tried to sneak a second blooper pitch by Monarchs player-manager Herm Green.[14]

**Roy Campanella's Brooklyn Stars and the Negro American League at Ebbets Field, 1959**

| Date | Action |
| --- | --- |
| 7/12 | Brooklyn Stars vs. Memphis Red Sox |
|  | Detroit Stars vs. Memphis |
| 7/26 | Brooklyn Stars vs. Memphis Red Sox |
|  | Birmingham Black Barons vs. Memphis |
| 8/2 | Brooklyn Stars vs. Detroit Stars |
|  | Detroit vs. Raleigh Tigers |
| 8/23 | Kansas City Monarchs 3, Brooklyn Stars 1 |
|  | Havana Cubans 6, Kansas City Monarchs 4 |

Source: *New York Times*

Yet even after the Cubans' victory had faded into autumn, a flicker of life was still visible. The Hakoah soccer club scheduled a series of four Sunday doubleheaders. As it turned out, though, only three were played. Thus the last known sporting event at Ebbets took place on October 25, 1959.

Literally at the center of the action was Lloyd Monsen, Hakoah's star striker and a member of the National Soccer Hall of Fame. Monsen was born in 1931 to Norwegian parents and grew up in the Bay Ridge section of Brooklyn. He states, "The Ebbets Field soccer scene was a large part of my career." For example, he scored a goal and two assists in the May 12, 1957, match between Hapoel F.C. of Israel and an ASL all-star squad, which also presented Marilyn Monroe and Sammy Davis Jr. as entertainers.

A trove of photographs and other items remains in Lloyd's possession, including a series of ASL newsletters. The November 1, 1959, issue explains what happened to that fourth Sunday outing. The games had been slated for November 8, but were rescheduled for Thursday the 5th and then canceled.

"Not that the American Soccer League would like to leave the confines of Ebbets Field, but circumstances beyond our control make it so. For instance, the Sunday blue law that ball games not commence before 2:00 P.M., the end of Daylight Saving Time and no lights if a twin bill is scheduled, makes it imperative for the ASL to call it quits at the Brooklyn park. Maybe if Ebbets Field is still around next year and not knocked down for a housing project, the ASL will again consider staging shows there next spring."

Monsen adds, "Ebbets was better than any of the other stadiums we used. Crowds were in the thousands, quite good for us—but probably not good enough to support business." He further recalls, "The dirt infield was still there in the right-hand corner of the field. The groundskeepers had leveled the mound and removed the rubber."

Indeed, during this time the most loyal Brooklyn foot soldiers were still at their posts. This is a chance to salute the most diehard retainer of them all—a man who may not have gotten even a line in any of the books about the team. Joseph Julius "Babe" Hamberger started as a clubhouse boy in 1921 and worked his way up to assistant traveling secretary. Although a number of club employees went west, Babe couldn't bear to leave the only workplace he'd

## Soccer at Ebbets Field, 1958–59

| Date | Score | Remarks |
| --- | --- | --- |
| 5/25/58 | Hearts of Midlothian 6, Manchester City 5 | Attendance: 20,606. Rainy and muddy.<br>Sir Hugh Stephenson, the British Consul General in New York, handled the kickoff. |
| 3/15/59 | Halsingborg (Sweden) 2, Hakoah 2<br>Prelim: Ukrainian Nationals 4, Brooklyn Italians 2 | Attendance: 6,500<br>Rainy, windy, and muddy. |
| 5/24/59 | Dundee 2, West Bromwich Albion 2<br>Prelim: Newark Portuguese 5, Uhrik Truckers 4 | Attendance: 21,312 |
| 5/30/59 | Legia (Poland) 8, Hakoah 1<br>Prelim: Empire State Junior Cup semi-finals<br>Hakoah Juniors 1, Segura 1 (2 OT) | Attendance: 5,241 |
| 6/14/59 | Dundee 3, Legia (Poland) 3<br>Prelim: Lewis Cup<br>Ukrainian Nationals 2, Hakoah 1 | Attendance: 12,429 |
| 6/21/59 | Napoli 6, ASL All-Stars 1<br>Prelim: Newark Portuguese 2, Fall River SC 2 | Attendance: 14,682<br>1,000 Napoli supporters run onto field before match to greet their club; dispersed by Babe Hamberger. |
| 6/28/59 | Two-game series for Fernet-Branca Cup<br>Rapid (Vienna) 1, Napoli 0<br>Prelim: Brooklyn Italians 2, Hakoah 2 | Attendance: 18,512<br>Heavily pro-Napoli crowd is in bad temper.<br>Fans spill onto field and fight in first half, causing 10-minute delay. Hundreds more riot after late goal decides game. Three officials and policeman injured. |
| 7/1/59 | Napoli 1, Rapid (Vienna) 1<br>Prelim: Bayside Boys Club 0, Hakoah Juniors 0 | Attendance: 13,351<br>Extra details of city and special police keep crowd subdued in return match, though one chair is thrown from left field stands. |
| 7/16/59 | Real Madrid 6, Graz Sports Club (Austria) 2 | Attendance: 13,500<br>P.A. announcements in Spanish, German, and English. |
| 7/19/59 | Real Madrid 8, Graz/New York Hungarians select 0<br>Prelim: NY Hungarians reserves 10, Austria F.C. 2 | Attendance: 9,056 |
| 8/8/59 | Palermo 5, ASL All-Stars 0 | Attendance: 5,457<br>Steady downpour, muddy turf. |
| 8/12/59 | Palermo 2, Rapid Soccer Club (Vienna) 1<br>Prelim: Bayside Boys Club 2, Hakoah Juniors 1 | Attendance: 12,598 |
| 8/16/59 | Palermo 7, Italia (Toronto) 0<br>Prelim: Metropolitan League Cup final<br>Colombia S.C. (Bronx) 2, Orsogna F.C. (Astoria) 1 | Attendance: 5,000 |
| 9/27/59 | Hakoah 2, Newark Portuguese 1<br>Brooklyn Italians 5, Uhrik Truckers 2 | Attendance: 1,500 |
| 10/18/59 | Ukrainian Nationals 2, Brooklyn Italians 1<br>Hakoah 8, Elizabeth Polish Falcons 2 | Attendance: not available |
| 10/25/59 | Hakoah 4, Uhrik Truckers 0<br>Brooklyn Italians 2, Colombo 0 | Attendance: not available |

*Source: New York Times, American Soccer League News (Vol. 26, No. 4, November 1–8, 1959)*

ever known. So he served as superintendent in the twilight phase, along with a skeleton crew that included a part-collie, part-chow watchdog named Angel.

Gay Talese, who was a sportswriter for the *New York Times* before becoming a best-selling author, visited Ebbets Field after the L.A. Dodgers won the World Series that October. Always a writer who pursued the offbeat, Talese filed a brief but arresting report that captured the ghostly feel of the place.[15] The decay would hasten after the Dodgers declined to pick up the two-year option on their lease in 1960 and the property reverted to Kratter. There is a visible difference in the number of broken windows on New Year's Day and several weeks later.

As late as January 29, 1960, lawyer William Shea continued to dangle the possibility that Ebbets might host a team from the Continental League, albeit temporarily.[16] (The permanent site in Flushing, Queens—which Robert Moses offered and Walter O'Malley rebuffed—later became Shea Stadium, home of the New York Mets.) Of course, Branch Rickey's would-be third major league never got off the ground. It folded in August of that year. And less than a month after Shea held out that last faint hope, the wreckers descended.

Jane Leavy's biography of Sandy Koufax refers briefly to a charity game played that final morning, when Campy, Carl Erskine, Ralph Branca, Tommy Holmes, Otto Miller (catcher from the inaugural season, 1913), and 200 fans gathered to bid their old home adieu. However, newspaper accounts don't mention anything of the sort, and it would seem doubtful on a winter day. The closest thing may have been "Oisk" posing with the baseball-painted wrecking ball that also leveled the Polo Grounds four years later.

Relics of Ebbets Field have survived in New York City. Marvin Kratter donated 2,200 seats to the diamond that bore his name at Hart Island, the spooky prison/potter's field site east of the Bronx in Long Island Sound. Downing Stadium on Randall's Island in the East River got the lights. Ironically, that park had been built by Robert Moses, who commanded his city makeovers from the nearby Triborough Bridge Authority headquarters. Over the years, though, nature overran Kratter Field, while the original fixtures at Downing had grown scarce by the time it was demolished in 2000.[17]

Yet the center-field flagpole, also donated by Kratter Corp., has stood for more than four decades at 1405 Utica Avenue in East Flatbush. The most ardent supporters had hoped to transplant it to Borough Hall in October 2005, as part of the 50-year celebration of Brooklyn's lone World Series championship. In another irony, this spot is just a Carl Furillo throw away from the old location of the team offices. Sad to say, though, the current owners are holding out for $50,000. Lucre vs. friendly allure—Ebbets Field's past still resonates in its prolonged afterlife.

### Notes

1. Joseph McCauley *Ebbets Field: Brooklyn's Baseball Shrine.* Bloomington, IN: AuthorHouse, 2004. Bob McGee *The Greatest Ballpark Ever.* Piscataway, NJ: Rutgers University Press, 2005.
2. "'Feeler' Received for Ebbets Field" *New York Times,* October 17, 1957, 35.
3. Jeane Hoffman "O'Malley Loaded with Baseball Parks" *Los Angeles Times,* May 6, 1958, C5.
4. Roscoe McGowen "Dodgers Sublet Brooklyn Home" *New York Times,* March 5, 1958, 41.
5. *New York Times,* August 26, 1958, 48. The Polo Grounds was considerably more successful than Ebbets Field after its prime tenant pulled out. The National Exhibition Company (corporate name of the New York Giants) continued to focus on business at the Manhattan stadium under its lease there. Events included mammoth gatherings of Jehovah's Witnesses, as well as long-running stock car racing and rodeo series. See Roscoe McGowen, "Polo Grounds Is Still Profitable to the Giants," *New York Times,* March 16, 1958, S1.
6. Gordon S. White Jr. "Soccer Fans Riot and Injure Three Officials and Patrolman at Ebbets Field" *New York Times,* June 29, 1959, 37.
7. William R. Conklin "New Pro Eleven Needs Field Here" *New York Times,* August 16, 1959, S6.
8. Philip Benjamin "Stark Acts to Force Forest Hills to Drop Bias or Cup Matches" *New York Times,* July 11, 1959, 1.
9. "Schreiber's Two-Run Circuit Drive Enables St. John's to Beat Manhattan" *New York Times,* April 25, 1958, 38. In a related curiosity, Schreiber's final major league at-bat on September 18, 1963, (he lined into a double play) was the last regular-season out in the Polo Grounds. However, a Latin All-Star Game that deserves to be better known took place on October 12.
10. Michael Strauss "Van Buren Defeats Curtis for P.S.A.L. Title with Rally in Eighth" *New York Times,* June 24, 1958, 42.
11. "Roosevelt Beats Curtis Nine by 6–5" *New York Times,* June 6, 1959, 16.
12. "Memphis to Meet Stars' Nine Today" *New York Times,* July 12, 1959, S4. This article notes that baseball entertainer "Prince Joe" Henry was scheduled to appear between games that day. However, Mr. Henry has stated to this author that he was (a) out of the game in 1959, (b) never appeared at Ebbets Field in his career, and (c) always appeared in game action, not between games.
13. "Negro Twin Bill Today" *New York Times,* July 26, 1959, S2.
14. "Paige Fans 4 Men and Allows 3 Hits in 3 Innings Here" *New York Times,* August 24, 1959, 25.
15. Gay Talese "Brooklyn Displays Little Enthusiasm After Dodgers Win" *New York Times,* October 9, 1959, 34.
16. Joe Reichler "Buffalo 8th Club in Rickey League" *Washington Post, Times Herald,* January 30, 1960, 12. Shea was quoted twice floating the same idea in July 1959.
17. Daniel J. Wakin "Ebbets Lights Dimmed Again" *New York Times,* September 27, 2000, B1.

# Was Roy Cullenbine a Better Batter Than Joe DiMaggio?

## by Walter Dunn Tucker

In Bill Borst's article "A St. Louis Harbinger: The 1942 Browns," in SABR's *Road Trips*, a statement by Bill DeWitt about the reason for the trade of Roy Cullenbine to Washington leaped off the page. "Cullenbine wouldn't swing the bat! Sewell would give him the hit sign and he'd take, trying to get a base on balls. Laziest human being you ever saw." Borst went on to write that in his 10-year career Cullenbine amassed 1,072 hits and 853 walks, an amazing ratio for a player who didn't lead off or hit for power.

*The 2006 ESPN Baseball Encyclopedia* revealed that Roy Cullenbine was a player ahead of his time. Through the close of the 2005 season, he was tied with Jeff Bagwell for 37th place on the all-time leaders in on-base percentage (at least 1,000 games) at .408. Hard-hitting Hall of Famers trailing Cullenbine's OBP were:

| | | |
|---|---|---|
| Arky Vaughan . . . . . . . .406 | Ralph Kiner . . . . . . . . . .398 | Bill Terry. . . . . . . . . . . .393 |
| Charlie Gehringer . . . . .404 | Johnny Mize. . . . . . . . . ..397 | Joe Morgan . . . . . . . . . .392 |
| Paul Waner. . . . . . . . . .404 | Richie Ashburn . . . . . . .396 | Honus Wagner. . . . . . . .391 |
| Luke Appling . . . . . . . .399 | Earl Averill . . . . . . . . . .395 | Joe Cronin . . . . . . . . . . .390 |
| Ross Youngs . . . . . . . . .399 | Hack Wilson . . . . . . . . .395 | Frank Robinson. . . . . . .389 |
| Joe DiMaggio. . . . . . . .398 | Rod Carew . . . . . . . . . .393 | Willie Keeler . . . . . . . .388 |

There were five seasons in which both Roy Cullenbine and Joe DiMaggio played more than 100 games. On base percentages for those five seasons and for their careers were:

| CULLENBINE | YEAR | DIMAGGIO |
|---|---|---|
| .369 | 1940 | .425 |
| .452 | 1941 | .440 |
| .405 | 1942 | .376 |
| .477 | 1946 | .367 |
| .401 | 1947 | .391 |
| .408 | CAREER | .398 |

Does this show that Roy Cullenbine was a better hitter than Joe DiMaggio? Of course not. Two things are revealed. Cullenbine was underrated, and there's a lot more to hitting than OBP.

WALTER DUNN TUCKER's *fate as a Cardinals fan was sealed on his 11th birthday by Whitey Kurowski's ninth-inning homer to win the 1942 World Series.*

Roy Cullenbine

NATIONAL BASEBALL LIBRARY, COOPERSTOWN, NY

# The 1945 All-Star Game
## The Baseball Navy World Series at Furlong Field, Hawaii

### by Bill Nowlin

THERE was no All-Star Game in the summer of 1945. But in late September, the service stars of the American League and those of the National League squared off in what might be called a combination all-star game and world series. It was a scheduled, best-of-seven game series, played at Honolulu's Furlong Field in the 14th Naval District. Furlong Field had been built in 1943, right near Pearl Harbor where, less than two years previously, Japanese aircraft had wreaked such destruction.

World War II had ended with the surrender of Japan on September 2, but few of the ballplayers in the service had yet been demobilized. There was a high caliber of players participating, and the games included Ted Williams, Stan Musial, Billy Herman, Bob Lemon, Johnny Pesky, and Bob Kennedy. The *Honolulu Advertiser*'s Gayle Hayes wrote that the Navy series would "present more individual stars than even the world series on the mainland . . . a titanic battle between some of the best known players in baseball" [September 23, 1945]. Herman, Musial, and Dick Wakefield had all been selected for the 1943 All-Star Game.

The first game was set for Wednesday, September 26, at 3:30 P.M. Additional stands had been erected, programs were printed, and all military personnel were "invited to the battle." The National Leaguers worked out at Peterson Field's Aiea Barracks, under the leadership of manager Billy Herman. A future Hall of Famer, Herman already had 13 major league seasons under his belt, playing for the Cubs and Dodgers, but his team was up against a squad of American Leaguers skippered by Schoolboy Rowe. Rowe's men drilled at the Sub Base.

BILL NOWLIN *is the current Vice President of SABR, and author of more than a dozen books on Ted Williams and the Red Sox. His two books in 2006 are* Day By Day with the Boston Red Sox, *and* The 50 Greatest Red Sox Games, *co-authored by SABR member Cecilia Tan.*

The announced starting lineups give some idea of the quality of play that could be expected. Most of the men were in decent form, having played a number of exhibition ball games during their time in the service. The 14th Naval District baseball league season had ended on the 16th, and Billy Herman had been voted the league's MVP, with 83 points, with Johnny Pesky of NAS Honolulu coming in second, with 50 points. Charley Gilbert edged out Eddie McGah by just one point for third place. Leading vote getter among the pitchers was the Aiea Hospital (and former Brooklyn Dodgers) star Hugh Casey.

The Naval District's All-Star team featured three unanimous choices: Herman, Pesky, and Ship Repair Unit's Stan Musial.

Ted Williams had played in only four games, as had fellow Marine Flyer teammate Bob Kennedy. Both had been stationed in Hawaii later than many of the others. "I'm still a little rusty, but I hope to be ready for this big series," Williams said. "I think every man on our squad is anxious to win, and every one of our boys will be ready to go Wednesday afternoon. It should be quite a series." Bill Dickey agreed. Dickey, the athletic officer of the District, declared that the teams were well matched and that he was "looking forward to seeing seven games of the best baseball you'll have a chance to see anywhere this year" [*Advertiser*, September 25].

### Game One: September 26

NL 6, AL 5 (WP: Casey, LP: Lemon): The *Advertiser*'s Hayes picked the American League as favorites. The starting lineups were:

| National League | American League |
|---|---|
| Charley Gilbert CF | Jack Conway 2B |
| Jim Carlin 3B | Johnny Pesky SS |
| Billy Herman 2B | Chet Hajduk 1B |
| Stan Musial RF | Ted Williams RF |
| Whitey Platt LF | Dick Wakefield LF |
| Wimpy Quinn 1B | Jack Phillips CF |
| Ray Lamanno C | Bob Kennedy 3B |
| Ray Hamrick SS | Rollie Hemsley C |
| Clyde Shoun P | Freddie Hutchinson P |

An overflow crowd of around 26,000 fans watched game one of the "All-Star Baseball Series." The match-up was a good one. Hutchinson was a key prospect for the Tigers, who had paid the then-enormous sum of $75,000 to purchase him in 1938. Shoun had thrown a no-hitter for Cincinnati against the Boston Braves a year earlier, on May 15, 1944. Ted Williams, incidentally, wore #23 and Musial wore #14.

The first scoring came in the second inning when Stan Musial led off with a line-drive home run over the right-field fence. After two outs, Ray Lamanno "smashed a towering drive over the right-center field stands." Clyde Shoun surrendered the 2–0 lead he'd been handed, walking Williams in the bottom of the second and giving up a single to Dick Wakefield, and then Bob Kennedy hit the first pitch into the left-center field seats for a three-run homer. Both teams put men on base throughout the middle innings, but the only run scored was when the AL got one in the sixth. Williams singled to lead off and moved up to second on a walk to Wakefield. Ned Harris had not

started in center for the Americans; Phillips had, and his single would have meant a run—except that Lamanno's throw from behind the plate picked off Ted at second. Kennedy walked, to load the bases. Rollie Hemsley's single to left just scored one, and neither Hutchinson nor Conway could push a run across.

That score held, 4–2 AL, until the eighth inning, though the *Advertiser*'s Hayes noted a couple of "fancy double plays to halt budding National League rallies." The NL tied it in the top of the eighth. After Charley Gilbert doubled to left, Jim Carlin doubled to right, but Gilbert had to hold at third. Herman hit a sac fly to Williams in right, and Platt lined a single to center, scoring Carlin. Bob Lemon, who had yet to pitch in the major leagues, came in to relieve, and threw one pitch to shut down the side. In the ninth, though, Lamanno singled off Lemon's glove, then took second on a sacrifice by Hank Schenz. Up stepped Hugh Casey, who'd come in to pitch the eighth, and Casey doubled to center, driving in Lamanno. Lemon's wild pitch allowed Casey to take third, and he scored moments later on Gilbert's sac fly to Ned Harris, who'd taken over for Phillips in center. It was a close play at the plate, and Casey hurt his leg sliding. Lou Tost replaced Casey on the mound, and nearly gave it back to the American Leaguers.

In the bottom of the ninth, now down 6–4 to the NL, Packy Rogers pinch-hit for Lemon and walked, but was forced at second on an Eddie McGah grounder. McGah was safe, and took second when Herman's throw to Quinn went wild. Johnny Pesky's Texas Leaguer moved him to third, and there were runners at the corners with just one out. Another NL error, this time by Carlin, saw McGah score, with Pesky taking second and Hajduk safe at first. Up stepped Ted Williams, who'd beaten the National League in the 1941 All-Star Game with a dramatic home run. This time he hit the ball sky-high but straight up, and Lamanno camped under it to make the catch. "In disgust, [Williams] hurled his bat 40 feet in the air, and it almost struck a photographer on the way down," wrote Joe Anzivino for the *Star-Bulletin*. Dick Wakefield struck out swinging on a pitch out of the strike zone for the last out.

### Game Two: September 28

NL 4, AL 0 (WP: Wilson, LP: Harris): AL manager Schoolboy Rowe expected more from Harris. Pitching for Barber's Point in the 14th Naval District regular season, he had twice had no-hitters going until the eighth inning. The left hander Wilson, though, had run off a string of seven straight victories for NAS Honolulu, and the AL had not fared well against either southpaw Shoun or Tost in the first game. Wilson won, and won handily, holding the AL to just one hit, a third-inning single by Johnny Pesky which barely landed in front of Musial's glove in right; Musial's throw cut down Johnny as he tried to stretch it to take two bases. The Nationals scored twice in the fourth, once in the fifth and again once in the ninth. Both The Kid and Stan the Man posted identical 0-for-3's at the plate.

### Game Three (September 29)

NL 6, AL 3 (WP: Tost, LP: Feimster): The third game was postponed a day due to heavy rains, but when the two teams played on September 30, it began to look like a National League rout, particularly when they scored four times in the top of the first. The four runs were enough to put the game away, and the AL stars did not score until the bottom of the ninth. Lou Tost threw a complete game for the Nationals, the big blow off him being a Ted Williams two-run homer completely over the right-field bleachers. Hajduk had singled before Ted. "We ain't whipped yet," Rowe announced. Even if the Nationals wrapped it up in

less than the full seven games, the plan was to play all seven contests. Wakefield had missed games two and three with an injured hand.

### Game Four: October 3

AL 12, NL 1 (WP: Hallett, LP: Shoun): After another rainout, the AL seemed to summon up the bats and knocked out 14 hits, scoring three times in the bottom of the first to take a lead that pitcher Jack Hallett did not let them relinquish. Shoun had walked Conway and Pesky, and then intentionally passed cleanup hitter Ted Williams after Hemsley had moved both runners up with a sacrifice. Bob Kennedy's single to right-center knocked in two. Leading batter on the day was Boston's Johnny Pesky, who went 3-for-3, with a single, a double, and a fifth-inning two-run homer into the right-field bleachers. Barney Lutz also hit a two-run homer into right in the same frame. Both home runs were hit off reliever Wes Livengood. Wakefield was back and went 3-for-4. Musial went 2-for-3, and Williams was 0-for-1. Rowe put himself in the game and knocked a long single off the fence in center. Players in those days cared deeply about their league, so it was perhaps true that "the victory had a slight taint" since Hallett was Pittsburgh Pirates property at the time, despite having broken in with the AL White Sox.

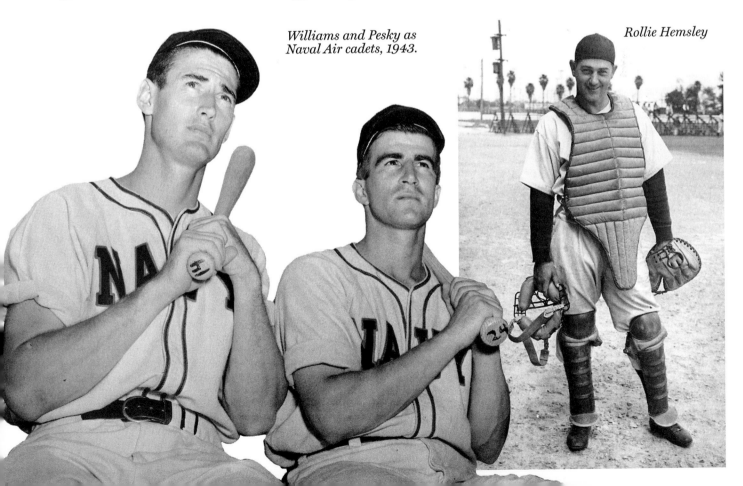

*Williams and Pesky as Naval Air cadets, 1943.*

*Rollie Hemsley*

### Game Five: October 5

AL 4, NL 1 (WP: HARRIS, LP: WILSON): Now the silent bats were those of the Nationals. Luman Harris went the distance, doling out just three hits and one run, a home run by Carlin in the top of the ninth. He'd had a no-hitter going for 6⅔ innings. The Americans scored three times in the bottom of the sixth on first baseman Ken Sears' three-run homer with Pesky on third and Kennedy on second (Pesky had bunted safely and Kennedy had doubled). Musial went hitless in four at-bats. Wiliams did not play and, suffering from a bad cold, had lost his voice. The doctor confined him to quarters. Uncharacteristically quiet, Williams whispered that he hoped to be able to play in the sixth game.

### Game Six: October 6

NL 4, AL 1 (WP: TOST, LP: WEILAND): This was a hard-fought game, with Lou Tost winning his second game of the series (and the series itself) over Ed Weiland. Scoreless through four, the NL scored once in the top of the fifth and once again the next inning. The Americans came back with one in the bottom of the sixth, and tied it with another in the seventh. After eight full, the score stood 2–2. Hamrick led off with an infield single to deep short, and Pesky's

*NL manager Billy Herman made a critical decision about the game six lineup and pulled . . . himself!*

throw to first went astray, letting him take second. Tost sacrifice-bunted him to third. Gilbert took four pitches and walked. Billy Herman had been 0 for his last 11, and after going 0-for-3 on the day, the manager had taken himself out of the game. Hence it wasn't Herman but Hank Schenz who batted next. Schenz tried to squeeze Hamrick across but fouled off the pitch. The next pitch was a called strike, so he was hitting away on the 0–2 count and banged a two-RBI double into right-center. The American Leaguers fought back in the bottom of the

ninth. Al Lyons, who had homered in the seventh, hit a terrific drive to center, but Gilbert hauled it in at the barrier. Phillips pinch-hit for Bill Marks, and was robbed by Quinn at first. Quinn had made a similar play on Pesky earlier in the game, squelching a rally. Down to their last out, American League manager Schoolboy Rowe put himself in, to hit for Weiland. A decent-hitting pitcher, Rowe connected and drove a home run over the left-field bleachers. Conway, though, whiffed and the game was over.

### Game Seven: October 7

AL 5, NL 2 (WP: LEMON, LP: SHOUN): The Americans left feeling a bit better, scoring a decisive 5–2 win in the anticlimactic final game on October 7. Both Phillips and Joe Glenn homered for the AL. Gil Brack supplied a homer for the Nationals leading off the ninth inning.

Composite batting statistics, minimum 10 at-bats:

| AMERICAN LEAGUE | | | | NATIONAL LEAGUE | | | |
|---|---|---|---|---|---|---|---|
| PLAYER | AB | H | BA | PLAYER | AB | H | BA |
| HEMSLEY | 15 | 6 | .400 | LAMANNO | 14 | 6 | .428 |
| PESKY | 26 | 9 | .346 | QUINN | 27 | 9 | .333 |
| HAJDUK | 12 | 4 | .333 | CARLIN | 25 | 7 | .280 |
| KENNEDY | 21 | 6 | .286 | PLATT | 24 | 6 | .250 |
| SEARS | 14 | 4 | .286 | HAMRICK | 20 | 4 | .200 |
| WAKEFIELD | 18 | 5 | .278 | MUSIAL | 20 | 4 | .200 |
| WILLIAMS | 11 | 3 | .272 | GILBERT | 27 | 4 | .148 |
| LYONS | 12 | 3 | .250 | HERMAN | 20 | 2 | .100 |
| PHILLIPS | 12 | 3 | .250 | | | | |
| MARKS | 17 | 4 | .235 | | | | |
| CONWAY | 25 | 5 | .200 | | | | |

HOME RUNS
**AL**: Glenn, Kennedy, Lyons, Lutz, Pesky, Phillips, Rowe, Sears, Williams. **NL**: Brack, Carlin, Gilbert, Lamanno, Musial.

RBI
**AL**: Kennedy 5, Sears 4, Lutz 3, Pesky 3, Glenn 2, Hemsley 2, Rowe 2, Wakefield 2, Williams 2, Lyons 1, Phillips 1. **NL**: Gilbert 3, Lamanno 2, Musial 2, Platt 2, Schenz 2, Brack 1, Carlin 1, Casey 1, Hamrick 1, Herman 1, Quinn 1, Scheffing 1, Tost 1, West 1, Wilson 1.

### Acknowledgments

Thanks to Duff Zwald for researching both the *Honolulu Star-Bulletin* and *Honolulu Advertiser* at my request.

NATIONAL BASEBALL LIBRARY, COOPERSTOWN, NY

# The First Unknown Soldier
## General Emmett O'Donnell, Baseball Commissioner

### by Bob Bailey

WHEN General William D. Eckert was elected to the office of baseball commissioner in 1965, Larry Fox of the *New York World-Telegram* is reported to have been one of the first to utter the phrase, "They've named the Unknown Soldier." But Eckert, a retired three-star Air Force general, was not the first military man elected to the position of commissioner. That honor falls to General Emmett O'Donnell, who was unanimously elected the third commissioner of baseball in 1951. Needless to say, he never served one minute of his term.

This story had its genesis in the attempt of then-Commissioner A. B. "Happy" Chandler to get an early extension of his contract in 1949. Chandler had been a surprise selection as the successor to Kenesaw Landis in 1945. In 1949, four years into his seven-year contract, Happy attempted to get a commitment to renew his contract. He apparently told the owners that he had several other opportunities to consider but would prefer to stay on as commissioner if a suitable extension could be worked out. Although Happy may have thought he was just being prudent in considering his future, several owners took it otherwise, thinking they were being pressured prematurely to commit to Chandler for another seven-year term. The owners begged off the request, noting that the current contract did not call for such a decision to be made before the close of 1950.

Happy returned to his Cincinnati office and for the next year handled a string of problems confronting baseball with skill and astuteness. The press and fans were generally favorably impressed with his handling of the return of banned players from the Mexican League, governmental examinations of how major league baseball handled granting rights to radio and television contracts, and various court challenges to baseball's reserve clause. Ed McAuley of the *Cleveland News* called Chandler's performance "a shining success." H. G. Salsinger of the *Detroit News* calmly predicted Chandler's efforts would surely be "offered a new seven-year contract." *The Sporting News* called his actions "a personal triumph." The owners made little comment.

But all was not sweetness and light for the former senator from Kentucky. In addition to these decisions that smoothed the baseball waters for the owners, he had made individual decisions about trades, signings, and the general chicanery that is part and parcel of the baseball owner fraternity. "We all cheat, if we have to," is what Cleveland owner Alva Bradley reportedly told Chandler not long after his election as commissioner. This should not have surprised Chandler. After the better part of a lifetime in the rough and tumble of Kentucky politics, he knew that men like the baseball club owners were used to getting their way and were not going to sit still if they didn't.

When Chandler was rebuffed in his effort to get an early extension, several owners sensed a weakness in the commissioner's position. The leaders of the "Replace Happy" movement were Fred Saigh of the Cardinals, Lou Perini of the Braves, and Del Webb of the Yankees. Saigh made no secret of his antipathy toward Chandler. It was not difficult to find others of a like mind among the team owners. There was no single overriding issue that coalesced the anti-Chandler group. To paraphrase Leo Tolstoy, "Happy owners are all alike, every unhappy owner is unhappy in his own way." Some had had their activities investigated by Chandler, some saw his increasing Landis-like independence as something to be avoided, some believed Chandler played favorites and they were on the wrong side, and some just did not like his image.

BOB BAILEY *lives in Newtown, PA, where he researches and writes on a variety of historical baseball topics when he is not visiting his grandchildren Anthony, Dominic and Matteo.*

While no owner would come out and say Chandler's Southern-politician style wasn't their cup of tea, Del Webb, who became the key force in the anti-Chandler camp said, "I don't dislike Chandler. I simply think we could get a better Commissioner." The antipathy to Chandler's style shows up more clearly in the way many New York newspaper writers would describe him. Even when praising his actions he would be identified as: "the sweet-singing tenor from Kentucky," (Arthur Daley); "the Blue Grass baritone," (Joe Williams); having "a penchant for autographing scorecards while warbling 'My Old Kentucky Home'" (Jimmy Powers). The techniques that stood him in such good stead on the Kentucky campaign trail did not play well in the big city. Bill Corum in the *New York Journal-American* wrote, "Without intending it in any sense as a back-handed slap at Senator Chandler, it seems to this column that there are any number of men in the United States who are qualified for the job of Commissioner." He may not have "intended" that comment to demean Chandler in any way, but Corum's "intention" probably did not give Happy much comfort.

By the time the vote on Chandler's retention came up at the winter meetings in December 1950, the minority had grown to seven votes and denied Chandler the necessary two-thirds he needed to claim a second term. Happy made some feisty comments about continuing the battle, and Washington owner Clark Griffith took it upon himself to lead the charge to overturn Chandler's dumping. In April all pretense of returning evaporated as the opposition held their seven votes, and Chandler began negotiating his early exit from the commissioner's office.

So who would be the next commissioner? Dozens and dozens of names were floated. It had become a baseball tradition for writers and owners to create long lists of distinguished candidates that were under consideration. These names kept appearing in the press even though everyone from the deepest baseball insider to your Aunt Minnie knew most would accept the position only if it was the sole way to escape a prison sentence. Politicians, elected and appointed, judges, businessmen, and baseball insiders dominated the lists. But all the lists always included at least one military name.

*Above: Major General Emmett O'Donnell in 1951. Below: O'Donnell arriving at Castle Air Force Base in 1953.*

This inclusion of the military as a source of candidates was getting to be a tradition in baseball. In 1920, when baseball was debating how to overhaul the National Commission in the wake of the Black Sox scandal, among the names put forth were Generals "Black Jack" Pershing and Leonard Wood. In 1945 it was more difficult to put forward a creditable candidate with World War II in progress. But someone listed Coast Guard Admiral Robert Donohue among the candidates. By 1951, even with the Korean War raging, multiple military names came out. General Douglas MacArthur had recently been relieved of his position by President Truman and so was added to the list. General Dwight Eisenhower saw his name appear in print as a candidate, as did Major General Maxwell Taylor, General Clifton F. Gates, and Major General Emmett O'Donnell. O'Donnell's name first surfaced in the *Los Angeles Times* story of August 22, 1951. The crux of the story, however, was that all uniformed military candidates had been eliminated due to the Korean War. This report notwithstanding, *The Sporting News* reported in its August 29, 1951 edition that General Emmett "Rosy" O'Donnell had been unanimously elected baseball's third commissioner in an owners meeting in New York on August 21.

While O'Donnell's name seemed to suddenly appear as a potential commissioner, he was not some unknown quantity. Born in 1906 in Brooklyn, New York, he graduated from West Point in 1928. While at the military academy Rosy, whose nickname apparently stemmed from his habit of blushing excessively when embarrassed, was a 155-lb. halfback for Army.

O'DONNELL PHOTOGRAPHS COURTESY OF THE NATIONAL MUSEUM OF THE U.S. AIR FORCE

Seldom used, he was reputed to be very fast and elusive. Over the years as he attained higher military rank, his football reputation also increased. During the next decade O'Donnell served in the Army Air Corps and from 1934 to 1938 he was an assistant football coach at West Point. A major by 1941, O'Donnell led a large contingent of planes from Hawaii to the Philippines in an effort to reinforce MacArthur's troops. Immediately after Pearl Harbor he was stationed at Clark Field in the Philippines. While the field was under Japanese air attack, his bomber squadron took to the air to attack enemy naval targets. During the battle Major O'Donnell was credited with shooting down four Japanese planes and damaging several Japanese naval vessels. He was later awarded the Distinguished Flying Cross for this action.

O'Donnell remained in the Pacific Theater, being stationed at Java and India before assuming command of the 73rd Bombing Wing out of Salina, Kansas. He was promoted to brigadier general in 1944 before taking his unit to Saipan. In November 1944 he led B-29 bombers on the first attack on the Japanese homeland since the Doolittle raid of 1942.

After the conclusion of World War II, General O'Donnell was part of the newly formed United States Air Force and became the commanding general of the 15th Air Force at Colorado Springs in 1948. He had received the rank of major general in 1947. The 15th Air Force moved to Japan in 1950 as the Korean War started, and O'Donnell set up the Far East Bomber Command. General O'Donnell returned to the United States in early 1951.

O'Donnell's passage through the military to the rank of major general had not been without some controversy. Along with Lieutenant General Jimmy Doolittle and Major General Curtis LeMay and others, O'Donnell was an outspoken advocate of a separate Air Force. Saying in December 1945 that the United States had "no air force worthy of the name" did not endear him to many. Comments while in Japan in 1950, noting that his bomber

group had not been allowed to bomb "the real strategic targets" above the Yalu River, immediately preceded his transfer back to the United States. At March Air Force Base in January 1951 he responded to a reporter's question by advocating use of atomic weapons in Korea. He was immediately called to the Pentagon. Upon emerging from this visit, he returned to his California base and was publicly instructed to "use care" in what he said.

During this controversy Rosy O'Donnell was criticized harshly in the press. Add to this his June 1951 appearance before a Senate investigating committee looking into the dismissal of MacArthur by President Truman, and we might be looking at a man seeking a new outlet outside the military.

Rosy O'Donnell was a novice in the world of sports politics when the major league baseball owners approached him, but he was not unknown in sporting circles. He was often mentioned in sports reports, attending various sports functions from banquets to games to speaking engagements before press groups. In the 1930s O'Donnell became friends with Detroit manager Mickey Cochrane and was often a visitor at the Tigers training camp in Lakeland, Florida. It is from this Detroit connection that Tigers owner Spike Briggs became his champion among the owners. He was friends with writers Red Smith and Arthur Daley. Smith called him "one of the good people," and Daley considered him "one of our gang."

Published reports of the process leave several questions unanswered. How did O'Donnell become a candidate for Commissioner? How did he garner enough votes to be elected and then never serve as Commissioner? *The*

*Sporting News* of August 29, 1951, reported that 10 days before the election O'Donnell was offered the commissionership. The reports also notes that the week before O'Donnell's selection, Spike Briggs visited Washington to find out if the general could be released from duty to accept the baseball position. The story goes on to say that President Truman refused, citing the current Korean conflict as taking precedence. If this is true, why did the owners subsequently even bother to take a vote on O'Donnell, let alone elect him? To confuse matters further, an item in the *New York Times* on September 10, 1951, has Spike Briggs giving the story of the process, saying that first the owners elected O'Donnell and then sent Briggs to approach him about accepting. "Rosy never batted an eye," Briggs said, and told that the general immediately declined the position because of the "international situation." Was he elected and approached or approached and elected? Did he decline or was he interested enough to allow baseball to inquire of his availability? Reports of the time stop with the *Times* story, and nobody seemed interested in sorting out the correct chronology.

But if we can speculate just a bit, it seems unlikely that baseball would put itself in a position of electing a commissioner without knowing if he would accept the position. So I would put forward that General Emmett O'Donnell would have accepted the position had he been released from his military duties, and Briggs' September interview was an attempt to put the best face on the situation. O'Donnell had served honorably and well for over two decades, and perhaps this was a way out of the political arena he found himself. From the owners' perspective, he would have been a good fit to follow Chandler, who saw himself as the boss of the owners rather than the other way around. O'Donnell would be educated in the business of baseball by the owners and would carry the aura of war hero into the office. The owners might have seen O'Donnell's hero status as beneficial in Washington circles, as there were whispers of baseball being curtailed during the Korean War. Coincidently, this same argument was put forward as a reason for selecting Chandler in 1945. But it remains strange that the owners would not have secured agreement for General O'Donnell's release before going through the election process.

A month after O'Donnell's premature election, the baseball moguls selected National League President Ford Frick as commissioner. This came after a tempestuous four weeks of politicking where Frick, Cincinnati President Warren Giles, former Postmaster General James Farley, and Ohio Governor Frank Lausche were all declared sure-fire winners in the race. If the owners had thought that O'Donnell might be a malleable commissioner who would not interfere with what were viewed as owners' prerogatives, they got the next best thing in Frick. He was a baseball man whose first speech at a baseball function after his election contained this quote: " I am not a monitor on high, ready to swing the big stick." But that would be unnecessary, as he described his bosses as "honest men, eager for the right, engaged in an honest business in an honest way." The threat of another commissioner acting like Landis was past.

General Emmett O'Donnell did not quietly fade from the military or sports scene after his brief flirtation with the commissioner's position. He continued to serve in the Air Force until his retirement in 1963 with the rank of full general. In the late 1950s he had an ongoing feud with Senator Margaret Chase Smith of Maine. The dustup started over O'Donnell's support of the nomination of actor James Stewart to the rank of general in the Air Force Reserves. Smith felt Stewart's nomination a mere publicity stunt while other, more deserving candidates were passed over. In 1959 she loudly opposed his fourth star when he was appointed commander of the Pacific Air Forces.

In the sporting world, Rosy O'Donnell's name started to appear with more regularity in press stories. In March 1952 he was part of the administration of the military's involvement in the Pan-American Games in Mexico City. He took a verbal shot at International Olympic Committee President Avery Brundage. Brundage had mused publicly that he had some question about the amateur standing of those in the military who took extensive foreign tours to compete in world athletic events. Rosy served on the United States Olympic Committee for several years in the mid-1950s and in 1961 was named an honorary delegate to the Amateur Athletic Union. At his death in 1971 O'Donnell's considerable obituaries made no mention of his brief flirtation with major league baseball.

### Acknowledgment
Thanks to Bill Marshall, author of *Baseball's Pivotal Era*, for his kindness in sharing his insights and research into this period of baseball history and for his suggestions that have improved this article.

# This Is Your Sport on Cocaine
## The Pittsburgh Trials of 1985

### by Steve Beitler

In the '80s we had a terrible cocaine problem. Did we have a policy? Did anything happen? No. We have a (steroid) policy.

–Commissioner Bud Selig, July 13, 2005, in the *San Francisco Chronicle*

Lonnie Smith had batted leadoff in hundreds of major league games, but on September 5, 1985, he was at the top of a very different lineup. On that day in Pittsburgh he was the first of seven major league players (six active and one retired) to testify in the cocaine-trafficking trial of Curtis Strong, a 39-year-old chef and caterer from Philadelphia. In four hours on the witness stand, Smith described meeting Strong through former Phillies teammate Dick Davis, and he named Davis, Gary Mathews, Dickie Noles, Keith Hernandez, and Joaquin Andujar as players with whom he had used cocaine on the Phillies and Cardinals.

The Strong trial, along with that of Robert McCue that followed it, was the culmination of baseball's cocaine immersion in the 1980s. In those years, dozens of players were arrested, suspended, and suspected. There was a torrent of public hand-wringing with two themes: players as role models and the threat that drugs posed to the game's integrity. Commissioner Peter Ueberroth sought to preserve that integrity, and his involvement was an element of the press coverage that was extensive and sometimes overwrought.

"Fidgety Keith Tells Coke Horror Story" screamed the *New York Post* on September 7 after Hernandez's first day of testimony in Pittsburgh. Ueberroth believed that stepped-up drug testing and tougher penalties were the heart of the solution. He also saw

Steve Beitler *has been a Houston Colt .45's–Astros fan since 1962 and a student of American drug policy since the late 1980s. He lives with his family in Palo Alto, California.*

the players union as the biggest obstacle to progress against drugs. Finally, there was skepticism among fans and observers. How could owners and officials not know about behavior that was so rampant? If baseball was truly intent on addressing drug issues, why were amphetamines beyond the scope of their efforts?

In Pittsburgh, Smith was followed on the witness stand by Hernandez, Enos Cabell, Dale Berra, Dave Parker, Jeff Leonard, and the retired John Milner. All the players had been granted immunity from prosecution, and they recounted their various contacts with Strong, which usually took place in hotel rooms and had been arranged over the phone, often the one in the clubhouse. Among the players alleged by these witnesses to have used cocaine were Rod Scurry, Steve Howe, Lee Lacy, Tim Raines, Derrel Thomas, Dusty Baker, Manny Sarmiento, and Eddie Solomon.

Some of the most spectacular testimony in Pittsburgh focused on amphetamines. According to the *New York Post* of September 11, 1985, Dale Berra said he had gotten amphetamines from former Pirates teammates Willie Stargell and Bill Madlock. Berra described the use of "greenies," as the pill form is called, as common on the team and said he didn't see anything wrong with amphetamines since so many established players were using them. Milner, a former Pirate and New York Met, created a stir when it was learned that, in his testimony to the grand jury that indicted Curtis Strong, he said that former teammate Willie Mays had the "red juice," a concoction of amphetamines dissolved in liquid, in his locker. Milner said he had never seen Mays ingest the juice. On September 20, the jury convicted Strong of 11 counts of cocaine distribution, and on November 4 he was sentenced to four to 12 years in prison.

The Pittsburgh trials were hardly baseball's first brush with cocaine. As reported in the *New York*

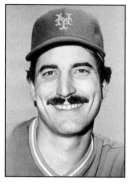

*The drug abuse scandal of the 1980s tainted the careers of several baseball players. Above, from top: Keith Hernandez, Lonnie Smith, and Vida Blue.*

*Times*, on June 9, 1983, before a game with the Cubs, Lonnie Smith, then with the Cardinals, felt "too jittery and nervous to play." He told manager Whitey Herzog that he had a cocaine problem and wanted help. Four days later the team announced that Smith had entered drug rehab. On June 20, state agents and FBI personnel arrested Mark Liebl at his home in Overland Park, outside Kansas City, as Liebl was getting ready to go to the Royals game. Liebl, who had managed sporting goods stores and had owned a liquor store, had befriended players on the Royals and other teams as their cocaine connection. The basement of his house, dubbed the "Hall of Fame room," was home to a growing collection of baseball memorabilia and was the frequent site of cocaine get-togethers by members of the Royals and other teams. The *Kansas City Times* reported that wiretaps installed on Liebl's home phone earlier in June had recorded about 100 calls on one day, including inquiries from three Royals players about buying cocaine. Four members of the 1983 Royals—Willie Wilson, Vida Blue, Willie Aikens, and Jerry Martin—would eventually go to prison, where Aikens remains to this day due to a subsequent 1994 conviction for drug trafficking.

Similar cases centered in Milwaukee and Baltimore in 1982 resulted in arrests and featured prominent players as alleged customers of those arrested.

The Pittsburgh trials in 1985 were also the culmination of a season that provided a sharp contrast between great moments on the field and less stellar ones off it. In *Baseball's Milestone Season* Morris Eckhouse and Clarke Carmody put together a day-by-day chronicle of the season that culminated in Pete Rose breaking Ty Cobb's record for career base hits (on the same day as Dale Berra's testimony on amphetamines), Phil Niekro and Tom Seaver notching their 300th victories, and Nolan Ryan becoming the first pitcher to strike out 4,000 hitters. The cocaine counterpoint to these highlights began well in advance of the pennant races. On February 13, Oakland A's pitcher Mike Norris was arrested in northern California for cocaine possession. Claudell Washington, Darryl Sconiers, Scurry, Alan Wiggins, and Howe all took their turns in the headlines thanks to their issues with drugs during the season.

In mid-May of 1985, two weeks before the grand jury in Pittsburgh handed down its indictments of Strong, McCue, and five others, Commissioner Ueberroth announced mandatory drug testing in the minor leagues and for major league owners, executives, field managers, and umpires. He couldn't mandate this program for the players because of that pesky matter of collective bargaining. Ueberroth often said that his targets were drugs, not players, and he worked behind the scenes to try to move the players union to collaborate on a plan for random drug testing. Ueberroth believed that Latin America was a key to the cocaine problem, and he tried to extend mandatory drug testing to the winter leagues in that region. He told the *New York Times*, "there are places where players play where people look the other way."

Mainstream accounts of the Pittsburgh trial portrayed Ueberroth as the beleaguered champion of integrity and fairness. A *Newsweek* story of September 16, 1985, somehow concluded that the events in Pittsburgh "provided powerful, if unwelcome, vindication of the hard-line anti-drug position of Commissioner Peter Ueberroth, whose call for random testing has so far been resisted by the players' union." Writer Pete Axthelm noted, "Ever since he accepted his job, he has viewed this matter as one of elemental right and wrong." But Ueberroth had sent several signals that he was not eager to punish players. Earlier in the season Ueberroth had been asked if he would take action against players implicated in a future Pittsburgh trial. "I'd have to think about it long and hard and study it," he replied. "I don't want to attack baseball players. . . . I don't see my main role as commissioner to punish people." In an interview with *GQ* after the 1985 season, Keith Hernandez recounted a late-September visit Ueberroth had made to the Mets clubhouse. "We went into Davey's office [Johnson, the Mets manager], and he [Ueberroth] told me not to worry about getting suspended, just play ball." On September 24, 1985, the *New York Post* reported, "A source close to the trial of Curtis Strong

BLUE: TRANSCENDENTAL GRAPHICS
OTHERS: NATIONAL BASEBALL LIBRARY, COOPERSTOWN, NY

says that [Ueberroth] will take no disciplinary action against Keith Hernandez."

As 1985 turned into 1986, Ueberroth summoned 23 players and one coach who had been implicated in Pittsburgh to his office for one-on-one meetings. (John Milner declined the invitation.) Frank Dolson reported in the *Syracuse Herald American* on March 2, 1986, "Those interviews were little more than routine. Nothing new. Just a rehashing of old information." So there was much surprise on February 28 when Ueberroth announced detailed punishments that divided 21 players into three categories. Group 1 players (Andujar, Berra, Cabell, Hernandez, Leonard, Parker, and Smith) received one-year suspensions without pay unless the player agreed to (1) donate 10% of his 1986 salary to a drug-abuse prevention program or facility, (2) perform 100 hours of drug-related community service in each of the next two years, and (3) participate in a random testing program for the rest of his career. Players in other categories received similar but less severe punishments.

Hernandez was livid. Before Ueberroth announced the punishments, Hernandez had noted, "He could have made the decision a month ago; then you'd start

the season without a cloud. Does he care about the game?" Long-held suspicions that Ueberroth cared deeply about promoting himself resurfaced quickly. "Apparently, Peter Ueberroth would rather have people talking about drugs and Peter Ueberroth, not necessarily in that order," wrote Dolson. "Ueberroth is being seen by many today as the champion drug buster of the free world . . . [he] has done everything but dress himself in tights and a cape with his initials on his chest."

Skepticism about the motives and competence of baseball's management was not limited to Ueberroth. John McHale, president of the Montreal Expos, said baseball's cocaine problem "slipped in the back door and you didn't even know it was in the house." That door was apparently ajar for a long time, since McHale also opined that cocaine had cost his Expos the 1982 division title. Players went to great lengths to hide their use of the drug, but it's still hard to believe that cocaine was so invisible. It did not single out cocaine, but a 1973 report of a House of Representatives Investigations Subcommittee had described drug abuse among pro athletes as "widespread and rampant at all levels," adding that the degree of "improper

TRANSCENDENTAL GRAPHICS

*Dale Berra*

drug use—primarily amphetamines and anabolic steroids—can only be described as alarming." In 1980, Terry Pluto of the *Cleveland Plain-Dealer* reported on that newspaper's survey of baseball players, coaches, and executives, which estimated that 10–12% of baseball players used cocaine.

Many of the teammates of players who had testified in Pittsburgh had not exactly been in the dark. After Hernandez's time on the witness stand, infielder Wally Backman told Jack Lang of the *New York Daily News*: "As far as what he might have revealed in court, I haven't read his testimony. But all of us knew of his involvement . . . He told me he had used it (cocaine) three times." Pitcher Ed Lynch told Lang, "We all knew. He didn't call a team meeting or anything like that to tell us, but he did talk to some of us." None of this, or any of the other dozens of incidents through the 1980s and early '90s, prevented Bud Selig, then acting commissioner, from saying this to *The Sporting News* in July 1995 when asked about steroids: "If baseball has a problem, I must candidly say that we were not aware of it. It certainly hasn't been talked about much. But should we concern ourselves as an industry? I don't know, maybe it's time to bring it up again." What a difference a decade makes!

Another difference between the '80s and today is that back then players were more open about their cocaine experiences and were willing to talk about the drug's allure. "Why should I be sorry? It's something I did," Parker told the *Pittsburgh Press*. In August 1986, Al Holland told Michael Kay of the *New York Post*, "I don't regret that it happened because I learned a lot from that." Asked why he tried recreational drugs, he said, "I liked it. It was nice." Tim Raines, who would slide headfirst so as not to break the vials of cocaine he kept in his back pocket, said, "It made me feel real good. I had to keep cool because of who I was, but it was a great experience. I was sorry it felt so good. In a sense the drug experience didn't hurt but helped because I discovered what I can and can't do." Enos Cabell testified in Pittsburgh that he "snorted cocaine as many as 100 times between 1978 and 1984 and that he usually performed well, getting two or three hits in games the day after using the drug."

Players may have been more willing to talk candidly about their drug experiences in the 1980s, but one element of baseball's drug scene that hasn't changed is the belief that the current crisis is the prelude to a drug-free future. In August 1986, Holland was asked about the recent cocaine-related deaths of basketball star Len Bias and National Football League player Don Rodgers. "It could have been me," Holland said, adding, "Baseball is done with drugs. It's not like that anymore in baseball. . . . You do it now and you're nobody." Keith Hernandez agreed. In April 1986 he told the *New York Post* that "baseball is drug-free."

Holland and Hernandez may have taken their cues from Peter Ueberroth. Eckhouse and Carmody's book recounts the events of October 30, 1985, when Ueberroth spoke at a luncheon in Washington, D. C. Earlier that day, Robert McCue had been sentenced to 10 years in prison and three years probation for his conviction on seven counts of cocaine distribution to Dale Berra and John Milner. Ueberroth was in Washington at a tribute to first lady Nancy Reagan and to help launch the Girl Scouts' drug-abuse program. He took the occasion to announce that he would guarantee the total elimination of drugs from professional baseball. There's little doubt that Ueberroth was genuine in his belief that he could lead an effort to achieve that goal. In 2005, though, Ueberroth's pledge looks like Hall of Fame-level grandstanding. History shows that drugs are deeply rooted in baseball and in America, in part because they are an object of great ambivalence in the sport and society. Today it remains an open question as to how much progress we are making in banishing them to the sidelines.

### Sources and Acknowledgments

*The Sporting News Official Baseball Guide.* St. Louis: The Sporting News, 1986.
*New York Times*, August 19, 21, 22, 23, 1985.
*The Sporting News*, September 16, 23, 1985.
Eckhouse, Morris and Clark Carmody. *Baseball's Milestone Season.* Pittsburgh, PA: M&M Publications, 1986.

For invaluable research assistance, thanks to Eric Enders, Triple E Productions, Cooperstown, NY, and Bobby Plapinger, R. Plapinger Baseball Books, Ashland, OR.

# Sound BITES

## by Darryl Brock

A .357 Magnum fired at arm's length slams your eardrums with 168 decibels of volume. Rumbling car subwoofers can pump out as much as 176dB. A police siren logs in around 140dB, a rocker's wailing guitar at 120dB. Of course, it matters how far you are from the source, but even at a distance, any of the above can easily swamp normal human conversation, which occurs at roughly 70dB.

What about noise in big league ballparks? Increasingly unable to talk to somebody even in an adjacent seat without leaning close and yelling, I decided to check for myself. Armed with a sound-pressure meter purchased at Radio Shack, I took measurements from my field-level seat during an afternoon A's game at McAfee Coliseum, where the high outfield enclosure of football seats and glass-fronted boxes (known with scant affection locally as "Mount Davis," after the Raiders owner responsible for the structural abomination) traps sound with a resulting resonance that seems greater than across the Bay at the Giants' ball yard—although things are hardly quiet there—or at Cincinnati's Great American Ballpark and other parks I've visited lately.

Though the late-summer weather was gorgeous and the A's were locked in a pennant race, the crowd was relatively modest—some 25,000, mostly placid souls. Ambient crowd measurements "at rest" ranged between 68–78dB. A brass-lunged heckler six rows behind me registered 79–82dB. Cheering during rallies reached the high-middle 80s and spiked up over 90 on a Nick Swisher home run.

What issued from the powerful ballpark speakers was another story: player introductions, 79–81dB; PA announcer promotions, 81–85dB; prerecorded baseball highlights and up-tempo music, 87–91dB; Dot Racing, 92 dB. Keep in mind these are *averages*. When I set the dial at "max" to measure volume peaks, the results pushed 100.

All of which confirmed my suspicions: *everything* coming from the speakers reached field-level seats at well over conversational level. When you consider that *each increase of six decibels represents a doubling of volume*, it becomes plain that most of the amplified noise is maintained at levels well above even the loudest of crowd sounds.

Not only does this tend to drown out conversation, it definitely produces stress. "At 90 decibels and above is where human damage begins," says bioacoustic expert Dr. Bernie Krause, who has witnessed the incursions of human noise into shrinking natural soundscapes around the globe. "Glucocorticoid enzyme levels shoot up at those levels, and the heart rate speeds," Krause says. "It's a deliberate concentration of acoustic energy to promote the illusion of action."

Ironically, this "action," along with the excitement (i.e., stress) it produces, occurs in ball games precisely when there is no action. And conversely, since the speakers still have to be silenced while the game is actually being played, moments of real baseball action occur in relative quiet—or at least not yet supplemented with manufactured noise. It seems that the game's ambience is ever more in the hands of disc jockeys and marketers. Therefore, the times when you most want to track events on the field are the only times you can easily talk and be heard.

*"Noise is power."* Bernie Krause is fond of wryly repeating this statement by James Watt, former Interior Secretary. As Krause elaborates the assumptions behind it, I see his point. That guy with the 808s blasting in his car is asserting his kingship over the jungle—including your audio space. Why do we raise

---

DARRYL BROCK *is the author of the historical novels* If I Never Get Back, Havana Heat, *and* Two in the Field. *He lives and writes in Berkeley, California.*

our voice in arguments? To dominate, of course, to impose *our* notion of how things should be. Which is exactly what enormous speakers do in ballparks. Yes, they may provide information. Yes, they may enhance a game's drama. But above all they dominate.

"What happens is that somebody installs a system or uses new techniques to get certain effects," says Jack Freytag, an acoustic engineer whose San Francisco firm has shaped soundscapes from the Hollywood Bowl to small restaurants (where noise levels can produce quicker turnover at tables, or promote intimacy by blocking neighboring conversations), "and the next year they want to do even greater things. The trouble is, at some point they go over the top." Freytag concludes: "Louder isn't always better."

In years gone by, I would occasionally bring rough pages and writing notes out to the Coliseum hours before the first pitch, spreading out comfortably in the bleachers and taking in the sounds of the place coming to life: the cracking impacts of BP, the thud of balls against the fence, the players' laughter and wisecracks, the vendors' cries, the kids' shouts.

Some 45 minutes before game time, the scoreboard screen would come to life. "Hello there, everybody," a dulcet voice would say. "This is Mel Allen bringing you *This Week in Baseball*." Highlights followed, narrated at reasonable volume, especially when compared with today's amplified frenzy.

Why does adrenaline have to be pumping every minute now? Sometimes the results are beyond ludicrous. A few years ago, I was at an A-league game in Charleston, West Virginia: Alley Cats vs. the visiting River Dogs. A thunderstorm sent the teams rushing off the field. The delay continued so long that most fans left. Hours passed. At half past midnight, driving past the ballpark with my family, I realized that the game was still in progress. I got out and went up to the gate. Bottom of the eighth. Fewer than ten people in the stands. And *still* the sound system was sending out peal after peal of "DAAAAAAY-OHs," drum rolls, bugle calls, exhortations to "*charge!*" and so on. The effect was eerie. A haunted ballpark, amped up for nobody.

In 1934, when the Chicago Cubs installed Wrigley Field's first public address system (presumably megaphones were employed till then), Ruth Reynolds reported in the *New York Daily News* that Cub manager Charlie Grimm strongly opposed the new system, fearing that "music records" would be played on it, as in some other ballparks. "Grimm contends that miscellaneous records would clash with the rhythm of baseball procedure," Reynolds wrote, "and that records would not be selected to meet the tempo of the varying movements in practice workouts."

I think Jolly Cholly Grimm's worries were dead-on. Can't the game itself be enough?

A resounding *no* comes from Mike Veeck, baseball executive and promoter non pareil, who has written, "So-called baseball purists always say, 'The game is enough to bring fans out to the park. It doesn't need embellishing.' Well, those people never owned a ball club. If you catered only to the purists, 75% of your seats would remain empty. When people come to the ballpark, we should celebrate the three hours that we have them."

Okay, point taken; maybe so.

Let's all celebrate, if we must, while games unfold before us.

But couldn't we turn down the relentless white noise? Please?

# Death in the Ohio State League

## by Craig Lammers

The year 1906 was one of change for minor league baseball in Ohio. The previous season, independent teams from Ohio and western Pennsylvania had joined organized ball as the Class C Ohio Pennsylvania League. By early spring, the unmanageable number of teams was reduced to eight, six of them in Ohio.

New Castle was one of two Pennsylvania cities represented in the O–P League for its first full season of play. New Castle had a long history of baseball excellence, and recognition of that heritage was planned as part of the opening-day ceremonies. Charlie Bennett, one of the great catchers of the 19th century, was invited back to be honored as part of the 1878 team.

Almost overshadowed in the excitement over opening day was a battle for the Nocks' second base job. One candidate was Charles "Buster" Brown, a 23-year-old player on option from Buffalo of the Eastern (now International) League. Brown had left college and joined Buffalo after his play attracted the attention of Bisons manager George Stallings. He had also played for Augusta of the South Atlantic League, a team that included young Ty Cobb. After contracting malaria, Brown returned north and finished 1905 with an independent team in Warren, Ohio. He was expected to win the New Castle job easily.

Brown's competition was a 17-year-old from the village of Collinwood, now a part of Cleveland. Charles Pinkney, the youngest son of a railroad engineer, was better than expected. Brown was in the lineup when the team opened on the road, but Pinkney soon won the job.

A 3-for-3 day with two doubles at Lancaster, Ohio

on April 30 would turn out to be a key to Brown's baseball future. When the Ohio team went to New Castle for the Nocks' long-anticipated home opener, a shakeup was planned. After another infielder initially balked at joining the team, Brown was purchased by Lancaster management. He debuted with his new team on May 11, initially playing third base. After a few weeks the other infielder reported and Brown was benched.

Meanwhile after an impressive debut, Pinkney endured a slump. A late May report said he had been released. But the release, if it occurred, was short-lived and Pinkney became a key to the success of the team. His role was even more important after the New Castle manager resigned in mid-season to take the job at East Liverpool, Ohio, taking some of the Nocks better players with him. At the time of the defections, Pinkney led New Castle batters with an average of .297. His play drew comparison with former Cleveland second baseman Clarence "Cupid" Childs, and Pinkney soon received the same nickname.

In mid-June, Charles Brown finally gained a regular job at Lancaster. After an injury to the Lanks first baseman, their second baseman shifted to first and Brown was able to play his strongest position. His defense immediately made a difference. Typical was a play described in the *Lancaster Gazette*. "Little Brown brought the crowd to a standstill in the 8th when he leaped into the air and pulled down a terrific line drive with two men on bases retiring the side."

The Lancaster press in 1906 chronicled both the serious and not so serious moments in Brown's season. In July he was hit by a flying bat and knocked unconscious, but after ten minutes he regained consciousness and stayed in the game.

That same week also offered a little comic relief and demonstrated Buster's fondness for hats. A report in the *Gazette* said, "He entered a restaurant at

CRAIG LAMMERS *is country music director at WBGU radio in Bowling Green, Ohio. His main research interests are the Deadball Era and minor leagues of Ohio and Kansas. He also plays for the Wood County Infirmary Inmates Vintage Baseball team, and batted .333 last year.*

suppertime, putting a new straw hat, which cost him a big price, on the rack. After supper he picked up a hat, which he supposed was his own, never noticing the difference until he had walked up the street when his attention was called to it by a fellow player. He looked and found the name W.W. McCoy written in lead pencil several times on the inside. He tried in vain to locate McCoy until Saturday evening when he learned that McCoy had left at 4:30 for Oklahoma with the hat."

The *Gazette* related the story of another hat that Brown couldn't give away. "[Brown] purchased a gray felt hat with a blue silk band. Almost immediately the team started down the toboggan. When Mansfield was here recently, Pitcher [Harvey] "Doc" Bailey was looking for a mascot. He espied the hat and asked Brown for it and got it. Since then he has lost a 15 inning battle with Lancaster and an 18 inning game with New Castle. Brown received word this morning that the hat had been shipped back. When it arrives it will be placed in a fiery furnace. Nobody can make Brown believe there is nothing in luck."

By season's end, both Brown and Pinkney had been keys to their teams' successful seasons. New Castle finished third, just three percentage points ahead of Lancaster. Pinkney was sixth among league regulars in batting at .278. He played in 133 of his team's 139 games and stole 35 bases. Brown hit .229, about average for the league, and stole 22 bases. Defensively Pinkney led regular second basemen with a .965 fielding percentage. Brown was fourth at .945.

A report in the *Cleveland Plain Dealer* said Brown had been drafted by the St. Louis Browns, and Bob Quinn of the American Association's Columbus Senators was also impressed with his play. Brown for his part, expressed an interest in leaving Lancaster and playing farther east, closer to his home in Albion, New York. Nothing came of the rumors and Buffalo didn't exercise its option, so both Brown and Pinkney returned to the Ohio Pennsylvania League for 1907.

Pinkney suffered through a sophomore slump in 1907, hitting .202 in 57 games. His fielding was strong and he stole 17 bases, but he sprained an ankle in July and didn't return to New Castle. Brown played in all of Lancaster's 134 games and hit .236. His .960 fielding percentage was second among O-P second basemen.

Much like 1906, 1908 was marked by changes in Ohio minor league baseball. A split occurred in the Ohio Pennsylvania League. The four western and southern teams—Lancaster, Mansfield, Marion, and Newark—left to form the Ohio State League. Lima and Springfield (soon to be replaced by Portsmouth) rounded out the new league.

The spring of 1908 also brought national attention to Charles Pinkney's hometown. On the morning of March 4, smoke was noticed under a stairway at the Lakeview School in Collinwood. In the resulting panic 173 students and two teachers died at the school Pinkney had attended a few years before.

The season of 1908 was a good one for Charles "Buster" Brown, as Lancaster won the pennant. The Lanks' pitching staff threw six no-hitters that season, and the team's defense was key to the pitching success. Four of those no-hitters were thrown by Walter "Smoke" Justis, and the sports editor of the *Newark American Tribune* later said, Brown "more than anyone else [was] responsible for the splendid showing made by Justis for he alone could bring the Big Smoke back to earth after an ascension." Brown played in 152 games for the league champs, hitting .258 and stealing 34 bases. He led Ohio State League second basemen with a .957 fielding percentage.

Cupid Pinkney was released by New Castle during the middle of 1908. The 19-year-old was signed by Newark as a utility player but soon took over the second base job, becoming a favorite of the fans in the Ohio State League's roughest town. He hit .253 in 42 games and committed just four errors.

The 1909 season began as a year of promise in both Lancaster and Newark, but by season's end both teams would fold, scattering their players to other teams. The two cities would return to organized ball the following season, but by opening day 1910, Charles "Buster" Brown and Charles "Cupid" Pinkney were dead.

The normally durable Brown missed almost half of Lancaster's 1909 games with an injured ankle suffered in a game at Newark. According to the *American Tribune*, he was avoiding a play where he would have spiked Pinkney. After Lancaster folded in late August, he'd finish the season with York, Pennsylvania, of the Tri State League.

The financial situation in Newark was even more precarious. Cupid Pinkney and his teammates were sometimes not paid, and the team was taken over by the league, playing some of their home games in Columbus. A couple of weeks before the league gave up and disbanded the Newark team, Cupid Pinkney left the league.

Dayton of the Class B Central League was going through a miserable season, and was looking for players to plug major holes in the team. They'd already acquired a few players from the Ohio State League, and on August 7 the *Dayton Journal* announced that owner Elmer Redelle had acquired Pinkney "for a cash consideration said to be $300." The Central League was a promotion for Pinkney, and at age 20 he was one of the league's youngest players.

Pinkney joined Dayton during a road series at Evansville, Indiana. He first appeared for his new team on August 10 after an injury to the starting second baseman. He remained in the Veterans lineup, and when the team returned home he soon made an impression on the fans. On the 16th, the *Journal* described a key play. "Dick Grefe sent a whisper to the right of first base. Pinkney is the only one of the numerous second basemen Dayton has had this summer who would have even looked at the ball. With one hand he grabbed the fleeting sphere and threw the batter out at first holding the runner at third." The eighth-inning play helped save a 3-1 Dayton win.

In his first eight games with his new club, he hit .435, and the *Journal* said, "How the midget can get on base. If he does not slam the ball or beat out a bunt, he's sure to be passed or else some fielder foozles the ball. He's a regular little wizard." The article was probably exaggerating only a little when it said that John J. McGraw and Connie Mack would soon be at Dayton's Fairview Park scouting Pinkney.

After a game in which he had two doubles, a single, scored two runs, and stole two bases in four at-bats, the Journal dubbed him "Little Hans" after the great Pirate shortstop.

Although he slumped briefly at the plate, strong defensive play continued. On September 2, he went 3-for-4 with two runs scored, but a defensive play was the key. South Bend manager Angus Grant, according to the *Journal*, "was laughing wickedly as he went to the plate determined to break up the siesta then and there. And he smote the first offering over second with all his might and a little bit more. Up goes Little Pink, no one having any idea he would shake hands with the pellet. But the midget is bigger than he looks and when he descended from his aeroplane he was clutching the ball in his gloved hand. All he had to do was hurl it to (first baseman) Bunny (Pearce) and the game ended with a double play."

September 14 must have been a day Cupid Pinkney looked forward to. Dayton was starting its final series of the season, hosting the Grand Rapids Stags. His father was on the way from Cleveland for a visit before the trip home and a planned welcoming party. Pinkney led off the first game of the day's doubleheader with his only home run of the season, off a 22-year-old right hander, Kurt "Casey" Hageman. Hageman allowed four runs and was removed in the second inning of Dayton's 10-0 win.

As was common in the Deadball Era, Hageman returned to start the second game. Charles Pinkney Sr. arrived at Fairview Park in the fifth inning, and between innings briefly visited with his son on the field. By that time it was rapidly growing dark, and the *Journal* commented the game should have been called after five. It was decided the seventh would be the last inning. Grand Rapids led, 5-3. Hageman walked the first batter and retired the next, bringing Pinkney to the plate. As the *Journal* described it, "Pitcher Hageman threw three balls to Pinkney and the fourth appeared to be a ball which would entitle the batter to his base. It was a swift shoot, which approached the home plate like a swift shot from a rifle. It was growing very dark and before Pinkney could dodge, the ball had hit him square in the head just back of and above the left ear. The report was so loud it was heard by practically all present. The athlete fell to the ground like one shot."

Pinkney's father was one of the first to reach his side after the beaning, and "players of both teams rushed to the side of the stricken young man and doctors who were hastily summoned by President Elmer Redelle worked over him."

The young second baseman was rushed to Dayton's St. Elizabeth Hospital, where reports were contradictory. The physician in charge was quoted that Pinkney would pull through, but it wasn't to be. He died shortly after noon on September 15, 1909. Pinkney's father, who fainted shortly after helping carry his son to the ambulance, remained at the hospital, and the *Journal* expressed concern about how the young player's mother would react to the news. "Her whole life has been wrapped up in her children, and our youngest Charles was only a boy." Charles "Cupid" Pinkney was buried in Cleveland's Lakeview Cemetery. A decade later, Cleveland shortstop Ray Chapman was buried in the same cemetery.

No blame was placed on pitcher Hageman. The *Journal* said, "He deserves the sympathy of every person in the city. Since the accident proved to be a fatality he has refused to be comforted. He has been absolved from all blame, yet he seems to think he is branded for life." The following season Hageman refused an offer to play in the Central League, reportedly because he didn't want to return to the scene of the tragedy. He appeared in the major leagues with the Red Sox in 1911-12 and the Cardinals and Cubs in 1914, playing in 32 games, 11 as a pitcher.

Charles "Buster" Brown returned to his home in Albion, New York, after finishing the 1909 season. His sister later remembered that Brown was "rather nervous" when he returned home. Financial concerns were an apparent factor, as he was still owed money by the defunct Lancaster team. He was the primary support of a widowed mother and intended to spend the off-season in Albion.

Those plans changed when he was asked to come to Buffalo to work as a clerk for the Pullman Company. Family members said, "He wouldn't leave his room in Buffalo after coming home from work. He said the fellows were standing on the corners talking about him." His sister told a friend, "Every night he would tell me that he wanted to tell me something and then he wouldn't. He said he hadn't slept in three weeks."

Just after Christmas 1909, Brown was persuaded to commit himself to a private hospital in Batavia, New York. In conversations with his family he expressed thoughts of suicide. Still, there were hopes of recovery and even talk he'd be offered the job as manager of Canton in the Ohio Pennsylvania League.

On Saturday March 12, 1910, Charles Brown left the hospital at three o'clock to mail a letter. His sister said he walked 20 miles to Albion including a walk through a swamp, arriving at eight o'clock Sunday evening. "No one being home he entered through a rear window and took off his wet clothes. About nine o'clock his brother came and found him shivering. He was wet up to his shoulders." After putting on dry clothes, Brown remarked that "he wished he could die." When asked how he'd gotten there, Brown remarked, "It doesn't matter. I am home and that is all that is necessary."

His sister described the events of March 14 to a friend in Lancaster. "On Monday morning early, I phoned over to the hotel in Albion and they said come over at once, as Charlie is very sick, and needs someone to take care of him. Charlie didn't want his friends to know he was at a hospital, and I arrived at Albion just a few moments after he hung himself."

Charles Brown was 27 years old when he committed suicide. A third second baseman from the 1909 Ohio State League also died young. Cincinnati native Ed McKernan had been a teammate of Brown's in the South Atlantic League, and spent part of 1909 with the Ohio State League's Portsmouth team. He later managed in the Kentucky-based Bluegrass League and at Battle Creek of the Southern Michigan League. McKernan had an eye for talent and soon reversed the fortunes of the Battle Creek club. He was thought to have a bright future as a manager and scout, but was taken seriously ill after leading his team to the 1913 pennant. It was initially thought that he had typhoid fever, but it turned out to be cancer and McKernan died in Cincinnati in May 1914.

### Sources

Several Ohio newspapers were used to research this article: the *Lancaster Eagle*, 1906–1910; *Lancaster Gazette*, 1906–1910; *Newark American Tribune*, 1906–1908; *Newark Advocate*, 1909–1910; *Dayton Journal*, 1909; *Zanesville Signal*, 1909–1910; and the *Battle Creek* (MI) *Enquirer*, 1913–1914.